A Practical Guide to Hospitality Finance

A Practical Guide to Hospitality Finance

John M. Tarras

Associate Professor
Michigan State University
East Lansing, Michigan

VNR VAN NOSTRAND REINHOLD
_____ New York

Copyright © 1991 by Van Nostrand Reinhold

Library of Congress Catalog Card Number 90-33434
ISBN 0-442-31885-5

Manufactured in the United States of America

Published by Van Nostrand Reinhold
115 Fifth Avenue
New York, New York 10003

Chapman and Hall
2-6 Boundary Row
London, SE1 8HN

Thomas Nelson Australia
102 Dodds Street
South Melbourne 3205
Victoria, Australia

Nelson Canada
1120 Birchmount Road
Scarborough, Ontario M1k 5GA, Canada

16 15 14 13 12 11 10 9 8 7 6 5 4 3 2 1

Library of Congress Cataloging-in-Publication Data
Tarras, John.
    A practical guide to hospitality finance / John Tarras.—1st ed.
        p.   cm.
    Includes bibliographical references.
    ISBN 0-442-31885-5
    1. Hospitality industry—Finance.   I. Title.
TX911.3.F5T35   1990
647.94'068'1—dc20   90-33434
                                                        CIP

This book is dedicated to my two children
Samantha and Christine. I love you both very much.

Contents

Preface

I wrote this book primarily for students interested in financial development of the hospitality industry. Entrepreneurs who are thinking of starting their own hospitality business will also find this book a good starting point for learning the financial aspects of developing a hospitality business.

This book guides the student through the topics that are of the most concern to the hospitality developer or investor. The hospitality industry is changing rapidly, and obtaining financing is also changing. With changing tax laws, inflation, the savings and loan crisis, foreign investment interest, etc., the hospitality executive must be creative in locating affordable sources of capital. These changes make it difficult for any textbook to be current in all areas at all times. However, this text concentrates on the important concepts that underlie financing a hospitality project and then discusses the relevant financial tools available to the developer (whether they are currently popular or not). For instance, soon after the Tax Reform Act of 1986, limited partnerships became a less important way to finance purchasing or building hotel properties. However, a change in the tax law could re-establish their popularity.

This book is meant to be an introduction to hospitality real estate development. Key economic and legal concepts are introduced to help students understand how financing development operates. I have kept financial calculations to a minimum, concentrating instead on the concepts. Many times in practice I have noticed that young professionals do not understand what they are trying to accomplish, even though they know how to perform the mathematical calculations.

With increased competition between companies in the hospitality industry, it is important for today's developer to keep tight control on the financing costs of building or purchasing a hospitality property. Today's developer must be aware of the many different aspects of raising capital to increase his or her chances of funding a project. This book is divided into chapters that discuss these important financial issues.

Chapter 1, "Overview of Hospitality Finance," discusses the hospitality industry in general and the need for careful financial planning before developing hospitality property. Key legal terms are also introduced.

Chapter 2, "Forms of Ownership of Hospitality Properties," discusses which business entity is appropriate given the business and tax needs of the developer of a hospitality property.

Chapter 3, "Key Tax Consideration in Hospitality Development," discusses the overall tax considerations that a hospitality developer must consider when operating and developing a hospitality property.

Chapter 4, "Feasibility Studies," discusses the importance of planning and site selection before selecting a location on which to build a hospitality project.

Chapter 5, "Measuring Rate of Return," discusses several techniques to aid the hospitality developer accurately measure a return from a project.

Chapter 6, "Financing Procedures and Costs," discusses how a hospitality project is financed and the cost of developing a property.

Chapter 7, "Raising Capital," discusses the different sources from which the hospitality developer may raise the necessary financing for a hospitality project.

Chapter 8, "Leasing," discusses the importance of leases as a financial tool in the hospitality industry and key terms and strategies.

Chapter 9, "Franchising-Management Contracts," discusses the franchise process in the hospitality industry. In addition, management contracts in the hotel industry are discussed along with special management contract opportunities in hotel condominiums and time shares.

Chapter 10, "Buying and Selling of Hospitality Properties," discusses the process of buying and selling hospitality properties and the associated problems and opportunities.

Readers who have already had basic accounting and finance classes will get the most use from this book. The concepts in this book, while often complex, will aid the student for many years as a reference.

I hope that you enjoy this book and the exciting field of hospitality development that this book introduces. I wish to close by thanking my teaching assistants Michael Anderson and Kelly Collister for their patient research efforts in gathering material for this book.

John M. Tarras

A Practical Guide to Hospitality Finance

Chapter 1

Overview of Hospitality Finance

INTRODUCTION

Obtaining financing for a hospitality project is usually quite difficult for the developer or entrepreneur. Different projects have different financing needs. Opening a catering business requires less capital than opening a hotel. The developer or entrepreneur obtains the needed capital from traditional financing sources, such as commercial banks. However, the creative developer can use several sources of financing, including pension funding, government financing assistance, outside investors, or a combination of sources.

Larger hospitality projects, such as major hotels, often tap into large institution financing sources, including life insurance companies, pension funds, and investment banking. In addition, the larger hospitality projects may obtain investor financing by offering limited partnership offerings to a select group of wealthy investors. This is known as a "private placement." Or the large hospitality firm may finance a project using contributions from a large number of small investors. This is known as a "public offering." (See Chapter 7 on raising capital for a complete discussion of this topic.)

Today, hospitality firms must finance projects creatively because financing is becoming more difficult to obtain and, if attainable, increasingly expensive. For example, when interest rates for loans exceeded 20 percent in the early 1980s, many hospitality developers turned to participation loans to make a project economically feasible. Although interest rates have fallen since then and caused a decline in participation loans, there is no assurance that rates may not rise again in the future.

Another factor is that as the market becomes saturated with fast food restaurants, hotels, and similar businesses, lending institutions may be more reluctant to loan funds to the hospitality industry. Financial institutions may increase their interest rates to be compensated for the increased risk of loaning funds in a highly competitive market. (See Chapter 6 for financing techniques available to the hospitality developer.)

Hospitality firms also must be aware of law changes to maximize saving through proper tax planning, which is important to determining what business entity a hospitality firm should adopt. (See Chapter 2 on choosing a business entity.)

Hospitality developers have to be constantly aware of how tax laws affect not only their operations but also their ability to raise capital. For instance, the massive changes brought about by the Tax Reform Act of 1986 (TRA 1986) have severely restricted the use of tax shelters as a method of raising capital by the hospitality industry. (See Chapter 3 on tax laws that affect most hospitality firms.)

Many entrepreneurs have a restricted amount of money to invest in a project. For example, those who desire to run a restaurant often do not have sufficient capital available to finance both the purchase of equipment and a building. However, the entrepreneur may be able to finance the restaurant if he or she is able to lease a suitable site. Thus, leasing actually becomes a method of financing the restaurant. There may be other reasons for leasing space other than for using it as a financing device. For instance, a desirable location may not be for sale but available only for lease. (See Chapter 8 on leasing for a detailed discussion).

Before financing a hospitality project, many lending institutions first require that the developer conduct a feasibility study to prove that the project has a reasonable chance of being profitable. In a feasibility study, an independent consultant examines the local market for economic viability, competitive environment, demand for the service in the area, site analysis, and the potential for future growth. The study consists of financial statements showing the projected income or cash flow from the project. The more costly the hospitality project, the more likely the lender will insist on a feasibility study. (See Chapter 4 on feasibility studies for a more detailed discussion.)

The developer of any hospitality project must forecast as accurately as possible the expected return on the original investment. The developer measures the risk associated with a given project and then determines what rate of return will compensate him or her for the risk taken.

The developer focuses heavily on the expected cash flow from the project. Cash flow is often more important then the financial income statements. In order to analyze expected cash flow from a project using today's dollar figures, the developer will probably apply some discount technique to arrive at a present value for the cash flow. One of the more popular discounting techniques is the internal rate of return calculation. (See Chapter 5 for a detailed discussion of how to measure rate of return.)

In today's competitive market, many lenders shy away from lending funds to independent operators. Lenders frequently insist that developers hire professional managers to run their properties as a condition to lending any funds. This requirement by lenders and the fact that many hotel companies focus on operating properties rather than owning them has led to the rapid growth of management companies in the past two decades.

For many years, the restaurant industry has been a rich area for franchising. The growth of restaurants such as McDonalds, Burger King, and Wendy's has been accomplished through franchises. A franchise offers the parent company an opportunity for rapid growth, while the owner of a franchise has the advantage of a proven method of operation. The failure rate for franchise operators is lower than that for independent restaurants. Thus, it is generally easier to obtain financing for franchise operations than for independent restaurants. (See Chapter 9 on franchising and management contracts for further details.)

Finally, buying and selling existing hospitality properties is discussed in Chapter 10. A hospitality owner must consider numerous factors when purchasing a hospitality project. The main advantage for the buyer in purchasing an existing property is the operating history to guide him or her in the purchase negotiations. The seller of a hospitality project, on the other hand, attempts to maximize the sale price.

However, numerous details must be worked prior to any sale. The buyer has to obtain accurate information about sales, expenses, and the seller's reasons for placing the property on the market. The seller must assess the buyer's ability to purchase the property and may have to offer incentives to make the property more attractive to the buyer. For instance, the seller may offer to finance part of the sale price with an attractive below-market interest rate.

HOSPITALITY INDUSTRY AND DEVELOPMENT

There is no single definition of the hospitality industry. Rather, it consists of a series of related service industries that have in common the pampering and comfort of guests. Under this broad category, some of the businesses considered hospitality would include but not necessarily be limited to the following:

- Hotels
- Restaurants
- Resorts
- Clubs
- Contract food services (hospitals, airlines, etc.)
- Clubs
- Travel agencies
- Theme parks
- Institutional (military, nursing homes, etc.)

Many separate subcategories to each of the above items make the hospitality industry diverse. Each of the general categories listed above has its own financing needs. The following list includes some of the possible lodging segments; each has its own unique financing requirements.

- Luxury hotel
- Full-service hotel
- All-suite hotel
- Mid-priced hotel/motel
- Economy or budget motel
- Resort hotel

Each of these categories can in turn be segmented. For example, some budget motels offer full services, while others offer nothing more than a room for rent.

Financing a resort hotel can run into the hundreds of millions of dollars, while financing an economy motel can be accomplished for less than a million dollars. Therefore, the larger properties usually obtain financing from the largest financial institutions, while the number of potential lenders for the economy motel would be much larger.

The restaurant industry is also segmented. The following list contains the major segments in the restaurant industry:

- Full service
- Fast food
- Theme
- Coffee shop
- Cafeteria
- Catering

As with hotels, the restaurant industry also includes subsegmentation within the general categories shown above.

A full-service restaurant is more complex and requires greater capital investment than does catering, which may be operated in someone's home kitchen. There are also a wide range of capital needs in purchasing a franchise operation. An investor may purchase a McDonald's franchise for hundreds of thousand of dollars, while a newer and lesser known franchise restaurant may cost only a few thousand dollars.

Clubs, contract food service, travel agencies, theme parks, and institutional businesses carry the same range of prices. The key determinant is that no matter how sophisticated the project, the developer must often finance part of the project with either debt financing or equity contributions from outside sources.

The remainder of this text focuses on the hospitality industry as a special form of real estate development. Although the industry is geared to the entrepreneurial developer (in contrast to the large national chains), the financing analysis could apply equally in most cases to both types of owners.

The hospitality industry is different from other types of real estate developments because providing service plays such an important part in determining the value of a particular property. For instance, an office center primarily rents space to others for rent, and the tenant and managers of the building interact relatively little. A hotel, on the other hand, may have a highly desirable location, but if its provides poor service to its guests, it will not likely remain profitable for long.

Because of the sheer number of hotels and restaurants in this country, this book will focus on these two businesses. A hotel often requires a substantial capital investment to be built. This is because a hotel's major selling point is rooms, which are very expensive to build and furnish. Therefore, the thrust of this book will apply to the hotel industry directly.

A restaurant usually requires less capital for construction and usually is financed by a local lender. In addition, a restaurant owner is more likely to lease space than a hotel operator. Therefore, the chapter on leasing is geared to the restaurant industry.

Having selected the type of hospitality business to build, the developer will then select the site where the property is to be located. Although a more thorough discussion of site location is given in Chapter 4 on feasibility studies, some general comments about location are appropriate here.

It has often been said that three things count when selecting a property: location, location, and location. This emphasises the importance of selecting the right site if the operation is to be successful. For instance, a fast food operation located away from the main traffic pattern of a community is almost destined for failure before it even opens its doors. Fast food restaurants require large traffic flow to provide enough potential customers to be profitable.

On the other hand, a good location is desirable for, but may not be as necessary for, a destination-type restaurant. (A destination restaurant is one where the food and service are sufficiently unique to motivate customers to go out of their way to get there.) Here, the restaurant thrives despite its less-than-desirable location.

However, for almost all hotels, property location is of prime importance. The competition among lodging properties for desirable location around the country is quite intense, with as many as five or more companies bidding on the same parcel of land in some locations. In fact, many properties owe their increase in value not so much to being a well-run hotel property but to operating in a rapidly increasing real estate market.

A hotel's property value may increase due to the removal of negative factors. For instance, many cities have rehabilitated their downtown business districts in an effort to attract people back into the city. Many of these rehabilitation projects have resulted in older hospitality properties getting a new lease on life.

Another important characteristic of site selection is that once a site is selected, the property cannot be moved. Thus, great care must go into selecting a site because once the decision has been made to locate at that site, there is no inexpensive way to change the location.

Because a hospitality firm is at a fixed location, it is also considered unique. This uniqueness has given rise to the legal concept of specific performance for enforceability of the sale of land. Generally, a person can only obtain monetary damages if another party breaches a contract for sale of goods or services. However, because each parcel of real estate is considered unique under the law, the purchaser may insist that the seller go through with the sale of the land. Courts will enforce that request.

TYPES OF OWNERSHIP INTEREST

The discussion of any hospitality real estate interest requires the reader to understand the different methods of owning property. To begin with, it is important to understand what is considered "real property." Real property is defined as land and any structures that are permanently attached to the land. For instance, a building is considered real property because it is attached to its site by a physical foundation. A mobile Burger King outlet would not be considered real property because it is not permanently attached to its site.

The other major category of property is "personal property." Personal property is defined in the negative as all property that is not real. However, a general guideline for defining personal property is that it can be removed from the real property with little or no damage done to the real property. For example, in the mobile Burger King example, the mobile unit can be driven to a particular site and set up there for the day and then be hooked up and driven away with very little difficulty. Furniture can be removed from a building without any difficulty and thus is considered personal property.

The question of whether property is real or personal is very important in leases. Generally, major improvements added to a rental facility belong to the landlord when the lease is terminated.

Furniture, on the other hand, is considered personal property and may be removed by the tenant at the termination of the lease. One test to determine whether an addition is an improvement or personal property centers on the intentions of the parties. If a restauranteur plans to add valuable additions to the property, the tenant should get a written agreement with the landlord that the fixtures will be considered personal property if the tenant wants to retain the additions. The agreement could cover any monetary damages that may occur upon the removal of the additions.

Freehold Estates

A person may have different ownership interests in real property. Below is a list of three possible methods of owning real property:

1. Fee simple absolute
2. Defeasible fees
3. Life estate

Fee Simple Absolute

The fee simple absolute gives the holder of the real estate the most complete set of rights in the real property. In this country, most property is owned under the fee simple absolute.

The owner has the unequivocal right to use property and dispose of it. Legal and government restrictions may be placed on the property, such as liens and community zoning laws.

Defeasible Fees

Defeasible fees are less common and are of two types: the fee simple determinable and fee on condition subsequent. Basically, under a defeasible fee, the owner has a fee simple absolute unless a condition stated in the deed is not met. This has the effect of tying up property for only certain uses. The courts dislike these restrictions on the transfer of property and are not likely to find a defeasible fee unless the language is absolutely clear.

The fee simple determinable is found when a required condition is not met and the owner will lose the property. Under the fee simple determinable, property automatically goes back to the original owners if the condition is not met. For instance, if a person leaves property to the city to be used only as a library and, years later, the city converts it to a city hall, the property would automatically revert to the original owners' heirs.

The fee on condition subsequent creates a defeasible fee that may be lost if the condition is not adhered to. The main difference between a fee simple determinable and fee on condition subsequent is that under the latter, the property may revert back if the original owner or his heirs brings suit. It does not, however, revert back automatically. The language on fee on condition subsequent specifies that the holder of the fee has the property on the condition that he or she use the property for a stated purpose.

Life Estate

The life estate is an interest created in a property that ends with the death of the life tenant (or the life of a third person so designated). This often occurs when property is left to a widow to use as long as she lives and then is transferred to the other heirs. The life tenant can convey her interest to a third party, but the interest of the third party terminates upon the death of the life tenant.

The person who has an interest in the property upon the death of the life tenant has a remainder interest in the property. The remainder interest permits the holder to sue the life tenant if the life tenant fails to maintain the property in reasonably good condition.

Leasehold Estates

The freehold estates create ownership, and the leasehold estate creates rights to possession to the property only. The leasehold interest can be for a specific period of time or left open by the parties. However, the tenant realizes from the beginning that he or she has no ownership interest in the property. The common types of leasehold estates are as follows:

- Estate for years
- Estate from period to period
- Estate at will
- Estate at sufferance

(They are discussed in detail in Chapter 8 on leasing.)

Concurrent Estates

When more than one person owns interest in a hospitality property, the property is held under one of the following concurrent estates:

- Tenancy in common
- Joint tenancy
- Tenancy by the entirety

Tenancy in Common

Under tenancy in common, each party holds an undivided proportional interest in the hospitality property. Each owner can sell his or her undivided interest to a third party, and the third party will then have a tenancy in common with the other owners. Upon the death of the tenant in common, his or her proportional share is passed to the heirs and does not automatically go to the other tenants in common.

When tenants in common own a property, an owner who no longer wishes to be in the tenancy in common can demand a partition of the property. A partition is a division of the property among the tenants. If parties cannot agree on how to divide the property, the courts will partition the property for them.

Joint Tenancy

Joint tenancy is differentiated from tenancy in common by the fact that ownership carries with it a right of survivorship. This means that upon the death of the joint tenant, the property automatically, by operation of law, vests complete ownership in the property to the other tenant(s). The courts will find a joint tenancy only if language that specifically states a right of survivorship exists. Otherwise, the courts will hold that property was held as tenants in common. Finally, if a joint tenant sells his or her interest to a third party, the joint tenancy is converted to a tenancy in common.

Tenancy by the Entirety

Tenancy by the entirety is a special joint tenancy in which the parties own the property equally, and this tenancy can only be created between a husband and wife. The main difference between a tenancy by the entirety and the joint tenancy is that one spouse cannot sell his or her interest to another party without the consent of the other spouse.

Nonpossessory Interests

A nonpossessory interest is created when a party wants or needs to use the property of another but does not take possession of the property. The most common forms of nonpossessory interest are easements, licenses, and profits.

Easements

An easement is simply the right of a third person to use part of someone else's property. The most common easement is the right of utility companies to use part of a property owner's land for power, gas, or phone lines.

Another type of easement is known as the easement appurtenant. This easement is created when one of two properties located next to each other and owned by the same person is sold. The seller specifies in the deed a positive easement so that the property sold will have access over the other property to the main road. A negative easement can also be created in an easement appurtenant when the previous owner of the property agrees not to construct any structure or limited the height of any structure in order to not interfere with the use of the property sold.

Easement in gross is the most common easement. The easement in gross benefits the person who is given the easement but has nothing to do with another parcel of land. A common of example of easement in gross is that of the telephone company running its lines across a property. The easement benefits the telephone company and is usually granted in the deed.

Easement can also be implied. An implied easement usually arises when the owner of a property creates an easement over part of his property to another part. Under common law, when an owner sells one or both of the parts of the property, under common law an easement still exists between the properties even though it was not specifically granted in writing.

If a property is subdivided and some of the land sold becomes land locked (i.e., it has no access to the outside), an easement by necessity is created over the seller's remaining property to public access.

Finally, an easement may be created because of someone's use of another property over an extended period of time (usually 10 years) without any pretense of having the owner's permission. This open and notorious use of another property in such a manner is known as an easement by prescription.

License

A license is permission given by the owner of a property to another for a specific purpose. It conveys a narrower set of rights to the person using the land and does not convey any ownership interest in the property. For instance, if a hotel rents a ballroom for a wedding, the parties renting the room have a license to enter the property for the specific purpose of holding a wedding.

Profits a' prendre

Profits a' prendre is the right given by a property owner (usually through sale) to remove minerals or timber from the property. This right is given to individuals to remove property fom the land. In the case of minerals (oil, gas, ore, etc.), the purchaser pays a royalty for the removal of property.

LEGAL TRANSACTIONS INVOLVING HOSPITALITY PROPERTY

Generally, there are complex legal requirements in the purchase of a suitable site for hospitality development. This section explores some of the more common legal requirements in contracting for the purchase of property.

Contract Requirements

In order for there to be a valid contract between two parties for the purchase of a property, four requirements must be met:

1. Offer and acceptance
2. Consideration
3. Capacity of the parties
4. Agreement contained in writing

Offer and Acceptance

Before a valid contract can be formed, there must be an offer to sell and an acceptance to buy. The offer states the seller's terms and conditions for the sale. If the potential buyer accepts the terms of the contract in its entirety, a contract is formed. If, however, the potential buyer changes the terms of the contract, there is no acceptance. The buyer may not accept the contract in its entirety, but instead changes some of the terms (e.g., the price of the property). In this case, the buyer is deemed to have rejected the contract and to have made a counteroffer. The seller then is in the position of having to accept the offer of the buyer in order to have a valid contract if other aspects of the contract are valid.

Consideration

In order for a contract to be formed, consideration must pass between the parties. Consideration does not have to consist of money; it can be a promise of payment at some future date. In fact, consideration is anything that incurs a legal determinant to one of the parties or the forgoing of some legal benefit. The purchase of property clearly involves consideration between the parties.

Capacity of parties

For a contract to be valid, the parties to the contract must have the requisite capacity to enter into the contract. Thus, insane persons lack the capacity to understand the contract and are thus protected by the law from people who attempt to take advantage of their condition. Usually, a contract entered into by someone who lacks capacity is voidable at the option of the person lacking the capacity or by his or her guardian. A voidable contract is one in which the party lacking the capacity may elect to hold the other party to the contract if he or she so wishes. However, if that person elects not to honor the contract, he or she is required to return any consideration received from the other party.

The largest class of individuals protected under the law is children. Anyone under the age of 18 or 21 (depending on applicable state law) is deemed by law to be a minor and thus has the capacity to void any contracts entered into. However, it is unlikely that many minors have the money or resources required to purchase a hospitality property.

Agreement Contained in Writing

Generally, most valid contracts can be either oral or written. However, because of the importance of real estate in our history, the statute of frauds was developed. It requires the sale of real estate to be in writing in order to be enforced by the courts. Due to the danger of fraudulent actions on the part of parties and the high dollar value of real property, it was felt that there should be this additional protection of requiring the contract to be in writing to be enforced. The writing must indicate the intent of the parties for the contract to be enforceable. For example, the following statement would be acceptable under the statute of frauds: "I agree to sell my restaurant to Mr. Smith for $100,000."

As with most rules, the statute of frauds has an exception to the writing requirement. The courts may enforce an oral agreement if there has been a partial performance of the contract and the courts can infer the parties' intent from their actions. More has to take place than merely transfer money. For instance, if one party has taken possession and made substantial improvement to the property, the courts will have a basis to infer an agreement between the parties.

Title

After a valid contract has been entered into by the parties, the buyer wants to acquire good title. More specifically, the buyer wants to make certain the seller has no major liens or encumbrances on the property that would cloud the title. In other words, the buyer wants the seller to provide food and marketable title to the property.

To obtain the best possible protection against a defective title, purchasers of real property often take out a title insurance policy.   A title insurance policy is issued by a real estate insurance company and ensures that the title received is free of any deficiencies at the time it is transferred. This is a valuable service, and no property should be purchased without this protection. In fact, almost all lending institutions insist that the buyer obtain a title insurance policy as a condition for making a loan.

The insurance company issues the title insurance policy after it conducts its own search of the seller's title. The insurance protects against the possibility that the recording system has failed to indicate a claim on the property. The insurance company does not insure against all defects. Those defects shown in the title such as liens and easements are listed by the insurance company and are not covered under the policy.

Deed

The deed is the instrument that conveys the title from the seller (grantor) to the buyer (grantee). The title is represented by the deed document. A deed is not valid until delivered and accepted by the buyer. Also, a deed must be delivered to an entity or person who exists at the time of the transfer. A deed conveyed to a person who is deceased is void.

Each state has statutes that regulate what must be contained in the deed for it to be effective. However, a general requirement is that a deed be signed by the grantor to be valid. Also, the deed must indicate in sufficient detail the property being transferred; there must be no doubt on the face of the deed which property is involved. The language of the deed must also indicate conveyance of the property from the grantor to the grantee. Finally, most states require that to be effective the deed be registered according to applicable state law.

Several different types of deeds may be used to convey property. The following deeds are the most common:

- General warranty deed
- Special warranty or grant deed
- Bargain and sale deed
- Quitclaim deed
- Special use deed

General Warranty Deed

The most inclusive—and as such the most desirable—deed from the buyer's point of view is the general warranty deed. Depending on state law, the general warranty deed conveys the following five promises or covenants from the grantor to the grantee:

1. *A covenant against encumbrances.* A promise that there are no restrictions on the property other than what is stated in the deed.
2. *A covenant of seism or ownership.* A promise that the grantor has good title to pass to the grantee.
3. *A covenant of quiet enjoyment.* A promise that the grantee's ownership will not be disturbed by another party having a claim upon the property.

4. *A covenant of the right to convey.* A promise from the grantor that he or she has the right to convey the property.
5. *A covenant of the defense of title.* A promise by the grantor that he or she will always defend the title conveyed.

Special or Grant Warranty Deed

This is a popular deed arrangement in western states and is similar to the general warranty deed except for one important area. Under the special or grant warranty deed, the grantor conveys and makes promises about the covenants of title, but these promises relate only to the time period that he or she actually owned the property. The grantor makes no promises for the time period before he or she owned the property.

Bargain and Sale Deed

A bargain and sale deed generally contains none of the covenants listed above but instead contains the consideration paid for the property along with the conveyance of the property.

Quitclaim Deed

A quitclaim deed simply transfers any interest that the grantor has in the property to the grantee. The grantor makes no warranties whatsoever and the grantee takes only that which the grantor has the right to convey. For instance, if Smith transfers his interest in the XYZ Hotel to Jones, Jones takes only the interest that Smith had the right to transfer. If Smith had no interest in XYZ Hotel, Jones takes nothing and has no recourse against Smith under breach of warranty.

Quitclaim deeds are often used in divorce proceedings where one spouse transfers his or her interest in a property to the other spouse as part of the divorce settlement. Also, if the title appears clouded by a possible interest by another party, the buyer may insist that a quitclaim deed be conveyed by that other party so as to clear up the title.

Special Purpose Deeds

There are also numerous deeds issued by persons other than the owners of the property. For instance, an executor uses an executor's deed to transfer title held by a deceased person to his or her heirs. A tax deed is conveyed when the owner fails to pay property taxes. A sheriff's deed conveys title to property sold at a valid sheriff's auction.

SUMMARY

The hospitality industry is diversified and includes many different types of businesses, from multimillion dollar resorts to small catering businesses in someone's house. Each type of business has its own financing needs. Smaller hospitality firms are more likely to use the commercial banking system or Small Business Administration loans. Large hospitality projects have a variety of financing techniques (e.g., pension funds, investment banks, limited partnerships, etc.) to fund a project.

Probably the best that can be said for the state of hospitality financing is that it is always changing. Factors that affect the financing of any project include, but are not limited to, availability of capital, interest rates, market saturation, and tax laws. These and other factors make financing hospitality properties a challenging endeavor that requires the hospitality developer to think creatively to locate sources of financing.

The importance of providing quality service to the guest is critical to how the hospitality industry differs from other real estate ventures. For instance, a hotel derives its value not only from its desirable location but also on how well it serves its guests' needs.

It cannot be overemphasized that a good location is critical for the success of most hospitality properties. Except for destination restaurants, most hospitality properties depend upon a good location to attract the targeted customers to their properties. That is why companies spend so much time analyzing possible sites before they commit to building at a certain location. Once a hospitality business has been built, there is no inexpensive way of relocating that property to a more desirable site.

A hospitality property can increase in value if negative factors affecting the surrounding area are removed. For instance, many inner city hotels have been rehabilitated and are operating profitably after years of losses as cities commit resources to make their downtowns attractive again.

The hospitality industry is made up of several different types of businesses that cater to pampering and comforting of guests. Some of the businesses considered part of the hospitality industry include:

- Hotels
- Restaurants
- Resorts
- Clubs
- Contract food services (hospitals, airlines, etc.)
- Clubs
- Travel agencies
- Theme parks
- Institutional (military, nursing homes, etc.)

Each category of the hospitality industry has special financing needs. However, this textbook concentrates primarily on the hotel and restaurant industries. Even within these two industries, there is a wide range of financing needs that the developer will face.

It is important when studying hospitality development to understand some key legal aspects of real estate. The first is what constitutes real property. Real property is defined as land and any structures permanently attached to the land.

Personal property, on the other hand, is defined in the negative: it includes all property that is not considered real. The difference between real and personal property becomes very important when deciding what may be removed by a tenant at the end of a lease and what is considered an improvement that belongs to the landlord at the end of the lease.

A person can hold an interest in real estate by different methods. The most common freehold estate with the greatest ownership rights is the fee simple absolute. A person who owns real estate under fee simple absolute has the unequivocal right to use (subject to government regulations) and dispose of property.

Defeasible fees are rare and very seldom seen in this country. The fee simple determinable and fee on condition subsequent are the two types of defeasible fees, in which property reverts automatically to the heirs of the original property owner upon the failure to satisfy the condition in the deed. Under the fee on condition, the title to the property will revert back to the heirs of the original property owner only upon action by the heirs. It is not an automatic event.

The life estate gives the holder of the property the right to possess the property until his or her death or the death of some designated third party. The life tenant must take reasonable care of the property, or the person who has the remainder interest may intervene.

The leasehold estate gives the holder of the property the right to possess the property but not include any ownership interest. The common types of leasehold interest are:

- Estate for years
- Estate from period to period
- Estate at will
- Estate at sufferance

Concurrent interest is present when more than one person has an ownership interest in the property. The most common form of multiple ownership is the tenancy in common, where each party holds an undivided proportional interest in the hospitality property. Each owner may sell or dispose of his proportionate interest as he or she see fit. Upon the death of one of the owners, ownership interest is passed onto his or her heirs, not to the other owners.

In the joint tenancy form of property ownership, property passes to the other owners as a matter of law upon the death of one of the joint owners.

Tenancy by the entirety is a special joint ownership that can exist only between a husband and wife. Property owned under this relationship cannot be disposed of without the consent of the other spouse.

A nonpossessory interest in property is created when a party wants or needs to use the property of another but does not want to take possession of that property. The most common type of nonpossessory interest is the easement, which gives a third party the right to use part of someone else's property. Easement can be expressed in writing in the deed or be implied by the actions of the parties.

The most common easement is the easement in gross. Easement in gross gives someone the right to use the property in question but not any other parcel of land. Public utility easements are the most common example of the easement in gross.

A license is permission given by the owner to a third party to use his or her property for a specific event or activity. An example of a license an owner allowing someone to hunt on his property during hunting season.

Profits a' prendre is the right given by the owner for a third party to remove minerals or timber from the property.

In any transaction for the purchase of either an existing property or land for development of a hospitality property, the owner will enter into a contract for the purchase of property. To be a valid contract for the purchase of property, the elements of a valid contract must be met. The first requirement is a valid offer and an acceptance for the purchase and sale of property. The second is that consideration must be present (almost never a problem when dealing with unrelated parties in purchasing property). Third, the parties must have requisite capacity to enter into a valid contract. Finally, the sale of real estate must generally be in writing to be enforced in a court of law under the statute of frauds.

The purchaser will want to ascertain whether the seller has good title to the property being purchased. To protect himself from a defective title, the purchaser usually buys a title insurance policy, which protects the buyer from any defects not shown on the reporting records.

After the record has been completed, the transfer of title from seller to buyer is accomplished by a written instrument called a deed. The deed is valid only if the parties exist at the time of the transfer.

There are several different types of deeds. The warranty deed offers the greatest protection to the buyer. Under a warranty deed, the seller promises that there are no encumbrances on the property other than what is stated in the deed, that he or she has good title to the property, that no persons have a claim on the property, that he or she has the right to transfer the ownership, and that he or she will defend the title against any party claiming an interest.

The quitclaim deed conveys only the interest that the party giving the quitclaim deed has in the property. It carries no warranties, and the recipient takes only the interest that the conveying party had in the property. The quickclaim deed is a common form of transferring ownership interest in divorce proceedings or when there is a question of ownership interest in a property.

GLOSSARY

Acceptance   The method of agreeing to an offer made from the other party to a contract.

Capacity   In law, the ability to understand and comprehend the terms of a contract.

Concurrent estate   An interest in ownership of property held by more than one person.

Consideration   A requirement for a valid contract that requires that the parties incur a legal detriment or forego a legal right.

Contract   An agreement by the parties that is enforceable by law. It requires that a valid offer and acceptance take place between the parties.

Deed   A written legal document that transfers title in real estate.

Defeasible estate   An interest in real estate that may be lost upon the failure to honor the condition stated within the deed or an event that comes to pass that causes title to revert.

Developer   Someone who takes raw land and improves it through the construction of buildings, roads, utilities, and/or landscaping.

Easement   The legal right to use but not possess land owned by another.

Easement appurtenant   The right of an owner to use another's property in order to use his or her own property.

Easement by prescription   An easement created under law for someone who openly and notoriously uses someone's property for a period of time (usually 10 years).

Easement in gross   The easement created to benefit someone who may not own land adjoining the property.

Estate at sufferance   A tenancy that exists when a party fails to live on the premises at the termination of a lease.

Estate at will   A tenancy that exists at the will of the parties that does not specify the time termination.

Estate from period to period   A tenancy for a specific period of time that does not necessarily state the duration of the lease.

Estate for years   A tenancy for a definite period of time stated in years.

Fee simple absolute   The highest form of real estate ownership that gives the holder the greatest rights to the use and disposition of his property.

Fixtures   Property that is attached to real property in such a manner that makes it difficult to remove without damaging the real property structure.

Grantee   The person who receives the ownership interest in a real estate transaction.

Grantor   The person who conveys the ownership interest in a real estate transaction.

Joint tenancy   The multiple ownership of property by which the property transfers automatically to the other owners upon the death of one of the parties. Often called joint ownership with right of survivorship.

Life estates   Interests in real property that terminate upon the death of the recipient or some other designated third party.

Offer   The presentation of terms that bind the person making them into a valid contract if accepted by the other party.

Partition   The division of real property upon the ending of a tenancy in common, either by the parties themselves or by a court of law.

Personal property   Property that is not considered part of the real estate. One common test is whether the property may be removed from the real estate with little damage.

Quitclaim deed   A deed that conveys only the ownership interest (if any) that the conveyer has in the property without any warranties.

Real property   The land and permanent structures, fixtures, fences, and improvements attached to it.

Remainder interest   The interest that a party has in real property that entitles him or her to the property upon the expiration of the life estate.

Specific performance   A legal right of the buyer to have the owner convey the real estate as specified in the contract.

Statute of frauds   A legal requirement that the sale of property be in writing in order to be enforceable by the courts. It is designed to prevent fraudulent transactions.

Tenancy by the entirety   A joint tenancy that can exist only between a husband and wife.

Tenancy in common   Multiple ownership of property in which each party owns an undivided proportional interest in a property. The right of survivorship does not exist for this type of ownership.

Title   The legal right to ownership of property.

Warranty deed   A deed in which the seller promises that the title is good and that there are no defects in the title except as shown on the deed.

References

Gibson, Frand, Karp. *Real Estate Law.* Chicago: Real Estate Education Co., 1983.

Corley, Robert N., Shedd, Peter J., and Floyd, Charles F. *Real Estate and the Law.* New York: Random House, 1982.

Irverson, Kathleen M. *Introduction to Hospitality Management.* New York: Van Nostrand Reinhold, 1989.

Recommended Reading

Irverson, Kathleen M. *Introduction to Hospitality Management.* New York: Van Nostrand Reinhold, 1989.

Powers, Tom. *Introduction to the Hospitality Industry.* New York: John Wiley & Sons, 1988.

Brymer, Robert A. *Introduction to Hotel and Restaurant Management: A Book of Readings.* Dubuque: Kendall/Hunt, 1988.

Chapter 2

Forms of Ownership of Hospitality Properties

INTRODUCTION

One of the most important decisions a hospitality firm makes is choosing the form or entity it will use to conduct business. Generally, this decision is based on tax, business, and legal considerations. Five entities are available:

1. Sole proprietorship
2. General partnership
3. Limited partnership
4. Corporation
5. S corporation

The choice of a particular entity is not cast in stone. A firm should examine which entity is more favorable as circumstances, including legal environments, shift. For example, the Tax Reform Act of 1986 initiated the most sweeping changes in the income tax system in decades. As a result, top corporate tax rates are now higher than the top individual rates. Therefore, many closely held hospitality corporations may want to consider changing to the S corporation entity to take advantage of the lower individual tax rates. This is only one example of how changing circumstances can affect the choice of business entity in the hospitality industry.

Tax Considerations

When choosing a type of business entity, owners of hospitality properties should select the one that will best fit into their overall tax planning strategies. Usually, property owners will understand how they want their businesses structured for operational purposes. However, they usually have very little understanding of the different types of business entities available. Hospitality owners usually engage an attorney or accountant knowledgeable in tax law to explain the various options. For instance, owners of new hospitality properties may wish to select the S corporation as their initial business entity because most new businesses lose money at the beginning of operations. In the S corporation, owners can reflect these losses immediately in their individual income tax returns (Form 1040). In the regular corporation, owners cannot take advantage of these losses so soon and are forced to carry them forward until such time as the corporation shows a profit. Thus, the hospitality owner can reduce current income tax liability by initially choosing the S corporation as his or her choice of operating entity.

The following brief tax issues show why the hospitality owner must give serious consideration to choosing a business entity. It should be noted that the degree of tax planning required when choosing a business entity would require a separate textbook for adequate explanation. However, these issues should forewarn anyone in the hospitality industry to seek expert tax advice when contemplating the choice of entity.

Reducing Tax Liability

An example of the principal of reducing the owner's overall tax liability is the double taxation problem of corporations. Here, income is first taxed at the corporation level and then taxed at the individual level when dividends are distributed to shareholders. This problem can be alleviated by compensating the shareholders in the form of bonuses. However, if this form of compensation is judged unreasonable (see Glossary for definition of *unreasonable compensation*) by the IRS, it will be treated as dividend income. This problem does not exist in the S corporation entity because income is passed directly to the shareholders and is taxed on the individual level only (a more detailed discussion of the S corporation follows).

Tax Structure for Investors

The choice of the correct entity is particularly important when a hospitality developer wishes to raise outside funding through investors. If a hospitality firm wishes to sell its stock to the public, the corporate form of doing business is the only choice possible. However, if the developer wishes to raise a smaller amount of money and still control the operation, he or she may want to use a different entity. For example, developers of single hotel projects traditionally have favored the limited partnership entity because it is flexible; it allows income and losses to be allocated between the general and limited partners. This flexibility is unavailable in the corporation or S corporation entities because income and losses are allocated in direct proportion to their stock ownership percentage (detailed discussion of special allocations for the limited partnership in section IV follows). However, the Tax Reform Act of 1986 (TRA) requires investors to also consider the impact of passive loss rules on the deductibility of losses incurred (see Chapter 3, "Key Tax Considerations in Hospitality Development," for a more detailed discussion).

Estate Planning

The choice of business entity also plays an important role in estate planning. The corporation, with stock as the medium, can easily be divided among heirs. This contrasts with outright ownership in a sole proprietorship or a partnership interest. Also, buy-sell agreements for stock purchase buyouts in the event of the untimely death of a key owner is much easier in the corporation than in the partnership entity.

Fringe Benefits

Congress has passed many amendments to the tax code in recent years to equalize benefits between various business entities (especially in the area of pension law). However, many fringe benefits still remain that are available only to corporations. For example, medical reimbursement plans are limited to corporations, as is the Group Life Insurance exclusion up to $50,000. Perhaps the biggest fringe benefit available only to corporate employees is the 401(k) plan. If adopted by a corporation, the 401(k) plan allows employees another way to put money away for retirement in addition to any pension plans. Most corporations match a portion of the employee's contribution to the plan. The 401(k) plan is used by many hospitality corporations as an additional way to retain and motivate employees.

Business and Legal Considerations

Tax considerations should not be the only basis for choosing the proper business entity for a hospitality property. There should also be sound business reasons. Many hospitality firms choose the corporate entity without any adequate cost-benefit analysis.

It is important for owners of hospitality properties to realize that a business entity may be changed in response to a changing business climate. There have been cases where many small hospitality properties having significant liquor revenue were suddenly unable to obtain liquor liability insurance or could obtain such insurance only at a very high cost. In response, many of these businesses decided to create a corporation, which under normal circumstances is treated as a separate entity under the law. Then, the owners placed only business assets in the corporation so that in the event of a lawsuit their personal assets would not be at risk.

Hospitality developers may want to consider five additional business and legal considerations:

1. Ways to limit the liability of the principal owners or investors
2. Ease of transferring ownership interest
3. Type of owners of the hospitality firm
4. Number of owners
5. Flexibility of adding or removing investors

We have examined just some of the reasons why an owner may select a certain type of business entity for conducting operations. One could probably think of additional reasons. However, the main point is that careful consideration is necessary in selecting a type of business entity because one form may not suit the business needs of the owner as well as another.

SOLE PROPRIETORSHIP

The easiest and most popular type of organization in the hospitality industry is the sole proprietorship. A "sole proprietorship" is usually defined as a business that is owned and operated by one person. Its popularity is due to the ease with which a hospitality owner can form it. To establish a sole proprietorship, the hospitality firm needs only to obtain whatever licenses are necessary and then begin operations. No formal paper work must be filed with any government agencies. The hospitality owner merely opens the door to the public and is then in business. Thus, the main benefit of the sole proprietorship is its simplicity.

There is no separate legal entity when one chooses the sole proprietorship form of business. The sole proprietor reports all business income and expenses on Schedule C of his or her individual federal income tax return (Form 1040). Those amounts are then combined with the taxpayer's other income and deductions. The net amount is then taxed. Similarly, tax credits and other special character items (e.g., dividends, contributions, and tax preferences) retain their character on the owner's individual return.

Currently, the highest tax rate is 28 percent for most individuals, while the top corporate rate is 34 percent for corporations. For the first time in many years, the top individual rate is lower than the top corporate rate. Therefore, smaller properties may wish to consider maintaining the sole proprietorship. However, when one compares the corporate rates with individual rates, the hospitality business that generates income less than $75,000 may still find the corporate form of doing business more advantageous.

The sole proprietorship also has an advantage of allowing the owner to employ his or her children under age 18 in the business, and bona fide wages paid to them are exempt from social security taxes. Recent tax legislation has removed the spouse from the social security tax exemption.

Although recent tax law changes have reduced some of the tax benefits for all entities, there still remain several areas in which a sole proprietorship is at a disadvantage. For example, tax-deductible payments up to $50,000 for group term life insurance coverage, without any income to the insured, is only available through a corporate entity. Also, fully tax-deductible payments for medical insurance premiums and medical expense reimbursement plans are more advantageous under the corporate entity. TRA now permits sole proprietors to deduct without limitations 25 percent of the amount they paid for health insurance for themselves, their spouses, and their dependents. The remaining 75 percent qualifies as a medical deduction (subject to the 7.5 percent limitation on adjusted gross income) on their individual tax returns.

A major disadvantage of using the sole proprietorship entity is the owner's unlimited liability for all the firm's debts. This unlimited liability extends to all the owner's assets, including house and automobile. Although this appears drastic, the proprietor usually is in no more peril than a small hospitality businessperson who incorporates. Many liability risks can be minimized by adequate insurance coverage. Also, even if the corporation entity is selected by the small hospitality firm, any lending institution will insist on the personal guarantee of the owner before lending the business any funds. Thus, as far as the threat of business failure is concerned, the corporation or sole proprietorship entities would result in the owner being held responsible for any loans made to the business.

GENERAL PARTNERSHIP

The Uniform Partnership Act (UPA) defines a general partnership as "an association of two or more persons to carry on as co-owners of a business for profit." Not every association between two parties is treated as a partnership. For instance, the mere existence of joint or part ownership of property does not establish a partnership. Regardless of whether the co-owners share the profits obtained from the use of the property, a business must be conducted. However, if persons who are not partners but who by their conduct lead others to *believe* that they are partners, and they rely on that belief to their disadvantage, then a partnership will be created by estoppel.

The UPA states that "proof that an individual shares in the profits of a business is prima facie evidence that he is a partner in the business, unless he receives the profits as payment of (1) a debt (installment or otherwise); (2) wages; (3) rent; (4) an annuity paid on behalf of a deceased partner; (5) interest on a loan (even though the amount of the payment varies with the profits of the business); or (6) consideration for the sale of the goodwill of a business or other property by installments or otherwise."

Although there is no requirement that a partnership must be specified in writing to be effective, it is advisable to spell out each partner's rights and obligations in a partnership agreement. Since all partnerships end at some point, it is recommended that there be not only a formal operating agreement between the partners but also a buy-sell agreement in case of the subsequent death, disability, or withdrawal from the partnership by any of the partners.

Although the partnership agreement should be tailored to the needs of the partners and the goals of the operation, the following guidelines will assist those contemplating forming a general partnership for a hospitality firm.

Name and Purpose of the Partnership

The partnership agreement should contain the name of the partnership and a statement of its general business purposes. The agreement should also specify any licenses that the partnership must obtain before business may commence. Also, the partnership agreement must specify whether the partnership is to continue for a specified number of years or exist at the will of the partners.

Contributions by the Partners to the Partnership

Contributions to a partnership can take the form of cash, property, and/or services. The partnership agreement must reflect the value to be credited to each partner for his or her contributions. The individual partners also must consider the tax basis of their partnership interest in any property they contribute because it will more than likely differ from the basis credited by the partnership. Services contributed may result in a taxable transaction, and the partner will have to consider its impact upon his or her individual tax situation.

Dividing Partnership Profit and Losses

One of the most flexible characteristics of the general partnership concerns the sharing of profits and losses. Generally, the partners share income and losses in proportion to their ownership interests in the partnership. However, partnerships may specifically allocate income and losses among partners as long as they have economic substance as defined in the Internal Revenue Regulations. An example of economic substance is when one partners contributes only his or her services while another contributes equipment. The partnership agreement may provide for the partner contributing the equipment to receive the depreciation expense.

Operating the Hospitality Firm

Unless provided for in the partnership agreement, all partners have an equal voice concerning management of the hospitality firm. It should be recognized that this can create conflict among the partners and also have a demoralizing effect upon the employees. The partners' duties and areas of responsibility should be spelled out. Also, each partner has the implicit right to bind the partnership if the transaction is one that an outsider would consider to be in the ordinary course of the partnership's business. The partnership agreement should clearly specify who is to represent the partnership in day-to-day operations and who is authorized to bind the partnership.

Withdrawal From the Partnership

Planning is extremely important when preparing for the voluntary or involuntary withdrawal by a partner. The partnership agreement should spell out in detail how a partner's interest is to be terminated. Because partnership interests usually are not very marketable to outsiders, how a partner's interest is to be evaluated should be spelled out in the agreement.

Salaries and Other Payments to Partners for Services Rendered

Generally, unless the partnership agreement provides for payment of services, a partner is not entitled to payment for those services. A salary paid to a partner is a deductible expense of the partnership and additional compensation to the partner receiving the payment.

Withdrawal of Partnership Income and Capital

The partnership agreement should establish when sufficient funds are available for withdrawal for the partner's personal use. It should also delineate procedures for withdrawing profits and/or capital from the partnership as well as the maximum percentages allowed. The agreement may also allow for withdrawals for specific purposes, such as a partner's proportioned tax burden due on his or her share of the partnership income.

Indemnification of Partner Payments Made on Behalf of the Partnership

The partnership agreement should allow for indemnifying the partners for legitimate payments made to others on behalf of the partnership.

Miscellaneous Provisions

Many additional provisions should be added to a partnership agreement simply to avoid disagreements among the individuals involved. For instance, property purchased with partnership funds will be considered partnership property unless written proof to the contrary is provided. Also, the agreement should require all partners to report any transactions relating to the partnership.

Advantages and Disadvantages

The chief advantage of the general partnership entity is its flexible structure both in terms of duties and obligations and financial allocations to the individual partners.

The partnership agreement can be structured to assign duties among the individual partners according to their expertise. Although the duties of the partnership are spelled out, the partners can decide independently on the voting rights of each partner. For example, in a partnership formed to operate a restaurant, one partner could be assigned managing day-to-day operations while another partner, better adapted to marketing, could be responsible for that area.

Flexibility in financial structuring is another major advantage of the general partnership. This flexibility could include permitting partners who contribute property to the partnership to receive the depreciation expense from those assets. Also, the arrangement of payments to each partner could vary in structure.

However, certain disadvantages make the general partnership inappropriate in some situations. The most common problem with this entity is that each partner has unlimited liability for partnership liabilities. A general partner is jointly and severally liable for all debts of the partnership. Thus, if a general partner is unable to pay his or her share of liabilities, creditors can seek payment from the other partners.

This fact, along with the right of active participation in management decisions by all general partners, makes the general partnership most suited for a small group of individuals who can work well together. The individual partners have the power to bind the partnership with outside contractors who, in the ordinary course of business, would assume that the partner who does the contracting has the authority to bind the partnership. Thus, remaining partners may have to pay for goods or services contracted by a partner.

One problem with any small business entity, and especially the general partnership, is the difficulty in selling one partner's interest. It is a well-established rule of law that no partner can transfer his or her interest and make the transferee a partner without the consent of the other partners. However, it is permissible to assign one's interest in the partnership's profits. The assignee, however, may not participate in the business of the partnership or vote in partnership matters.

Another potential disadvantage of the general partnership is the ease with which the partnership may be terminated. Generally, a partnership will be dissolved at the end of its specified term or upon the completion of a specified undertaking. The partnership can also be dissolved if one partner decides to terminate the partnership (unless prohibited in the partnership agreement) when all partners agree to do so or upon the expulsion of a partner pursuant to the terms of the partnership agreement.

If the partnership violates the partnership agreement, a partner can cause the entity to dissolve. Also, death, bankruptcy, or mental incapacity of a partner can result in the partnership's dissolution.

Tax Implications

The general partnership is treated as the sole proprietorship in that each partner reports his or her share of income or loss on his or her individual tax returns. Although the partnership is not a taxable entity for federal income tax purposes, it is a reporting entity, and Form 1065 must be filed to show overall income and loss.

Partnership income or losses will be allocable to each partner for the portion of the year in which the partner was a member of the partnership. A partner's share of income and losses can be allocated on a daily basis. Therefore, it is important to keep detailed records of when partners enter into the partnership.

Contributions by Partners

Generally, any property contributed by a partner to a partnership will not result in a taxable event for that partner. If a partner's only contribution consists of services rendered, he or she will be taxed on the fair market value of those services. The basis to the partnership from property contributed by the partners will be the same as if in the hands of the partner contributing the property. For example, if one partner contributes land for a hotel that originally cost him $125,000 but today is appraised at $275,000, the partnership would show $125,000 as the basis for the land for tax purposes on the partnership records. The contributing partner receives credit from the other partners for the appraised value of the property ($275,000), and the partnership's allocations of income and losses reflect the appraised value of the property.

There may be tax consequences to the partner who contributes property if the property is encumbered by debt that is assumed by the partnership. Any debt on property contributed by a partner reduces the basis of the property contributed. Thus, if property has a basis of $100,000 in the hands of the partner but is encumbered by a $30,000 mortgage, the partner's basis in the partnership is $70,000 ($100,000 minus the $30,000 mortgage assumed by the partnership). If the debt exceeds the adjusted basis of the property, the amount of the indebtedness that reduces the balance below zero results in a taxable gain to that partner.

It is very important to realize that a partner cannot deduct losses from a partnership in excess of his or her basis in the partnership. Basis is determined by the money, the partner's adjusted basis in property contributed, and recourse indebtedness of the partnership. A partner can increase his or her basis by making additional contributions before the end of the partnership tax year.

Basis is also reduced when cash distributions for the year exceed the taxable income of the partnership. If the basis of the partner has already been reduced to zero, the partner will have capital gain income for the amounts received.

Special Allocations of Partnership Income, Losses, and Credits

As previously mentioned, a partnership may make special allocations among partners for income, loss, and credits if the allocations are found to have economic substance. If an allocation is found to lack economic substance, the items specifically allocated will need to be reallocated on the same basis as the partner's interest in the partnership as a whole.

Economic substance will be determined from the facts at the time the transaction was entered into. The IRS will closely examine the facts to determine whether the only purpose for the special allocation was tax avoidance or evasion. Some of the criteria used by the IRS to determine whether there is economic substance include:

- Is there a business purpose for the allocation?
- Are related items subject to the same allocation?

- Is the allocation for a limited time?
- Was the allocation made only after its amount was ascertainable or could reasonably be estimated?

Sale or Exchange of Partnership Interests

When a partner sells or exchanges his or her interest in the partnership, a capital gain or loss is realized. This is measured by the difference between the amount realized from the transaction and the adjusted basis of the partnership interest, except to the extent that the proceeds of the transaction are attributable to this pro rata share of unrealized receivables or substantially appreciated inventory. The last condition is almost never a problem for a hospitality firm.

The initial basis of a partnership interest acquired by contribution is the sum of the money contributed plus the contributor's adjusted basis in any property contributed. When the partnership interest is acquired with the performance of services, the initial basis of the interest includes the amount of taxable income realized by the performer in connection with the receipt of the interest.

A partner's initial basis or partnership interest is increased by is or her distributive share of partnership taxable income and partnership tax-exempt income. The adjusted basis of a partner who makes additional contributions is increased by the amount of cash contributed to his or her adjusted basis for any property contributed.

A partner's basis for partnership interest is decreased (but not below zero) by three elements: (1) the amount of cash distributed to him or her; (2) the basis of any property distributed by the partnership; and (3) his or her share of partnership losses and nondeductible expenditures of the partnership not property chargeable to capital account.

LIMITED PARTNERSHIP

One of the most flexible forms of raising capital for a hotel or restaurant has been the limited partnership. This entity allows those (general partners) who wish to develop a hospitality project to be matched with the money sources (limited partners). The general partners are liable for the debts and obligations of the partnership, and the limited partners are at risk only for the amount of their contributions committed to the limited partnership.

To maintain limited partner status, an individual must refrain from participating in the management of the hospitality firm. For this restriction, the advantage is that the limited partner can only lose equity investment in the partnership.

This entity is defined by the Uniform Limited Partnership Act (ULPA) as having at least one general partner and at least one limited partner. Unlike the general partnership, the limited partnership must have a written partnership agreement. In addition, a certificate of limited partnership must be filed with the appropriate state agency. This certificate must contain the names and residential addresses of all the general and limited partners. Summary information from the limited partnership agreement is also required for the certificate. The certificate must be amended when there are changes in the partnership agreement or among the partners.

The advantages and disadvantages discussed in the general partnership section also apply to the limited partnership entity. Note that a general partner can also be a limited partner in the same business. However, this individual is treated as a general partner and receives no particular advantages over the limited partner other than being an additional investor in the project.

Status of Limited Partners

Unless stated in the partnership agreement, all limited partners are treated on an equal basis for sharing income, losses, and cash distributions in proportion to their ownership percentages.

Generally, limited partners cannot bind the partnership in any business transactions. The limited partner, if he or she indeed acts like a general partner, can be held liable to the partnership for such acts and may be reclassified as a general partner. Also, a limited partner is liable to outside creditors for contributions promised to the partnership. Creditors may also require that the limited partner return any distributions plus interest on amounts received by the limited partner as a return on contributions for creditors who had claims prior to the return of capital.

Unlike the general partners, the death of a limited partner will not result in the dissolution of the limited partnership. This is a practical rule because the limited partners are usually considered investors rather than active participants. The personal representative of the deceased limited partner steps in and assumes all the rights and obligations of the deceased, including liability for any outstanding contribution commitments.

The limited partner may, like the general partner, assign his or her right to receive profits, income, or return of contributions to someone else. If the partnership agreement provides or if the other partners agree, a limited partner can name another person as a substitute limited partner. In this event, the substitute limited partner will have all the rights and liabilities of the assignor. However, the assignor is not released from any liabilities owed to the partnership.

Under the ULPA, the limited partner is entitled to the following without being held to be a general partner:

- Inspect the partnership books at the partnership's place of business.
- Obtain an accounting of partnership affairs.
- Have the partnership dissolved and wound up by a court decree.
- Share in the partnership profits and income.
- Receive and return his or her contributions.

The more active the limited partner is in the partnership, the greater the likelihood that he or she will be considered a general partner by a court of law.

This limited involvement does not preclude the limited partner from transacting business or making loans to the partnership. However, the limited partner may be deemed to have committed a fraud on other creditors if he or she receives or holds property of the partnership as collateral. Also, under the ULPA, the limited partner is prevented from receiving payments on any obligations if at the time of payment the assets of the partnership are insufficient to discharge all liabilities to nonpartners.

Tax Considerations

Like the general partnership, the limited partnership is treated as a business entity form. The latter is a conduit through which general and limited partners report their share of profits, losses, and credits on their individual Form 1040.

Although the tax implications discussed in the partnership section apply to limited partnership returns, several considerations are more applicable to limited partnerships than general partnerships. The first consideration is whether the limited partnership is a true partnership or merely a disguised corporation. For years, the IRS has required that a limited partnership *not* meet more than two of the following criteria in order not to be treated as a corporation.

- *Continuity of life.* The absence of the entity's continuity of life points to a partnership, not a corporation. This test is met easily if a limited partnership agreement specifically limits the term of the partnership or states that the partnership will dissolve upon the death, disability, or insanity of a general partner.
- *Centralized management.* If centralized management is present, the character of the entity is more like that of a corporation. Since a limited partnership is by necessity run by the general partners and the majority of ownership interest lies in the limited partners, the management will necessarily by centralized. Thus, this test is likely to hold that the partnership more closely resembles a corporation.
- *Limited liability.* Generally, if the general partners have substantial assets or are personally liable for the nonrecourse debts of the partnership, the entity will be treated as a partnership, not a corporation. Because almost all general partners in a hospitality syndication have substantial assets, this test will not be met. Thus the entity will be treated as a partnership.
- *Free transferability of interests.* A common provision in most limited partnership agreements requires permission from the general partners before ownership interest can be transfered to a substituted limited partner. The mere right to assign rights to profits in a limited partnership should not be considered a free transferability of interest.

Because most limited partnerships fail to meet three of these four tests, partnership treatment can reasonably be assured under current IRS rules.

Another planning opportunity often used with the limited partnership entity is the inclusion of a corporate entity as the general partner. The use of the corporation is obvious, since the limited liability of the corporation, along with the limited liability of the limited partners, would make no individual fully liable for the partnership debts. The IRS has published several guidelines by which it recognizes the corporate general partner as having substantial assets in order to fail the limited liability test. The two-part test is as follows.

1. *Net worth requirements.* If the total contributions to the partnership are less than $2.5 million, then at all times during the life of the partnership the corporate general partner must have net assets equal to 15 percent of the total contributions or $250,000, whichever is less. If the total

contributions are $2.5 million or more, the corporate general partner must have net assets equal to 10 percent of total contributions.

2. *Ownership requirements.* The limited partners in the partnership cannot directly or indirectly own more than 20 percent of the stock of the sole corporate general partner.

One major concern for a limited partnership is that it not be considered formed merely for the purpose of reducing federal taxes and with no economic substance. Revenue Procedure 74-17 states the guidelines for determining whether the IRS will issue a letter ruling stating that the partnership is not formed solely to evade taxes. If the tests are not met, the taxpayer still can argue that the business aspect of the partnership is valid. However, the IRS will not issue a letter ruling (in effect, giving its blessing).

The IRS guidelines contained in Revenue Procedure 74-17 are as follows.

- All the general partners, in the aggregate, must have at least 1 percent interest in each material item of partnership income, gain, loss, deduction, or credit.
- The aggregate deduction of the limited partners during the first two years of the partnership's operations cannot exceed the amount of the equity investment in the partnership.
- No creditor who makes a nonrecourse loan to the partnership may acquire, as a result of having made the loan, any direct or indirect interest in the profits, capital, or property of the limited partnership, other than as a secured creditor.

With the passage of the Tax Reform Act of 1986, the investor was limited as to deductions he or she can claim. In almost all cases, losses are considered "passive" deductible only against other passive-type income of other limited partnerships, or they are deferred until the limited partnership generates income of its own or is sold. For a more in-depth discussion of passive loss rules, see Chapter 3—"Key Tax Considerations in Hospitality Development."

Use in Syndications

Probably one of the most popular forms of raising capital is through the syndicated limited partnership. This is especially true for hotel projects. For instance, Marriott's Courtyard is almost totally funded through limited partnerships. Although the syndication form saw its apex prior to the TRA, which limited deductions from hospitality limited partnerships, it still represents an effective method of raising capital for a hotel and, to a lesser extent, restaurant projects. For a detailed discussion of this topic, see Chapter 7—"Raising Capital."

CORPORATIONS

The corporation is the most complicated form of business; the sole proprietorship is the simplest.

Created by law, a corporation is generally recognized as a separate legal entity independent of its owners (shareholders). This provision allows the corporate entity to be liable for all debts and obligations, and the shareholders are liable only for their investments. However, this provision may be of little comfort to a smaller hospitality firm because lenders often insist upon personal guarantees when making loans to a corporate entity.

Because it is a separate legal entity, the corporate entity may:

- Engage in lawsuits in its own name as well as be sued in its own name.
- Own property in its own name.
- Maintain perpetual life unless dissolved by law or statutory limitations.
- Engage only in acts given to it within the scope of the powers expressly or impliedly granted under its state charter of certificate of incorporation.
- Raise money on its own through the issuance of stock, debt, bonds, or other securities.

Tax Consequences

Because the corporation is a separate legal entity, it is also taxed separately. See Exhibit 2-1 below to determine the tax rates for a regular corporation.

Although the top taxable rate for corporations exceeds that for individuals, lower-income hospitality firms still have a tax rate advantage if they are corporate entities. A corporation's income must exceed $75,000 to be taxed at the top rate, while an individual filing a joint return with his or her spouse would be in the 28-percent bracket on taxable income in excess of $29,750. Therefore, the corporate entity may be more efficient for accumulating funds for future expansion of smaller hospitality firms.

One disadvantage of the corporate form is that the same earnings are taxed twice: once for the corporation and again in dividends when they are distributed to the shareholders. To a certain extent, the double tax on corporate earnings can be avoided if payments can be made to shareholder-employees as deductible expenses (e.g., in the form of salaries). It is important that salaries not be excessive as defined by the IRS, or they will be treated as dividend payments. Also, to the extent that the regular corporation can justify the accumulation of earnings under Section 531 of the Internal Revenue Code, the double-tax problem can be postponed. However, as earnings increase, it becomes more difficult to remove them from the regular corporation without the double-tax problem. At this point, the owner of a closely held corporation may wish to consider switching to an S corporation entity.

If the decision to incorporate is made, closely held corporate shareholders will want to be able to deduct the investment losses as ordinary losses rather than as capital losses with their annual limitation of $3,000 per year if the venture fails. This can be accomplished by making certain that the

EXHIBIT 2-1
Corporate Income Tax Rates

Taxable Income	Tax Rate
Less than $50,000	15%
More than $50,000 but less than $75,000	25%
More than $75,000	34%

stock qualifies under Section 1244 of the Internal Revenue Code as small business stock so that any losses up to $100,000 (on a joint return) can be treated by shareholders as an ordinary loss.

Advantages and Disadvantages

The main advantage often claimed for the corporate entity is its limited liability. However, as previously mentioned, most hospitality firms can obtain insurance to cover most cases of liability. Also, lending institutions are often reluctant to make a loan to a corporate entity without the personal guarantees of the individual shareholders in closely held corporations.

As noted, many smaller hospitality establishments that are unable to obtain liquor liability insurance have incorporated in an attempt to limit their liability. Although it is debatable whether this technique is successful, the debate does raise the question of when a corporation will be recognized for legal purposes. Generally, in a lawsuit involving a closely held corporation, a plaintiff will attempt to show that the corporation is really a sham and that the shareholders/owner should be held personally liable for the debts of the corporation. This is what is known as "piercing the corporation veil."

No set formula can ensure that the corporate entity will not be disregarded, but certain steps can be taken in the ordinary course of business to demonstrate that the corporation is considered a separate entity by its shareholders rather than a mere instrument or alter ego of the shareholders. Shareholders should try to comply with the following steps as much as possible to demonstrate that the corporation and its shareholders are truly separate.

- Loans and other financial transactions between the corporation and its shareholders should be properly documented.
- The corporation should not deal exclusively with its shareholders.
- Third parties should realize that they are dealing with the corporation and not the individual owners.
- The corporation should maintain its own financial books and records and not comingle them with the personal records of the shareholders.
- The corporation should observe all corporate formalities and maintain corporate records.
- All equipment and other property of the corporation should be separated from the property of its shareholders.

Because the shares of a corporation are more freely transferable (unless restricted by the corporate by-laws) than those of a partnership interest, there is a tendency to favor the corporate entity when there is a desire to raise additional capital or change shareholders through the issue of stock.

The major disadvantage of using a corporation to own a hospitality firm is that the corporation is recognized as a separate entity for tax purposes. Thus, tax losses from corporate-owned hospitality firms may not be passed through to the shareholders, but can only be used by the corporation. If the corporation has no prior earnings, the losses can only be carried forward for up to 15 years.

Because of the complexity of establishing a corporation, an attorney is usually needed to draft the proper forms for incorporation. Also, there are additional expenses for filing annual reports with various state and local governments, for maintaining separate accounting records, for filing separate tax returns, and for maintaining certain corporate records (e.g., corporate minutes).

THE S CORPORATION

The Tax Reform Act of 1986 has had a significant effect on the hospitality industry, making the S corporation a very attractive operating entity for many hospitality firms.

An S corporation is a form of business entity that combines many of the tax advantages of partnerships with the legal attributes of a corporation, including limited liability for its shareholders. Its name is obtained fom a subchapter of the Internal Revenue Code. Except for tax purposes, the S corporation is treated in the same manner as any regular corporation. As with a partnership, however, income and losses for an S corporation are generally passed through directly to shareholders for inclusion on their individual tax returns. An S corporation thus avoids the double-tax problem facing regular corporations.

In order to qualify as an S corporation, a hospitality firm has to meet the following four criteria.

1. The corporation may not have more than 35 shareholders. (A married couple filing a joint return is counted as one shareholder.)
2. All shareholders must be U.S. citizens or residents, and they must be natural persons, estates, or certain types of trusts.
3. The corporation may have only one class of stock outstanding. (However, different voting rights are permitted for different shares of stock.)
4. The corporation may not own 80 percent or more of the stock of any other corporation.

If a hospitality firm can meet the above requirements, the S election can be made by filing Form 2553 with the IRS. Once an S election has been submitted, it is effective January 1 of the year it was filed if it was submitted before the 15th day of the third month of the corporation's taxable year. Otherwise, the election takes effect January 1 of the next taxable year.

After a valid election has been made, it remains in effect until revoked or terminated. An S election can be revoked only by a majority vote of shareholders. Once the election is terminated or revoked, a new election cannot be made for five years without the consent of the IRS. The IRS has ruled, however, that a corporation that revoked its S election prior to enactment of the TRA may make a new election at any time.

Advantages and Disadvantages

The main advantage of the S corporation is the avoidance of the double-tax problem of a regular corporation. As we have seen, regular corporations are taxed once at the corporate level and again at the shareholder level when income is distributed to shareholders in the form of dividends. Almost all closely held corporations initially avoid the problem by paying any excess earnings to the shareholders-employees in the form of additional compensation (usually year-end bonuses). However, a time will come when the compensation may exceed the amount that can be deemed reasonable. Any compensation that exceeds a reasonable amount will be treated as a constructive dividend for income tax purposes. Because a constructive dividend is a nondeductible item for income tax purposes, the double-tax situation would apply.

Under these circumstances, the S corporation can be a very valuable tool. Because the S corporation generally is not subject to any corporate taxes, it usually makes no difference whether distributions to shareholders of S corporations are characterized as compensation or dividends.

A regular corporation can avoid the double-tax problem by accumulating earnings within the corporation and thus avoid paying any dividends. This has often been an effective tool for corporations to accumulate money in anticipation of expansion. However, Congress prevents any accumulation of excess funds by imposition of the "accumulated earnings tax," which penalizes corporations that fail to distribute earnings not needed for the conduct of business operations. Since the S corporation passes all income and losses directly to its shareholders, an accumulated earnings tax would never be imposed on an S corporation.

Perhaps the most important reason to consider the S corporation is the downward revision of tax rates for both individuals and corporations. The TRA has lowered to 28 percent the maximum tax rate for most individuals. The real rate can go as high as 33 percent (a maximum rate of 28 percent with a 5 percent surcharge for taxable income between $71,900 and $149,250 for a joint filer and between $43,150 and $89,560 for a single filer). The maximum tax for corporations is 34 percent, but there is a 5 percent surcharge on taxable income between $100,000 and $335,000. For the first time in more than 50 years, the maximum tax rate for corporations is higher than the maximum rate for individuals.

Here is an example of how an S corporation can save on taxes to a greater degree than a corporation:

> In 1988, a restaurant with a sole shareholder (a joint filer with four dependents) generated $300,000 in taxable income. Taxes at the regular corporate rate were $100,250 ($22,250 on the first $100,000 and 39 percent on the remaining $200,000, following the Corporate Tax Tables for 1988). An individual's tax on the same $300,000 was $86,184 (28 percent of $300,000 plus 28 percent of $7,800 personal exemptions using the Individual Tax Tables for 1988). Thus, if this restaurant were organized as an S corporation, it saved $14,066 in taxes. (NOTE: Because this example is only intended to show the tax advantages of an S corporation, it ignores the issues of itemized deductions or other income.)

However, regular corporations are subject to only a 15 percent rate on taxable income on their first $50,000, and a 25 percent rate on taxable income between $50,000 and $75,000. Therefore, the regular corporate form of doing business may result in overall less tax than the S corporation for hospitality firms that do not generate a great deal of taxable income.

Another appreciable planning device for the S corporation is the start-up hospitality firm. Because losses are passed to shareholders in the same manner as income, start-up hospitality firm shareholders who are active in the business can generally benefit from the initial start-up losses usually incurred in new ventures. With regular corporations, such losses can only be used to offset prior or future corporate income. By electing S status at the very beginning, shareholders who are active in the business can claim business losses on their individual returns. (Of course, this assumes that the shareholders have sufficient income from other sources that utilize the losses generated by the S corporation.) After the corporation becomes profitable, the new venture may wish to consider revoking the S corporation entity, depending on anticipated income tax liability from operating as a regular corporation or an S corporation.

For shareholders who do not materially participate in the business, business losses will be deemed passive losses that can only be offset against passive income (subject to a five-year phase-in rule in certain cases under the TRA). Disallowed losses are carried forward to future years and are generally allowed in full when the corporation generates income or when the S corporation entity is revoked. Disallowed losses are also allowed in full when the shareholder disposes of his or her stock in a taxable transaction with an unrelated party.

As part of the TRA, Congress added a new corporate alternative minimum tax to replace the old add-on minimum tax. The application of this tax is similar to the individual alternative minimum tax that has been in effect for a number of years. What makes the new corporate minimum tax so troublesome is the so-called "book income" adjustment. Under the "book income" adjustment, corporations will now have to include in their alternative minimum tax calculations one-half of the amount by which their book income, as shown on their financial statements, exceeds their taxable income. This expanded concept of minimum tax means that more corporations will be subject to the alternative minimum tax. An S corporation is exempt from the alternative minimum tax rules (see Chapter 3—"Key Tax Considerations in Hospitality Development).

One of the important uses of an S corporation is the ability to shift income within the family unit to take advantage of the marginal tax brackets of different family members. This is usually accomplished by giving minority interest in the S corporation to family members (usually children of the principal shareholders). In the S corporation, family members can be treated as shareholders of the corporation. However, the IRS has the authority to reallocate income for failure to reasonably compensate shareholders (or their family members) for services or capital provided to the corporation.

The biggest disadvantage of the S corporation is the limitation of an S corporation to 35 shareholders, which may limit the corporation's future ability to acquire equity financing. Also, there are limits as to who may own stock in an S corporation. A corporation is ineligible to file an S election if any of the stock is owned by a partnership, another corporation, or any trust other than one of the specifically designated trusts.

The shareholder-employee of a regular corporation may receive tax-favored fringe benefits such as medical expense reimbursement, disability insurance, and group-term life insurance. On the other hand, an S corporation shareholder-employee may not. A "shareholder-employee" is defined as an employee or an officer of an S corporation who owns more than 5 percent of the out-standing stock.

Shareholders may deduct their pro rata share of an S corporation's losses and deductions on a per-share, per-day basis, but only to the extent of the total of their adjusted basis in the S corporation's stock and the adjusted basis in any indebtedness of the S corporation to them. Losses and deductions must be applied first to reduce stock basis; amounts exceeding stock basis are then applied to reduce debt basis. A shareholder is limited for loss allocation purposes to the adjusted basis of stock in the corporation, increased by the adjusted basis of direct loans advanced to the S corporation by the particular shareholder. (A shareholder's guarantee of third-party debt does not increase the shareholder's debt.) Restoration of basis is then applied first to the shareholder's post 1982 indebtedness and then to stock basis. If a debt is repaid before the debt basis is restored, the shareholder has a gain. The gain is treated as ordinary income if the debt is an open account. However, gain on debt evidenced by a bond or note is capital gain.

Comparison With Limited Partnerships

Although the S corporation has often been publicized as the equivalent of the limited partnership, the latter is more flexible than the S corporation. For instance, the limited partnership may specifically allocate income and loss amounts to the partners providing economic substance to the transaction. The S corporation must allocate income and losses to each shareholder in direct proportion to their percentages of stock ownership in the hospitality firm.

Also, the limited partnership can have any number of limited partners, while the S corporation is limited to 35 shareholders.

Passive loss rules may limit the deductions of the limited partnership, and they also apply to the S corporation. In addition, shareholders in the S corporation cannot increase their basis for their stock by a share of the corporation's mortgage liability for which they are not personally liable. In the case of a partnership, the loss equals the partner's investment in the partnership plus his or her allocable share of certain types of mortgage liability, even though the partner is not personally liable for the mortgage obligation. For this reason, the use of the S corporation entity may substantially limit the pass-through of losses and probably would not be chosen over a partnership entity where a hospitality firm is substantially leveraged with outside financing.

SUMMARY

The form of business entity selected by the hospitality firm will have a major impact on economic as well as tax planning opportunities. The sole proprietorship is the simplest method of doing business and is appropriate for the small hospitality entrepreneur because of its simplicity and that income is taxed directly on individual tax returns. The disadvantages are that it is inadequate if there are any partners or if the owner wishes to take advantage of certain fringe benefits that are only offered to corporations. If the single hospitality owner wishes to expand operations to more than one operation, he or she will want to seriously consider forming separate corporations for each location.

The general partnership can be similar to the sole proprietorship, except when there is more than one owner. A general partnership can be structured very simply, without any written agreement (although this is never recommended). The main advantage of the general partnership are its flexibility in allocating income, losses, contributions, and deductions among the various partners. The partnership agreement can be structured so that the responsibilities of the various partners is clearly spelled out to avoid confusion and disagreements. The big disadvantage of the general partnership is that individual partners have the authority to bind the other partners when acting on behalf of the partnership with firms that do business with the partnership.

The limited partnership derives its name from the fact that investors are not liable for debts of the partnership beyond their contributions if they agree not to be involved in the management of the hospitality business. This form of business entity has been one of the most popular methods of financing hospitality projects. The flexibility in how income and losses can be allocated to the individual partners is why this form of doing business is preferable to the corporate form of business, which also offers its shareholders limited liability.

The corporate business entity form is a separate legal entity. This makes the corporate entity separate from its owners (the shareholders). The corporate entity thus limits each shareholder's liability to the amount of equity invested. However, this is often more illusion than reality, especially since banks are likely to insist upon personal guarantees for any loans made to a start-up operation. Larger hospitality firms may be able to borrow money in the corporation's name, and thus the corporate form of business is more reasonable for this size of operation. Also, if the hospitality owner has more than one location, a separate corporation for each location may be a planning consideration until sufficient size is achieved to consolidate all the corporations into one company. The major disadvantage of the corporate form of doing business is that the corporation is treated as a separate business entity for tax purposes also. The corporation is taxed on its earnings, and then the shareholders are taxed on dividends distributed from the corporation. However, many closely held hospitality corporations can avoid the double taxation problem by paying out all earnings during the year as salary. The hospitality owners should be aware that any unreasonable compensation as defined by the IRS regulations could result in excess salary being treated as a dividend.

Since the passage of the TRA, the S corporation has received increased attention because corporate rates are now higher in certain circumstances than individual rates. The S corporation has the advantage of being treated as a corporation for all purposes except for tax purposes. The S corporation passes through all income and losses directly to the shareholders, much like a partnership, thus avoiding the double taxation problem of a regular corporation. There are a number of restrictions on the ability to qualify as S corporation. The most important is that not more 35 shareholders can own stock in the corporation. The S corporation is an excellent device for the new hospitality endeavour that wants the losses passed through to the shareholders' individual tax returns to offset income earned elsewhere. Also, if the hospitality corporation generates more income than it needs to accumulate, the S corporation is an excellent means of distributing income to shareholders and thus avoiding the double tax issue or the accumulated tax issues. Finally, shareholders of a corporation may find the lower individual rates more attractive than the higher corporate rate. The main disadvantages of the S corporation is the 35-shareholder limitation, that one class of stock is permitted, and that shareholders must be individuals except for certain trusts. Also, income and losses must be allocated according to the proportionate ownership interest of each shareholder, thus making the limited partnership more flexible in allocation of income and losses that could better reflect the economic realities of the various investments made by individuals.

The choice of business entity is a very important consideration for the hospitality owner. Careful planning maximizes both tax and legal aspects of operating a hospitality business in today's economy. See Exhibit 2-2 on page 38 for a summary of the various requirements for the business entities discussed.

EXHIBIT 2-2
Basic Factors in Selecting a Business Entity

	Sole Proprietor	Partnership	Limited Partnership	S Corporation	Corporate
Which tax rates apply	Individual	Individual	Individual	Individual	Corporate
Paperwork required	No organizational documents; no separate tax return	Partnership agreement desirable; separate tax return required	Partnership agreement required; separate tax return required	Incorporation papers; separate tax return	Incorporation papers; separate tax return
Allocation of income among owners	N/A	Possible	Possible	Must be in proportion to ownership share	Must be in proportion to ownership share
Character of losses in disposition of business	Ordinary or capital	Ordinary or capital	Ordinary or capital	Usually capital	Usually capital
Who may claim losses	Owner	Owners	Owners	Owners	Corporation
Character of gain at sale	Depends on assets sold	Depends on assets sold	Depends on assets sold	Usually capital	Usually capital

GLOSSARY

Basis   The value of property in the hands of the holder for tax purposes. Basis is usually the cost of the property. Basis is determined differently for gifts and inheritances.

Capital gain/loss   The gain or loss realized from the sale of capital assets. Capital assets include those used in the operation of a business, excluding inventory.

Closely held corporation   A corporation in which the stock is held by only a few stockholders. Usually found in corporations where family members hold the majority of stock.

Constructive dividend   A term used in tax law to describe when a taxpayer is deemed to have received a dividend even if an actual dividend was not declared. A constructive dividend is found when the IRS reclassifies compensation as a dividend because it has found the compensation to be unreasonable.

Corporation   A form of business that is owned by a group of individuals known as shareholders. The corporate form of doing business is granted the right to carry on business from the state in which it is located. It is considered a separate legal entity for both legal and tax purposes.

Cost-benefit analysis   An analysis conducted to determine whether the operation contemplated will be economically beneficial, given its economic cost.

Economic substance   An allocation of benefits in a partnership that has economic basis for the transaction other than for mere tax purposes.

Estoppel   A person who by his or her own actions has been prevented from asserting a claim against someone who has relied on such conduct and acted accordingly.

Form 1065   A tax form for partnership filings. This form is for reporting purposes only, as all income and credit allocations are reported on each partner's individual income tax Form 1040.

Form 2553   A tax form used as an election by shareholders to convert a corporation to a S corporation.

General partnership   A form of business where two or more persons carry on the business as co-owners for profit. The partners own all the assets and are personally responsible for the debts of the partnership.

Limited partnership   A form of business run by at least one general partner, who is personally responsible for the debt of the partnership, and that has as passive investors one or more individuals, known as limited partners. The limited partner is only liable for partnership debts up to the amount of his or her contribution to the partnership.

S corporation   A form of business that is considered a corporation for legal purposes but is treated differently from a corporation for tax purposes. Income and losses are passed through directly to shareholders (much like in a partnership), who then report such amounts on their individual income tax returns.

Small business stock   Stock that is held in a corporation and that meets the definition of small according to the Internal Revenue Code. The holder of small business stock is entitled to treat stock deemed worthless as ordinary loss and not as a capital loss.

Sole proprietorship   A form of business in which one person owns all the assets of the business. The sole proprietor is also responsible for the debt of the business.

Tax Reform Act of 1986 (TRA)   A comprehensive overhaul of the tax code signed into law in 1986. This act changed many of the established ways in which the income tax law is applied. Congress intended this law to tax individuals and corporations more fairly by lowering tax rates and by eliminating many tax deductions.

Uniform Limited Partnership Act (ULPA)   A uniform law that can be accepted by a state in its entirety or in part for the legal requirements in operating a business as a limited partnership.

Uniform Partnership Act (UPA)   A uniform law that can be accepted by a state in its entirety or in part for the legal requirements in operating a business as a general partnership.

Unlimited liability   A term used to describe an entity or person who is totally liable for debts of the business. For example, a sole proprietor is totally liable for any debts incurred by his or her business.

Unreasonable compensation   The Internal Revenue Code provides that compensation is deductible if it is reasonable. Reasonableness is determined on a case-by-case basis, and no one rule governs. One test used by the IRS is to compare a company's top executives' salaries with those paid other similar executives in the same type of business. Any compensation deemed excessive will be reclassified as a dividend, and is thus not deductible as compensation.

References

Tax Guide for Small Business, publication 334, IRS Tax Publication, 1989.

Tax Information on Partnerships, publication 541, IRS Tax Publication, 1989.

Tax Information of Corporations, publication 542, IRS Tax Publication, 1989.

Taxpayers Starting a Business, publication 583, IRS Tax Publication, 1989.

Tax Information on S Corporations, publication 589, IRS Tax Publication, 1989.

Tarras, John. "Effect of Fringe Benefits." *The Bottomline,* August, 1986, pp. 23–25.

Tarras, John. "Choosing a Business Entity: Part I." *Restaurant Management,* October 1987, pp. 26–27.

Tarras, John. "Choosing a Business Entity: Part II." *Restaurant Management,* December 1987, pp. 38–40.

Suggested Reading

Taxpayers Starting a Business, publication 583, IRS Tax Publication (1989).

Tarras, John. "Choosing a Business Entity: Part I." *Restaurant Management,* October 1987, pp. 26–27.

Tarras, John. "Choosing a Business Entity: Part II." *Restaurant Management,* December, 1987, pp. 38–40.

Chapter 3

Key Tax Considerations in Hospitality Development

INTRODUCTION

An important consideration in financing a hospitality property from either the developer's or the investor's point of view is the income tax ramifications of the financing techniques. Because tax consequences are very important in evaluating all types of financial returns, this discussion is included at this point in the book.

Federal income tax laws are very complicated and would require several volumes for an in-depth treatment. This chapter will discuss the major aspects of the more common tax problems facing hospitality owners. In addition, as specialized discussion is needed in subsequent chapters, tax laws that affect those chapters' topics will be discussed in those chapters as well.

The first section of this chapter covers depreciation rules. The change in the depreciation rate of new buildings from 19 years to 31½ years means that cash flow will be reduced as hospitality firms recover the cost of new buildings over a longer period of time. Some provisions that the hospitality industry took for granted have been eliminated under the Tax Reform Act of 1986 (TRA). Some tax benefits have been changed so that the investor or developer will have to evaluate these benefits' usefulness under new guidelines. For example, the Rehabilitation Credit now applies only to buildings constructed before 1936 instead of some credit for buildings that were only 30 years old under prior law.

These and other changes require that the investor or developer scrutinize the tax law carefully for opportunities to reduce their tax outlays.

One of the most comprehensive tax reform pieces of legislation ever enacted into law has dramatically changed the economics of how the hospitality industry will perform. TRA has virtually rewritten the tax code as it relates to the hospitality industry.

Congress attempted to make the tax law fairer, not simpler, when it passed the new code. Whether this code is fairer remains to be seen, but owners and managers have to cope today with the complex changes. This chapter concentrates on those aspects of tax law that most directly affect the hospitality industry.

DEPRECIATION RULES

When Congress slashed corporate and individual tax rates under TRA, it had to find a way to replace some of the lost tax revenues. To accomplish that, Congress overhauled the depreciation rules by increasing the length of time assets can be written off. As with many provisions under TRA, changes made by tax reform complicated a relatively simple system.

Many hospitality firms are still developing new properties, and these firms will be the big losers under the new modified accelerated cost recovery system (MACRS). Both residential and nonresidential real property must be depreciated using the straight line method. For nonresidential real property, the length of depreciation has been increased from 19 years to 31½ years, while the residential real property period has been extended to 27½ years.

In determining MACRS depreciation deductions for the tax year in which business property was placed in service, the mid-month convention must be used as under previous law. Under the mid-month convention, real property is treated as having been placed in service in the middle of the month regardless of what time is was actually placed in service. The same rule also holds for dispositions and sales of real property.

To illustrate the severity of the effect the depreciation rules will have on the hospitality industry, assume that it cost $15 million to build a hotel on January 1, 1989. Under the old ACRS rules, the first-year depreciation using the most generous deduction available would be $1.32 million using the accelerated cost recovery system (ACRS) table. Under MACRS, the same property would generate only a $456,200 depreciation deduction using the mid-month convention method. (See Appendix 2 for the IRS depreciation tables for real property and find the applicable percentage of 8.8 percent for ACRS and 3.042 percent for MACRS under column 1 for the first month the asset was placed in service.)

Alternatively, the new rules also provide that a taxpayer may elect to depreciate his or her property over a 40-year period using the straight line and mid-month conventions.

New rules concerning the writeoff of leasehold improvements will significantly affect the hospitality industry. Under the old ACRS rules, a lessee was to determine ACRS depreciation for leasehold improvements by taking into consideration the length of the lease. Under the TRA, the lessee is considered the owner for MACRS deductions. This means that the cost of leasehold improvements is recovered using the applicable ACRS recovery period. When the lease terminates, any remaining basis of the unamortized leasehold improvements can then be utilized. Any amortization of lease acquisition costs still are deductible over the life of the lease. However, if the lease contains renewal options that are likely to be exercised, then the amortization period will include the option period in most cases. For example, suppose a tenant leases a building for a restaurant. The tenant makes substantial internal improvements to the property classifiable as real property. The lease term is 15 years. The tenant must depreciate the improvements over a 31½ year basis. When the lease expires in the 15th year, the tenant can then write off the remaining basis of the improvements.

The number of cost categories under TRA have been expanded to six classes for personal property.

Depreciable assets for property in the 3-, 5-, 7-, and 10-year categories cannot be written off using the more favorable 200-percent declining balance method with an automatic switch to the straight line method to maximize the deduction rather than using the 150-percent method under prior law.

MACRS Property and Period
3-year property
5-year property
7-year property
10-year property
15-year property
20-year property

The depreciation method for 15-year and 20-year properties is 150 percent declining balance, with a switch to straight line to maximize the deduction.

3-Year Property

This class includes property with an Asset Depreciation Range (ADR) midpoint of four years or less. The Internal Revenue Code places all personal assets in various categories according to their useful life. A class life was given for each class of assets. The Internal Revenue Code in effect had assigned assets a range of years—ADR—in which an asset could be depreciated by a taxpayer with an upper limit, a lower limit, and a midpoint. However, automobiles and light-duty trucks are specially treated as 5-year property under the Tax Reform Act of 1986 (TRA). Small tools and special handling devices for manufacturing food and beverages are examples of 3-year property for a hospitality firm.

5-Year Property

This class consists of depreciable personal property with an ADR midpoint of more than four years but less than 10 years. This includes such property as computers, copiers, trailers, and typewriters. In addition, TRA specifically includes automobiles, light-duty trucks, and computer-based telephone central switching equipment as 5-year property.

7-Year Property

Included in this class is property with an ADR midpoint of 10 years but less than 16, and property that does not have a class life and is not specifically assigned to any other class. Examples are most office furniture, fixtures, and equipment.

10-Year Property

This class includes property with an ADR midpoint of 16 years but less than 20. Congress did not name specific types of property to be included in this category.

15-Year Property

This class includes property with an ADR midpoint of 20 years but less than 25.

20-Year Property

This class consists of property with an ADR midpoint of 25 years or more, other than real property with an ADR midpoint of 27½ years or more.

As under previous law, the half-year convention applies to all property in the personal asset classes. In addition, all property is treated as having been disposed of or retired from service in the middle of the tax year, thus allowing for a recovery deduction in the year of an asset's disposition (which was not permitted under previous law). There is no provision for salvage value as in previous law.

For illustration only, the following example shows how the depreciation methods differ for equipment that was depreciated under previous law as 5-year property but that is now classified as 7-year property. The equipment had an original cost of $20,000. The depreciation percent under the ACRS method was: 1st year (15 percent), 2nd year (22 percent), 3rd through 5th year (21 percent). Thus, the first year depreciation under ACRS was $20,000 × .15 = $3,000. The depreciation percent under the MACRS method is: 1st year (14.29 percent), 2d year (24.49 percent), 3d year (17.49 percent), 4th year (12.49 percent), 5th year (8.93 percent), 6th year (8.92 percent), 7th year (8.93 percent) and the 8th year (4.46 percent). (See Appendix 2 for a complete list of depreciation tables for personal property).

Year	ACRS	MACRS
1	$3,000	$2,858
2	4,400	4,898
3	4,200	3,498
4	4,200	2,498
5	4,200	1,786
6		1,784
7		1,786
8		892
	$20,000	$20,000

One new significant twist added under TRA is the "mid-quarter convention." This rule relates to the acquisition of personal property only when the aggregate bases of property placed in service during the last three months of the tax year exceed 40 percent of the aggregate bases of all the property placed in service during the year. If the mid-quarter convention is triggered, the first-year depreciation allowed is based on the number of quarters the asset was in service during the tax year. Property acquired at any time during a quarter is treated as having been placed in service in the middle of that quarter. The mid-term convention only applies to property depreciated under the new MACRS rules.

A hospitality firm may elect to depreciate assets using the straight line method over the applicable MACRS recovery period. Another option is for the taxpayer to use the alternative depreciation system (ADS) discussed below. In either case, the mid-year convention applies and salvage value is ignored. It is important to note that electing to use an optional recovery method for a particular class of property is binding for all property in that class acquired during the year. Once the election is made, it is irrevocable.

ADS is an alternative depreciation method that must be used in the following situations.

- To compute the portion of depreciation treated as a tax preference for purposes of the corporate and individual alternative minimum tax.
- To figure the earnings and profits of a domestic corporation or a controlled foreign corporation.

In addition to the above situations, one must use ADS when computing depreciation for the following types of properties.

- Property used predominantly outside the United States.
- Tax-exempt use property.
- Imported property restricted by Presidential Executive Order.
- Tax exempt bond-financed property.
- Luxury automobiles and listed property used 50 percent or less of the time in the business.

Generally, depreciation periods are longer under ADS than MACRS, resulting in lower depreciation deductions for hospitality firms electing to use this method. Also, depreciation is generally computed using straight line recovery without regard to salvage value. The one exception for using straight line is for purposes of the alternative minimum tax, in which case depreciation of personal property is computed using the 150-percent declining balance method.

Generally, a taxpayer can elect to treat a portion of the cost of qualifying property as an expense rather than as a capital expenditure. Congress increased the amount of this deduction from $5,000 to $10,000. However, Congress also placed four additional restrictions on its use.

1. The total cost of property that may be included as expenses for any tax year cannot exceed the taxpayer's total amount of taxable income that is derived from his or her active conduct of trade or business during the tax year. Any expensed amount in excess of taxable income is carried forward to future tax years and added to other amounts eligible for expensing.
2. If the cost of qualified property placed in service during the year exceeds $200,000, the $10,000 ceiling is reduced by the amount of such excess.
3. The qualified expense property must be property-purchased for use in the active conduct of the business.
4. An expense deduction will result in recapture income (the previously taken deduction added back as income) if at any time before the end of the property's recovery period the property is converted to personal use.

TAX CREDITS

Tax credits are subtractions from income tax owed in contrast to deductions, which are a sum subtracted from taxable income. Credits are more valuable than deductions because they represent a dollar-for-dollar reduction in the income tax owed, while the value of an exemption depends on the tax bracket of the taxpayer. For example, a taxpayer in the 28-percent tax bracket will save 28 cents of income tax on every deduction taken and will save one dollar for every dollar in tax credits.

Repeal of the Investment Tax Credit

TRA repeals the investment tax credit (ITC) retroactively for equipment placed in service after December 31, 1985. There is a transition rule for contracts entered into before 1986. The new law does provide that ITC carryovers be reduced by 35 percent for tax years beginning after July 1, 1987.

Rehabilitation and Historical Tax Credit

As part of TRA 1981, Congress restructured and increased the tax credit for rehabilitation expenditures. Congress was very concerned that the tax incentives provided to investments on new structures (i.e., ACR) would have the undesirable effect of reducing the relative attractiveness of the incentives in place as of 1981 to rehabilitate and modernize older structures. This might ultimately lead investors to neglect older structures and relocate their businesses.

As part of TRA 1986, Congress extended the depreciation for commercial real property to 31½ years and correspondingly extended the useful life of most personal property. Once again, Congress needed to examine the need for incentives to rehabilitate. Congress decided that continued incentives were needed because the social and aesthetic values of rehabilitating and preserving older structures do not necessarily figure into an investor's profit projections. Furthermore, Congress felt that a tax incentive was needed because market forces might otherwise channel investments away from such projects due to the extra costs of rehabilitating older and historic buildings.

However, significant changes were made concerning the rehabilitation credits allowed under TRA. First, Congress focused credits primarily on historic and certain older buildings. Second, Congress further tightened the requirements for what constituted "rehabilitation" to ensure that the credits accomplished their intended objective of actually preserving historic and older buildings. In addition, Congress felt that the existing credit percentages would be too high considering the drop in individual tax rates from 50 percent to 28 percent. Consequently, Congress reduced the credit on qualified rehabilitated property to 10-percent and on historical qualified property to 20 percent in order to approximate the same offsets to income under prior law.

Under prior law, the rehabilitation tax credit was 15 percent for nonresidential buildings at least 30 years old and 20 percent for nonresidential buildings of at least 40 years old. As mentioned above, there is only one 10 percent credit available for qualified rehabilitation. However, the new law does maintain the requirement that only nonresidential buildings can qualify for the rehabilitation credit. Furthermore, only property originally placed in service before 1936 will qualify for the rehabilitation credit.

Many existing provisions that determine whether rehabilitation expenditures qualify for the credit were retained under TRA. For example, a building will be treated as having been substantially rehabilitated for a taxable year only if the qualified rehabilitation expenditures incurred during any 24-month period selected by the taxpayer exceed the greater of (1) the adjusted basis of the building (and its structural components) or (2) $5,000. For rehabilitations completed in phases, the 24-month measuring period is extended to 60 months.

Qualified rehabilitation includes renovation, restoration, and reconstruction of a building. However, it does not include enlargement or new construction. Generally, the determination of whether expenditures are attributable to the rehabilitation of an existing building or to new construction are based upon consideration of all the facts and circumstances available.

However, Congress made substantial changes to the external walls requirement. Under prior law, 75 percent of the existing external walls of the building had to be retained in place in the rehabilitation process. An alternative test that could be adopted was also available. The new law replaces the 75 percent test with the alternative test provided under prior law. Thus, a building will not qualify for rehabilitation tax credit unless (1) 50 percent or more of the existing external walls are retained in place as external walls, (2) 75 percent or more of the existing external walls are retained in place as internal *or* external walls, and (3) 75 percent or more of the existing internal structural framework is retained in place. Congress intended to prevent a completely gutted building from qualifying for the rehabilitation credit.

The definition of external walls includes both the supporting elements of the wall as well as its nonsupporting elements (i.e., a curtain). The external wall includes any wall that has one face exposed to the weather, earth, or an abutting wall of an adjacent building. "External wall" also includes a shared wall (i.e., a single wall shared with an adjacent building), provided that the shared wall has no windows or doors that do have one face exposed to the weather, earth, or an abutting wall.

In general, a building's internal structural framework includes all load-bearing internal walls and any other internal structural supports, including columns, girders, beams, trusses, spandrels, and all other members that are essential to the stability of the building.

Congress felt that the Secretary of the Interior Standards for Rehabilitation ensure that certified historic structures are properly rehabilitated. Thus, the external walls requirement is not applicable to certified historical rehabilitation expenditures. Congress stated that although it wished to give the Secretary of the Interior more flexibility in determining historic rehabilitation, it wanted qualified expenditures to be true rehabilitations, not substantially new construction. Thus, Congress expects the Secretary of the Interior to continue to deny certification to rehabilitations in which less than 75 percent of the external walls are not retained in place.

Prior law required that the basis of the rehabilitated building be reduced by 100 percent of the rehabilitation earned credit and by 50 percent for the historic rehabilitation credit earned. Under TRA, the 50 percent basis reduction is deleted. Thus, a full basis adjustment is required for both the 10-percent and 20-percent rehabilitation credits.

Congress specifically stated that, for the most part, revisions under TRA determining whether rehabilitation expenditures qualify would not be different from those under prior law. Thus, no changes were made regarding the substantial rehabilitation test, the specific types of expenditures that do not qualify for the credit, the provisions applicable to certified historic structures and tax-exempt use property, or the recapture rules.

No expenditure is eligible for credit unless the taxpayer elects to recover the costs of the rehabilitation using the straight line method of depreciation. Further, expenditures incurred by a lessee do not qualify for the credit unless the remaining lease term, on the date the rehabilitation is completed, is at least as long as the recovery period under the ACR system (generally $27\frac{1}{2}$ years for residential real property or $31\frac{1}{2}$ years for nonresidential real property).

Finally, the development of hospitality properties by individuals, partnerships, and certain closely held corporations are subject to a further limitation on the amount of rehabilitation credit available in any given year. This limitation applies whether or not the taxpayer actively or materially participates in a real estate rental activity. The credit allowed is equal to the credit's deduction equivalent of $25,000. The following example shows the application of these rules.

In 1989, a partner in a hotel partnership received as his distributed share $12,000 of a qualified historical tax credit from the renovation of a downtown hotel. If the partner is a joint filer with taxable income of, say, $80,000, he or she may claim a $7,000 credit for 1988. This is because the partner is in the 28-percent tax bracket and the credit is restricted by its deduction equivalent ($25,000 × 28 percent = $7,000). The partner may carry over the remaining $5,000 unused credit to future years.

For purposes of the limitation of credits utilization as discussed above, the $25,000 limit (deduction equivalent) is reduced by 50 percent of the amount by which the taxpayer's adjusted gross income (without regard to passive activity losses) exceeds $200,000. It is eliminated when adjusted gross income reaches $250,000. In addition, the $25,000 deduction equivalent amount for application of the rehabilitation credits from passive activities against nonpassive income is also reduced by any passive activity loss from rental real estate activities. These are activities in which the taxpayer actively participates that have been utilized under the rules stated above to offset income from nonpassive activities before application of the credit. If the taxpayer in the preceding example generates $10,000 of losses from real estate rental activity in which he or she actively participates, he or she may then only claim credit for $4,200 ($25,000 − $10,000 × 28 percent = $4,200). The remaining $7,800 may be carried forward to future years.

Targeted Jobs Credit

Until 1985, hospitality managers had a very valuable credit for severely reducing payroll expenses in the Targeted Jobs Credit (TJC). Using the TJC, a manager could claim a credit of 50 percent of the first $6,000 of qualified first-year wages and 25 percent of the first $6,000 of qualified second-year wages of employees. Unfortunately, fewer employers took advantage of this program than Congress had anticipated, and subsequently, the credit was allowed to expire December 31, 1985.

The TJC has been given new life, however, because Congress restored a modified version of the program as part of TRA 1986. With certain changes, the TJC will apply retroactively for qualified wages paid after December 31, 1985 through October 1, 1990 unless extended again.

Under current tax law, an employer can claim a credit for 40 percent of the first $6,000 of qualified wages. In addition, a TJC is also available for employers who hire economically disadvantaged youths. The latter credit is equal to 40 percent of qualified wages, to a maximum wage base of $3,000 earned during the summer (May 1–September 15). In both cases, however, the employer must reduce the payroll expense by the amount of the credit claimed. Additionally, the qualified employee must be on the job for at least 90 days or complete 120 hours of service. For summer employees who qualify under the special youth provision, the minimum employment period is 14 days or 20 hours of service.

To qualify for a TJC, the employer must hire from one of the following eight designated groups:

1. Individuals who are defined as being handicapped for employment purposes and who receive vocational rehabilitation training for physical or mental disabilities.

2. Individuals who are at least 18 but no more than 24 years old and who are members of economically disadvantaged families.
3. Vietnam veterans who are members of economically disadvantaged families.
4. Individuals receiving federal or state supplemental security income during a month that ends within the 60-day period preceding the hire date.
5. Individuals who receive cash payments from a state or local general assistance program providing money on the basis of need during a period of not less than 30 days that ends within the 60-day period preceding the hire date.
6. Any economically disadvantaged persons between the ages of 16 and 19 who participate in qualified cooperative education programs.
7. Convicted felons from economically disadvantaged families who are hired not later than five years after their conviction or release from prison.
8. Eligible work incentive employees who qualify under Part A of Title IV of the Social Security Act.

To claim the credit, the employer first must obtain written certification that the employee does in fact meet the eligibility criteria of one of the eight target groups. If an employee is hired before the certification is obtained, the employer will be denied a TJC for that person. As stated earlier, the TJC has been made retroactive for 1986.

Generally, employers can obtain the proper certification through the local offices of the State Employment Security Agency. For students participating in a qualified cooperative education program, certification is made by the school administering the program. Keep in mind that managers will not be forced to hire an employee simply because that person belongs to a target group.

A comprehensive example shows the savings that can be realized under the TJC.

Assume that a hospitality firm hired a qualified employee on March 1, 1988, and then paid that person $8,000 in wages during 1988. The firm would be entitled to a credit of $2,400 in 1988 (40 percent of the first $6,000 in qualified wages). However, the firm has to reduce its wage deduction by the amount of credit taken. If that firm is in the 34 percent tax bracket, then the increased tax due to the reduction of wages would amount to $816 ($2,400 reduction in wages multiplied by the 34 percent bracket). The firm's net savings for 1988 would be $1,584 ($2,400 minus $816).

As the total savings in the preceding example demonstrate, there is a great opportunity for the hospitality owner to significantly lower the cost of payroll. In addition, the lower the firm's tax bracket, the greater the savings (subtracting TJC from wages will result in larger net savings). Note, however, that first year wages relate to the employment period of the individual, not the firm's tax year. For someone hired December 1, 1988, the employer would be able to count as first-year wages that employee's earnings (to the $6,000 limit) only through November 30, 1989. This results in a parietal credit in 1988 and 1989 for a calendar-year employee.

Another valuable aspect of the TJC concerns the special rules for summer youth employees. This provision allows employers to take a maximum TJC of $1,200 (40 percent of $3,000 of qualified wages). This program is designed for employers who hire economically disadvantaged youths who are at least 16 but not yet 18 years of age on the date they are hired. The credit applies only to wages paid for services performed during a 90-day period between May 1 and September 15, and the employee may not have previously worked for the same employer. The definition of "economically disadvantaged" is the same as for the regular jobs credit, except for the age requirement.

If management wanted to retain a qualified summer youth employee beyond the 90-day summer period, the firm may be able to obtain an additional TJC. First, the retained employee would have to obtain a second certification as a member of another target group. Second, the limit on qualified wages paid to that employee takes into account the wages paid to him or her as a qualified summer employee. For example, the maximum TJC an employer could receive for this type of employee would be $2,400 (40 percent of $3,000 plus 40 percent of $3,000).

Also, the TJC may be elected or revoked at any time before the expiration of the three-year period that begins on the due date (determined without regard to extensions) for filing the return for the tax year. If the tax credit is elected, the employer's wage deduction must be reduced by the amount of the credit in accordance with the rule discussed above, even if the credit cannot be currently applied.

Another concern when using the TJC is that it is combined with certain other credits, and the combined credit available for the year is limited. The credit cannot exceed tax liability. On the other hand, if liability is more than $25,000, the combined credit is limited to $25,000 plus 75 percent of the tax in excess of $25,000. If any portion of the TJC cannot be used currently, it may be carried back three years and forward for 15 years. It is applied on a first-in, first-out (FIFO) basis. The critical time is the three-year limit for revoking the credit and thus restoring the deducted wages. In many cases, management must pay careful attention to the prospects of future profits to determine which course of action is in the best interests of the firm.

In addition to the preceding rules for limiting the TJC, the employer is prohibited from taking the credit for the following individuals:

- The employers.
- Shareholders who own more than 50 percent of the value of outstanding stock in the employing firm.
- Beneficiaries, grantors, or fiduciaries of the employing estate or trust.
- Members of the employing partnership.
- Shareholders of an S corporation who are also officers of the corporation.

TAX SHELTERS

Basically, any legal plan designed to reduce tax liability can be considered a tax shelter. However, there are many different types of shelters, each having its own distinct advantages and disadvantages. Generally, there are three methods of reducing taxes: (1) permanently reducing taxes, (2) tax deferral, and (3) converting ordinary income into capital gain. The TRA has significantly reduced the benefits of the last two methods. However, valid planning opportunities still remain for the hospitality industry.

Permanently Reducing Taxes

The most common method of permanently reducing taxes is not to pay any taxes on the income received. The receipt of municipal bond income is an example of receiving tax-free income. This interest is exempt from federal taxation. However, this type of investment is usually characterized as one using after-tax dollars. For example, an individual will usually receive income from wages or other taxable sources and pay income tax on that income received. The income that is left over after the taxes have been paid then can be invested in tax-free municipal bonds.

Tax Deferral

Prior to TRA, the most beneficial method of reducing taxes was using pre-tax dollars to deferral tax liability until some future date. Thus, the taxpayer enjoyed the use of the money until the tax was paid in the future. The deferral resulted in an interest-free loan to the hospitality firm until the hospitality operations generated income exceeding the losses taken to date.

For the hospitality industry, and especially the heavily real-estate dominated hotel industry, depreciation has been the most significant deferral method of avoiding current taxation. This is because unlike more other expenses, depreciation is a non-cash item that is allowed as a deductible expense for tax purposes. With the lengthening of the depreciation rules and the addition of passive loss rules, the use of previous tax shelters are severely restricted (see discussion on depreciation and passive loss rules in section II and part E of this section).

Converting Ordinary Losses Into Capital Gain

Prior to TRA, a tax shelter for a hospitality firm existed if, in the process of deducting losses against ordinary income, the taxpayer could realize capital gain upon the sale of a hospitality property and the maximum rate of only 20 percent. (The maximum tax prior to TRA was 50 percent). In effect, the taxpayer got the federal government to absorb 50 cents of each dollar deducted, and when the property was sold the taxpayer only had to pay back 20 cents on the gain reported.

When Congress lowered the maximum tax rates for individuals from 50 percent to 28 percent for most taxpayers, it also limited the capital gain rate to 28 percent. Although Congress left intact the code sections dealing with capital gains, the gains are still being taxed at ordinary rates. Thus, the effect is to tax capital gains as ordinary income.

Capital losses are treated the same as ordinary losses, whether short- or long-term in nature. However, an annual limit of $3,000 in available capital losses to offset other ordinary income still exists. Any excess may be carried over to future years until it is utilized.

At-Risk Rules

Basically, the at-risk rules limit the amount of any loss that can be deducted by a taxpayer to the amount of capital (investment) that he or she actually has at risk. Taxpayers are allowed to deduct losses equal to their risk capital; this includes amounts of money or debt obligations for which tax-payers can be personally liable. If taxpayers exceed their risk amounts, they are required to suspend losses until such time as the project begins to show profits or the taxpayers increase their capital contributions. Thus, non-recourse type financing would not permit most taxpayers the additional basis needed to deduct losses outside their initial capital contributions. Most hotel developments are not subject to the at-risk rules due to the exception placed in the law for real estate developments.

TRA has modified the at-risk rules to include real estate, thus affecting hotels and other hospitality projects. However, the at-risk rules are not as severely applied under TRA for real estate as in other areas.

The taxpayer who invests in a typical hotel project would determine his or her at-risk position using the following criteria.

- The taxpayer's cash contributions to the activity.
- The taxpayer's tax basis in any property contributed to the hospitality project.
- The taxpayer's personal obligation on any indebtedness of the hospitality project or value of property used as collateral for loans made to the project.
- The taxpayer's interest in non-recourse financing in certain instances.

Generally, for the last item, non-recourse financing is allowed as basis for deducting losses if the loan is from one of the following:

- A qualified lender who is engaged in the business of making loans (e.g., a bank, savings and loan institution, insurance company, or pension fund), or any federal, state, or local government or instrumentality, provided the lender is not the promoter or seller of the property or a party related to either.
- A qualified lender who has an equity interest in the venture, so long as the terms of the financing are commercially reasonable and are substantially the same as loans involving lenders who do not have an equity interest in the venture.

It is important to note that lenders are also considered promoters—and thus will not be considered qualified lenders—if they receive fees based on the borrower's investment.

The terms of non-recourse financing are considered commercially reasonable if:

- The borrower executes a written unconditional promise to pay on demand or on a specified date;
- The amount to be paid is a fixed sum in money; and
- The interest rate is a reasonable market rate of interest, taking into account the maturity of the debt.

Generally, an interest rate is not considered commercially reasonable if any one of the following conditions exists:

- The interest rate is significantly below or above the market rate for comparable loans by qualified persons not related to the borrower.
- The interest rate is contingent. However, the interest rate may be adjustable or variable, provided that the interest is calculated with respect to a market interest index such as the prime rate charged by a major commercial bank, the London Inter-Bank Offering Rate, the rate on government securities, or the applicable federal rate. For example, an interest

rate floating at one point above the prime rate charged by a major commercial bank would not be considered contingent.

- The term of the loan exceeds the useful life of the property, or the right to foreclose or collect the debt is limited (except to the extent provided under applicable state law).

The at-risk rules will only apply to properties purchased or placed in service after December 31, 1986. This means that any hospitality property acquired before 1987 with no change in ownership can be refinanced without regard to the new at-risk rules.

Passive Activity Rules

TRA 1986 did more to change real estate development than any other provision within the law. Not only will development of hospitality firms be affected by TRA, but also the investment strategies of many upper-level managers and owners who have invested in real estate shelters to reduce their overall tax bills. Because much of the funds raised in the past few years for hotel development have been from limited partnerships, the hotel developer contemplating expansion will have to carefully consider the passive loss rules.

For years, Congress has favored real estate developments with generous tax advantages. With the generous depreciation rules and exception for the at-risk rules, developers of hotel properties enjoyed ample money from investors eager to participate in the development of hotel properties. Some experts contend that the overbuilding that has occurred in the hospitality industry could be directly related to these generous tax rules. Under TRA, the game has been completely changed. Investors in real estate can no longer deduct losses on real estate ventures against salaries and other types of active income.

Under TRA, all income is placed into one of three categories: (1) active income (i.e., salaries, bonuses, and business activities); (2) portfolio income (i.e., dividends and interest); and (3) passive income (i.e., limited partnership interests and income from rental property).

The provisions about what constitutes passive income are very broad and will have an impact on developers as well as on passive investors in real estate. Holding rental property will by its very nature be considered passive under TRA. However, Congress has stated that motels and hotels are not considered rental property. Thus, in most cases the hotel developer will be able to treat the property as a business activity not subject to the passive loss rules.

The general rule under the passive loss rules of Section 469 of the Internal Revenue Code states that the amount by which the aggregate losses from all passive activities for a taxable year exceed the aggregate income from all passive activities for that year may not be used as a deduction. Thus, losses from passive activities may not offset other income of the taxpayer (such as salary, certain interest, dividends, and active business income). The amount of any losses not used by the taxpayer may be carried forward indefinitely but only against any future passive income. If there are suspended losses from several activities, the losses would be determined on a pro rata basis in a manner to be determined by the IRS at some future date. The determination of whether a loss is suspended under the passive loss rules is made after the application of the at-risk rules. Thus, if a taxpayer is not at risk, the loss would be suspended under the at-risk provisions and not the passive loss rules.

TRA rules allow any remaining suspended losses (but not credits) from a passive activity to be taken in full when the taxpayer disposes of his or her entire interest in the activity in a taxable transaction. Any loss from a passive activity that has not been previously allowed can be deducted against other income by the taxpayer. This is done in the following order:

1. Income or gain from a passive activity for the taxable year (including any gain recognition on the disposition).
2. Net income or gain for the taxable year from all passive activities.
3. Any other income or gain.

However, the IRS will not permit sham transactions to qualify as bona fide sales for purposes of releasing passive losses not previously taken. For example, sales to relatives, transfers not properly treated as sales due to the existence of a put, call, or similar right relating to repurchase, and wash sales would not give rise to the allowance of suspended losses.

Another major limitation under the passive loss rules relates to the fact that income or loss from a passive activity is determined without taking into account any portfolio income (e.g., any earnings on working capital), any gain or loss from the disposition of assets producing portfolio income, or from property held for investment. This rule is designed to prevent taxpayers from combining portfolio assets with a passive activity to offset the loss against the income.

As indicated, an aggregate concept was adopted for the passive loss limitation. Thus, a net loss from one passive activity can be used to offset net income from another passive activity. In addition, the income from a passive activity includes income from the sale of such activity. Under this provision, gain or loss attributable to the disposition of property held for investment is not treated as income from a passive activity. However, any interest in a passive activity is not treated as property hold for investment. Thus, a taxpayer should be able to offset net passive loss against income generated from the sale of property considered a passive activity.

The passive loss rules apply to individuals, partners, shareholders of S corporations, trusts, estates, personal service corporations (except where the owner-employees own less than 10 percent by value), the corporation's stock, and closely held regular C corporations. A special rule provides that passive activity losses may offset net active income (but not portfolio income) in the case of closely held C corporations.

A key provision of the passive activity rules under the Internal Revenue (the Code) Code defines passive activity as any activity that involves the conduct of any trade or business and in which the taxpayer does not materially participate. The Code does not define what constitutes an "activity." The Senate Conference Report (the Report) on TRA provides that an activity consists of "undertakings" that involve "an integrated and interrelated economic unit, conducted in coordination with or reliance upon each other, and constituting an appropriate unit for the measurement of gain or loss." Reference is made in the Report to the rules under the "Hobby Loss Rules" of Section 183, and the traditional guidance of facts and circumstances applies.

A taxpayer is treated under the passive activity rules as materially participating in an activity only if he or she is involved in the operations of the activity on a regular, continuous, and substantial basis. It is presumed that a limited partnership interest is not an interest in which a taxpayer materially participates.

Material participation is determined on a year-by-year basis. However, there are special rules designed to prevent a taxpayer from triggering former passive losses by becoming a material participant in an activity. Under these provisions, any unused credits or deductions from a former passive activity retain their character as arising from a passive activity. The Report states that an individual who works in a line of business consisting of one or more business activities may be a material participant in each of the activities, even if the individual's role is in management rather than operations. In addition, a taxpayer may be a material participant in an activity if he or she plays a major role in the activity, even though the actual work done is minimal in comparison to other activities. For example, if a hotel developer arranges the bonding for a construction company that cannot operate without the developer's credit, the developer may be a material participant even if he or she hires a manager and is not active in day-to-day operations.

When applied to real estate, the passive loss rules emphasize the need for careful attention to the form and manner in which various real estate activities are undertaken. As stated above, passive activity includes any rental activity, whether or not the taxpayer materially participates. However, many real estate activities do not involve holding rental property and, thus, will not automatically be passive activities. As discussed, operating a hotel or similar transient lodging where substantial services are provided are not considered a rental activity. Accordingly, the hotel operation would be a trade or business, subjecting any owner who does not materially participate to the passive loss rules.

The passive loss rules involve other considerations as well. For example, a taxpayer who owns real property solely for investment (such as raw land) or for use in trade or business should not be subject to the passive loss rules. Thus, any interest expense incurred in carrying the land would be subject to the investment interest limitation and not the passive loss rules. As such, this expense would be deductible against portfolio income. In this regard, taxpayers who have separated the ownership of real property used in their trade or business in another entity and who have then leased it back may want to consider transferring the ownership back to the user entity to avoid the passive loss rules.

Certain technical rules are worth mentioning because of their potential impact upon investment decisions of hospitality owners and developers. For example, there is limited relief from the passive loss rules for middle-income taxpayers. Up to $25,000 of losses and credits from rental real estate activities may be used to offset other income if a taxpayer "actively participates" in the activity. Active participation is a lesser standard than material participation. Active participation can be satisfied without regular, continuous, and substantial involvement in operations so long as the taxpayer (1) is not a limited partner in a limited partnership; (2) participates in a significant and bona fide sense in such roles as making management decisions or arranging for outside contractors or vendors; and (3) owns 10 percent (by value) or more of all interest in such activity. This exception is phased out by 50 percent of the amount by which the taxpayer's adjusted gross income exceeds $100,000. Thus, the entire $25,000 exception is eliminated at $150,000 of adjusted gross income.

There is also a special provision of the passive activity rules concerning the rehabilitation tax credit and low-income housing credit. There is a special phase-out rule that applies to non-passive income, regardless of whether the taxpayer actively participates in the venture generating the credits. The phase-out is 50 percent of the adjusted gross income (disregarding passive losses) above $200,000 of adjusted gross income.

All the passive loss limitation rules discussed above are generally effective for all interests in passive activities for any taxable year beginning in calendar year 1987. There is no grandfathering for interests held before 1987, except that interests held on or before October 22, 1986, are subject to a phase-in over five years (allowing 65 percent of net passive losses against other income in 1987, 40 percent in 1988, 20 percent in 1989, and 10 percent in 1990). There is no phase-in for alternative minimum tax (AMT) purposes. Moreover, net operating loss carryforwards or credit carryforwards from taxable years before 1987 are not subject to the passive loss rules.

INTEREST EXPENSES

Like ordinary income and losses, there are different levels of interest expense deductions. Personal interest is all but eliminated except for mortgage interest, and limits are placed on investment interest. The only interest that is fully deductible without any limitations is business interest.

Business Interest Deductions

Interest payments in connection with any hospitality firm's business are deductible without any limitations. Knowing that their interest payments are fully deductible is a major advantage to highly leveraged hospitality firms.

Investment Interest Payments

There is a limitation on deducting interest payments that are considered investment interest. This rule was enacted by Congress to restrict interest expense deductions by investors to the amount of net investment income. If there is insufficient net investment income, interest may not be deducted currently but is carried over to a year when net investment income is generated.

Investment interest is defined as all interest paid or accrued by an investor on debt that is incurred to purchase or carry property held for investment. Generally, hospitality property would not be considered property held for investment because it is an income-producing property (trade or business). However, raw land held for future development of a hotel could be considered investment property and thus subject to the investment interest limitation rules because it is not currently a trade or business.

Net Investment Income

Net investment income can be defined as gross investment income minus investment expense.

Gross Investment Income

Gross investment income is a category of income that includes rents, dividends, interest, royalties, net capital gains from investment property, and recapture income on the sale of depreciable property. Gross passive income does not include income from passive activities (e.g., limited partnerships).

However, investment income in years 1987 through 1990 is reduced by passive losses that may be used to offset nonpassive income under the phase-in rule (see passive loss rules in Section IV, E for more details). This will result in many taxpayers having less investment income and thus the possibility of not being able to deduct in full all their investment interest expense until some future date.

Investment Expense

Investment expense consists of operating expenses, property taxes, bad debts, and straight-line depreciation.

Because TRA has eliminated the $10,000 exemption previously allowed investors in any given year, Congress decided to phase in any excess interest disallowed to mitigate the perceived harshness of the new law. The following phase-in schedule shows the amount of investment interest that will be allowed without any limitation:

Percentage	Year
65%	1987
40%	1988
20%	1989
10%	1990
0%	1991 and beyond

It should be noted that investment interest deductions not allowed in any given year can be carried forward indefinitely by taxpayers and used in any subsequent year in which they have net investment income.

Personal Interest

The deduction for personal interest has been curtailed for personal loans (e.g., car loans, student loans, and credit card finance charges) with a gradual phase-out that will eliminate the interest deduction completely for tax years beginning in 1991.

The only personal loans that remains fully deductible are mortgage loans secured by first or second homes. The interest deduction is limited to the cost of the property plus any improvements. Mortgages that are used to purchase a new home or to improve an existing one can not exceed $1 million in total for the interest to remain fully deductible. Also, any home improvement mortgages may not exceed $100,000 in any one year for the interest to be fully deductible.

CONSTRUCTION PERIOD INTEREST AND TAXES

Another significant change that TRA brings to the development of hospitality projects concerns modifications to the capitalization of construction period interest and taxes. The construction period generally starts when actual physical work begins on the project. Thus, interest and property taxes paid before construction activities begin are fully deductible.

TRA now provides that construction period interest and taxes must be amortized over the depreciable life of the project. Thus, for a hospitality project that would be 31½ years.

An additional requirement states that property taxes be allocated between land and the hospitality structure. The interest cost can be allocated solely to the building unless specific debt was incurred to purchase the land.

ALTERNATIVE MINIMUM TAX

The alternative minimum tax is an attempt by Congress to ensure that all taxpayers pay income tax if their taxable income is reduced by certain so-called preference deductions. The taxpayers who benefit from these laws have to pay at least a minimum amount of tax.

This additional tax is called the alternative minimum tax (AMT). Unfortunately, this tax requires many adjustments to taxable income in order to calculate the alternative taxable income. There is a separate AMT for corporations and individuals.

Corporate Alternative Minimum Tax

TRA 1986 contained some good news for corporations. It repealed the corporate add-on minimum tax after 1986. Unfortunately, TRA also contained some bad news. The add-on minimum tax was replaced by a new minimum tax called the AMT. This change was designed to ensure that no corporation with substantial economic income could avoid significant tax liability by using exclusions, deductions, and/or credits. Congress wanted corporations to pay tax equal to at least 20 percent of their income above the exemption amount.

Hospitality corporations are concerned about this change because the corporate AMT, which is similar to the individual AMT, applies to a broader income base than ever. The AMT base is equal to regular taxable income, plus or minus (1) adjustments and plus (2) tax preferences. This amount is reduced by the exemption amount, then multiplied by the AMT rate of 20 percent. This figure is compared to the corporation's regular tax liability and the corporation pays the AMT or its regular tax, whichever is higher.

Corporations are now compelled to make estimated tax payments with respect to tax liabilities under the corporate AMT system in addition to the regular tax. This requirement could frustrate most corporations due to the complexities of the AMT calculation.

Alternative Minimum Taxable Income

For a hospitality firm to determine if the AMT applies, the firm must first calculate its alternative minimum taxable income (AMTI). AMTI is determined by taking the taxable income of the corporation for the taxable year and making certain adjustments dictated by Sections 56 and 58 of the Code. In addition, taxable income will be increased by any applicable tax-preference items in Section 57 of the Code. Generally, adjustments require the recomputation of certain deductions under the regular tax. While pre-1987 tax law referred to all items taken into account for minimum tax purposes as "tax preferences," the Code now classifies those items requiring recomputation as "adjustments" and those requiring an increase to taxable income as "tax preferences." The key distinction between adjustments and tax preference items seems to be that an adjustment can either increase or decrease taxable income, while a tax preference item always increases taxable income.

The definition of regular tax includes the corporation's initial tax reduced by the foreign tax credit. Additional taxes paid, like the tax on lump-sum distributions from qualified retirement plans and investment tax credit recapture, are not included in the regular tax for minimum tax purposes.

Each corporation is allowed an exemption of $40,000. However, this is subject to a phase-out equal to 25 percent of the amount of the AMTI if the corporation's income exceeds $150,000. Accordingly, a corporation with an AMTI of $310,000 or more will not be able to use any of the exemption amount, as it would be fully phased out at that AMTI level.

An important limitation for most hospitality firms is that incentive tax credits like the targeted jobs credit and other general business credits may not be claimed against the corporate AMT. With the exception of the foreign tax credit and investment tax credits (discussed below), the new law has changed the way credits are used for regular tax purposes. Under previous law, credits such as the targeted jobs credit could be claimed even if they reduced the corporation's regular tax liability to an amount less than the minimum tax. Now, the amount of these credits may not surpass the excess of the corporation's regular tax liability for the tax year over the tentative minimum tax (TMT) for the year. Unused credits may be carried over.

Although new investment tax credits are no longer allowed, many firms still have some unused investment tax credits from previous years because of various carryover rules. These investment tax credits offset the greater of (1) either the regular tax liability for the year or the excess (if any) of the regular tax liability over 75 percent of the regular tax liability over 75 percent of the TMT, whichever is less, or (2) 25 percent of the TMT liability. There are additional limitations if the credit is combined with the foreign tax credit and net operating loss (NOL) deduction provisions.

Adjustments

As discussed earlier, the new AMT provisions distinguish between adjustments and tax preferences. The primary effect of treating items as adjustments to AMTI instead of preferences is that it permits netting. Netting occurs when, in a given year, an alternative deduction exceeds the regular tax deduction for the item for the year and thus is used to offset other adjustments. The adjustments applicable to corporations include several categories. Only five, however, will apply to the majority of hospitality firms:

1. Depreciation;
2. AMT net operation loss deductions (AMT NOL);
3. Installment sales;
4. Passive activity losses; and
5. Adjusted current earnings.

Depreciation

All corporations claiming accelerated cost recovery system (ACRS) on property placed in service after 1986 must recompute their depreciation deduction for AMT purposes under the alternative depreciation system. Generally, the depreciation method most corporations use is the 150 percent declining balance method, switching to straight line at the point where deductions are maximized. There are exceptions to the 150 percent declining balance method for real property and for any property that the taxpayer has elected or is required to elect the straight line method for regular tax purposes. The applicable recovery period will be the class life (determined by ADR midpoint) for most property and 40 years (using the straight line method) for nonresidential real property. To permit netting, the law treats all post-1986 ACRS property as one group for depreciation recomputation purposes.

In the case of pre-1987 property (except for early-elected revised ACRS rules), the regular depreciation for property placed in service prior to 1987 is treated as a tax preference only to the extent that it is constituted a preference under prior law.

AMT NOL

There is a condition in the law for an AMT net operating loss deduction (AMT NOL) in lieu of the regular net operating loss deduction (NOL). Usually, this computation takes into account the differences between the regular tax base and the AMT base. The starting point for calculating the AMT NOL is the regular tax NOL. The regular tax NOL is then subject to adjustments and reduced by items of tax preference to arrive at the AMT NOL.

Installment Sales

For AMT purposes, gain will be recognized in full in the year when the following are sold:

- Inventory;
- Property held primarily for sale to customers of the taxpayer's business or trade;
- Sales by real estate dealers;
- Sales of rental real estate; and
- Real estate used in a trade or business in which the sales price exceeds $150,000.

Passive Activity Losses

The determination of passive activity losses is another adjustment in the calculation of AMTI. (Passive activity losses were disallowed by the TRA 1986. However, TRA called for a five-year phase-in period of this rule.) This adjustment applies mostly to personal service corporations and certain closely held corporations in which five or fewer individuals own more than 50 percent of the corporation's stock.

Any passive losses denied for AMT purposes are carried forward and are deductible to the extent the taxpayer has AMTI that includes passive activity income or active business income in the case of closely held corporations. Any remaining loses are deductible in full in the year the passive activity interest is claimed.

Adjusted Current Earnings

The most controversial aspect of the corporate AMT must be the add back for the difference between adjusted current earnings and the corporation's AMTI. Basically, the AMTI of a corporation is increased or decreased by 75 percent of the amount by which its adjusted current earnings exceed AMTI.

The adjusted current earnings are the earnings of the corporation adjusted for tax preference items. The tax preference items are to be treated the same way for adjusted current earnings as they are for AMTI purposes.

Tax Preferences

The tax preferences of corporations that must be taken into account in computing AMTI include depreciation that is carried over from pre-1987 law. Accelerated depreciation or amortization on property placed in service prior to 1987 is treated as a tax preference only to the extent that it constitutes a preference under prior law. Therefore, for property placed in service before 1987, the only preference items allowed are: (1) accelerated depreciation on real property in excess of straight line depreciation and (2) accelerated depreciation on personal property only in the case of leased personal property in the hands of a personal holding company. Because depreciation is a tax preference and only increases AMTI, it is measured on an item-by-item basis, in contrast with the netting system used for the adjustments to property placed in service after 1986.

Minimum Tax Credit

To mitigate the burden in the AMT, Congress created the minimum tax credit. A corporation may offset its regular income tax liability in future years by the amount of AMT paid that is imputed to deferral preferences. Preferences and adjustments that are a result of a permanent exclusion of income from regular taxable income are not eligible for the credit. Deferral preferences and adjustments have the effect of deferring taxes. These preferences and adjustments will eventually reverse in a subsequent year. For example, book income adjustment is considered a deferral preference for minimum tax purposes.

The minimum tax credit may be carried forward indefinitely but may never be carried back. Once carried over, the credit can only decrease the taxpayer's regular tax liability to the extent that it does not exceed the excess of the regular tax over the tentative minimum tax (without regard to ITC) for the year.

INDIVIDUAL ALTERNATIVE MINIMUM TAX

The individual AMT includes the same preferences likely to be found in the corporate AMT for hospitality firms, except for the excess book income adjustment that is unique to corporations. The minimum tax rate for the individual is 21 percent instead of the 20 percent for corporations. The exemption for individuals is $40,000 for those filing joint returns, $30,000 for single taxpayers, and $20,000 for married couples filing separately. There is a phase-out rule of the exemption for high-income individuals similar to that for corporations. The exemption is reduced by 25 percent of the amount by which AMTI exceeds $150,000 on joint returns, or $112,500 for single returns. The exemption is fully phased out when AMTI is at $310,000 on a joint return and $232,500 on a single return.

Another significant difference in calculating the individual AMTI is the substitution of AMT itemized deductions for the regular income tax itemized deductions. The only itemized deductions allowed in calculating AMTI are (1) casualty, theft, and gambling losses; (2) charitable contributions; (3) medical expenses; (4) qualified interest; (5) the Section 691(c) estate tax deductions; and (6) certain estate and trust distributions to beneficiaries.

The following regular income tax itemized deductions are modified in calculating AMTI.

- *Qualified housing mortgage interest.* Mortgage interest on two homes is deductible for both regular tax and the AMTI. A special rule applies to homes that are refinanced. The amount of interest deduction allowed is limited to amortization of the original loan balance at the time of refinancing.
- *Consumer interest.* Even though there is a phase-out period for consumer interest deductions for regular income tax purposes, the AMT does not allow any consumer interest deductions.
- *Investment interest deduction.* Investment interest is deductible in the same manner for AMT purposes as for regular income tax purposes. However, no phase-in rule applies for the AMT, as in the case of the regular income tax.
- *Medical deductions.* Medical deductions are allowed for the AMT only if they exceed 10 percent of adjusted gross income, instead of 7.5 percent under regular income tax.
- *Casualty and theft losses and charitable deductions.* Casualty and theft losses as well as charitable deductions are treated in the same manner for AMT purposes as for regular income tax purposes.
- *State and local taxes.* The itemized deduction for state and local taxes is not permitted for the AMT. Thus, taxpayers in high-tax states may be subject to the AMT that they were not subject to under prior law.
- *Miscellaneous itemized deductions.* Miscellaneous itemized deductions are not allowed for AMT purposes.

Many more individuals will be subject to the AMT in the future because of the narrowing of the differences in tax rates between the top individual rates and the AMT rate. Careful planning by individuals contemplating an investment in the hospitality industry will be necessary to minimize the impact of the AMT on the investment decision.

OTHER IMPORTANT TAX RULES AFFECTING THE HOSPITALITY INDUSTRY

There were numerous changes made to the income tax code by the IRA 1986. Some of the more important changes affecting the hospitality industry are detailed below.

Corporate Tax Rates

Under TRA, the top corporate tax rate is reduced from the current maximum of 46 percent to a maximum of 34 percent. Congress did small business a favor by taxing the first $50,000 of corporate taxable income at 15 percent and the next $25,000 at 25 percent. The amount over $75,000 is taxed at the maximum rate of 34 percent. Congress did not want big business to profit by the lower rates, so taxable income between $100,000 and $335,000 are subject to an additional 5 percent tax (see Chapter 2, Table 2.1, for corporate rates).

Individual Tax Rates

Similarly, the individual tax rate for most individuals has been reduced from 50 percent to 28 percent. However, the maximum tax rate can increase to 33 percent for high-income persons. The following tables show the various rate percentages for married couples filing joint returns and single persons filing separately (there are also rates for heads of households and married persons filing separately that are not shown here):

Married Couples Filing Joint Returns	
Rate	Taxable Income Brackets
15%	0–$29,750
28%	$29,751–$71,900

Single Taxpayer Filing Single Return	
Rate	Taxable Income Brackets
15%	0–$17,850
28%	$17,851–$43,150

Business Meals and Entertainment

Under the TRA, firms may write off only 80 percent of the cost of business meals and entertainment. The pre-TRA law regarding substantiation of meals is retained. It makes no difference whether the taxpayer incurs the expense as entertainment or as part of a business trip away from home. However, the new law tightens the deductibility of meals by requiring that the meals have a direct relationship to the conduct of business. In addition, Congress is phasing out such entertainment devices as rentals of luxury skyboxes at sporting events.

Transportation and other travel expenses to the restaurant are still 100 percent deductible. Furthermore, the 80 percent rule does not change employee reimbursement policies. An employee can be reimbursed 100 percent by the employer with no tax consequences if the employee properly documents the expense.

Travel Expenses

As mentioned above, most travel expenses are deductible. However, deductions for travel on cruise ships are limited, while educational travel deductions (e.g., a tour to study various architectural styles of French homes) were eliminated. Likewise, travel and other costs associated with attending investment seminars are not deductible.

Miscellaneous

TRA made significant accounting changes that will impact upon the hospitality industry. Some of the more important include the following.

- Limitations have been imposed on the use of the cash method of accounting.
- Limitations have been imposed on the use of the installment sales method of deferring tax.
- Bad-debt deductions for hospitality firms will be allowed only for actual losses. The reserve method is being eliminated under the new law.
- Partnerships and S corporations are required to adopt the same tax year used by the principal partners or partners owning the majority of profits and capital, effective for tax years beginning after 1986. There is an adjustment made if this change results in income to the partners or shareholders over a four-year period.

SUMMARY

The chapter shows how important the tax law is in hospitality finance. The Government uses the Internal Revenue Code to set social policy as well as raise revenues. TRA 1986 has changed the way the hospitality industry operates. The longer write-off of assets will result in lowering the benefits of depreciation. Because many hospitality firms raise capital from outsiders, hospitality firms may not be as attractive an investment as they once were. Although the depreciation length has been increased for most personal assets, the shift to double declining balance rates in calculating the depreciation helps offset the longer asset lengths.

The tax credits allowed in the past have been eliminated (as in the investment tax credit) or sharply curtailed (as in the rehabilitation tax credit). However, the Targeted Jobs Credit still remains a valuable tax planning device for most hospitality firms that hire certain disadvantaged workers.

The elimination of the traditional tax shelter will impact the growth of many hospitality firms. With limitation of write-offs on tax shelter losses for most investors, hotel projects must be presented to investors as sound economic projects rather than as tax shelters.

The expanded AMT will result in many unsuspecting hospitality firms paying more taxes. This is especially due to the inclusion of the book income adjustment as part of the AMT calculation. Although not modified to the extent of the corporate minimum tax, the individual AMT will require careful planning on the part of the taxpayer in order to avoid the tax.

Most of the publicity about TRA has centered on the permanent reduction in both the corporate and individual income tax rates. But with the elimination or reduction of a number of previously allowed deductions, exemptions, and credits, many hospitality organizations and investors will pay more income tax than under the old law.

One change that will be eagerly followed in the hospitality industry will be the effect on restaurant sales brought about by the fact that now only 80 percent of the cost of meals can be deducted.

GLOSSARY

Accelerated depreciation rate A method that allows depreciation to be included as an expense more quickly than under the straight-line method. Double-declining balance method (DDB) is the quickest depreciation method allowed. An asset qualifying for DDB will be written off at twice the depreciation rate of the straight-line method. Another accelerated depreciation method is the declining-balance method (DB). An asset qualifying for DB will be written off at 150 percent of the straight-line method.

Alternative minimum tax An additional tax for those taxpayers who pay little or no income tax due to certain special deductions. Taxpayers who benefit from these laws must pay at least a minimum tax.

At-risk rule A limitation on the amount of loss from a project that a taxpayer may deduct on his or her tax return. Most real estate projects carry a major exception for investors.

Certified historic tax credit The income tax credit available to developers of commercial property who obtain a certified historical designation for either a residential or commercial property. The credit equals 20 percent of qualified expenditures.

Construction period interest and taxes All interest and property tax expenses that are incurred during the construction of a building. These expenses cannot be written off, but instead become part of the cost of the building. They are subject to depreciation.

Depreciation The obsolescence of property due to the economic decrease in the value of property. Also, the amount of assumed obsolescence allowed by the Internal Revenue Code depending on the type of property involved.

Half-year convention Personal property is deemed to be placed in service at the middle of a tax year regardless of when it was purchased, except if the "mid-quarter convention" (see definition below) is required.

Mid-quarter convention If more than 40 percent of all property acquired during the year is placed in service during the last quarter of the tax year, depreciation is calculated as if the assets were acquired in the middle of the quarter.

Modified accelerated cost recovery system A depreciation method required to be used by taxpayers under TRA 1986. It places assets in certain year classifications and designates the write-off period to be used by the taxpayer. For instance, cars are placed in a 5-year class, meaning that cars are written off over a 5-year period.

Passive activity losses Losses that result from an activity in which the taxpayer does not materially participate. Losses are limited in a particular activity to the extent that the taxpayer has passive income from other sources or until the activity begins to show a profit or is disposed of. All limited partners are considered to be involved in a passive activity.

Portfolio income Income generated by interest, dividends, annuities, and royalties. Portfolio income cannot be offset against passive activity losses.

Rehabilitation tax credit The income tax credit that is available to developers of commercial property who rehabilitate any nonresidential property built before 1936. This credit is equal to 10 percent of qualified expenditures.

Salvage value The residual value of an asset after it has been fully depreciated.

Straight-line method A depreciation method that results in writing off depreciation deductions evenly over the life of the asset.

Targeted jobs credit A credit allowed employers who hire certain disadvantaged persons, including but not limited to students, the handicapped, and the economically deprived. The credit is 40 percent of up to $6,000 in first year wages. Also, there is a special credit in hiring qualified students for the summer.

Tax bracket The percentage of income tax that one pays, based on where income falls in the income tax tables.

Tax credit For specified expenditures, a dollar amount that is allowed under the Internal Revenue Code as a reduction in the amount of income tax owed by a taxpayer.

Tax shelter A term used to describe any transaction, including holding of real estate, in which the owner is given certain tax advantages for participating. Tax shelters have been severely limited by the TRA 1986.

References

Explanation of Tax Reform Act of 1986. Commerce Clearing House, Inc, Chicago, Illinois: 1986.

Tarras, John. "Analyzing the Impact of the New Tax Law on the Hospitality Industry." *M.S.U. Hospitality Review,* Fall 1986 (pp. 8–9, 15).

Tarras, John. "New Law Tightens Deductions for Business Travel & Meals." *The Bottomline,* February 1987 (pp. 10–12).

Tarras, John. "Hospitality Firms Must Cope with New Depreciation Rules." *The Bottomline,* April 1987 (pp. 15–17).

Tarras, John. "Rehabilitation Credits Still Represent Opportunities for Hospitality Firms." *The Bottomline,* June 1987 (pp. 16–17, 22).

Tarras, John. "Hospitality Firms and the New Passive Loss Rules." *The Bottomline,* August 1987 (pp. 15–16, 8).

Tarras, John. "Many Hospitality Firms will be Liable under New Minimum Tax Rules." *The Bottomline,* October 1987 (pp. 9–11).

Tarras, John. "Managing Labor Cost with the Targeted Jobs Credit." *Cornell Quarterly,* May 1987 (pp. 18–19).

Tax Guide for Small Business, publication 334, IRS Tax Publication (1989).

Depreciation, publication 534, IRS Publication (1989).

Alternative Minimum Tax for Individuals, publication 909, IRS Tax Publication (1989).

Passive Activity and At-Risk Rules, publication 925, IRS Tax Publication (1989).

Recommended Reading

Explanation of Tax Reform Act of 1986. Commerce Clearing House, Inc, Chicago, Illinois: 1986.

Tarras, John. "Rehabilitation Credits Still Represent Opportunities for Hospitality Firms." *The Bottomline,* June 1987 (pp. 16–17, 22).

Tax Guide for Small Business, publication 334, IRS Tax Publication (1989).

The Tax Reform Act of 1986: How it Affects You. Prentice-Hall Information Services, Paramus, N.J.: 1986.

Chapter 4

Feasibility Studies

INTRODUCTION

As part of the Tax Reform Act (TRA) of 1986, Congress severely limited the financing of hotel developments. It eliminated the favorable tax status that real estate developers had enjoyed in the past. Congress wanted to deemphasize the tax advantages realized from investing in a hospitality project. This situation has resulted in a financing problem, one that makes it more difficult for developers to obtain financing. The problem is further compounded by the overbuilding of hotels and restaurants in many parts of the country. Thus, the need for quality feasibility studies to determine the practicality for construction has never been greater.

This chapter focuses on the strengths and weaknesses of a feasibility study and outlines the best ways to determine the relevance of the information obtained.

Although feasibility studies are conducted for restaurants, the majority of feasibility studies are conducted for prospective hotel properties. This chapter examines the hotel feasibility study, including discussion of differences from a restaurant, where applicable.

Feasibility studies are conducted for a number of very important reasons. Generally, they are undertaken at the request of lenders, franchisors, or investors to determine if a project is economically viable. With the recent overbuilding in certain hotel segments around the country, it is becoming increasingly important for developers to analyze the possible consequences of adding more rooms to a possibly overbuilt market.

A feasibility study containing positive results states that, given many inherent assumptions, a hotel is likely to succeed on a given site. Since the study is looking to the future, estimates as to average room rate, room occupancy, and operating costs are usually based on assumptions of the economy's stability. The developer, however, should not take this to be a guarantee. One need only look at the hotel industry in Texas to realize that assumptions about the local economy thought reasonable at the time of a study may later prove to be totally inaccurate.

A developer must first find a consulting firm to conduct the study. Although many firms claim that they can conduct feasibility studies, wise developers check out each firm they are thinking of doing business with. Firms such as Laventhol & Horwath and Pannell, Kerr, Foster specialize in feasibility studies for the hospitality industry, but many others have good reputations and the expertise to conduct professional studies. These firms range from large public accounting firms and specialized national hospitality real estate firms to regional and local consulting firms. Many times, developers pick the firm that the lender, franchisor, or investors have the most confidence in.

In today's competitive environment, a developer should solicit bids from more than one qualified firm when possible. As is the case when seeking other professional services, price alone should not be the sole criterion for making a decision, although many times a quality study can be obtained for a low price due to a number of valid reasons. For instance, some professional firms underbid their competition in order to dominate a certain market segment. A consulting firm may bid low because it has a number of qualified staff professionals temporarily out of work and whom the firm wants to keep busy.

It is important that the developer and consultant communicate closely during a feasibility study. For instance, will the consulting firm review local zoning laws for compliance? The developer must provide important information to the consultant about the project as a whole, emphasizing the type of hotel planned, its size, and why the developer thinks the hotel is needed. But bear in mind that even though it is very important for the consultant and the developer to work closely at all times, the feasibility study must be conducted independently by the consulting firm in order for it to have any validity with lenders, franchisors, or investors.

As noted earlier, it is also important to remember that a feasibility study does not guarantee the desired results for a proposed hotel. In fact, the developer should be able to negotiate a reduced fee if the consultant's initial findings are negative and if completing the study would serve no purpose. The report only presents conditional conclusions based upon the facts developed by the consultant. In any feasibility study, the consultant makes certain assumptions. The developer will have to study these assumptions closely to test the reasonableness of the conclusions.

There are many different types of feasibility studies. Many are economic and include both a market and an economic study. The economic study usually includes some form of rate of return analysis. An economic feasibility study should give the investor or lender sufficient information as to whether or not the project is feasible.

Another type of study is the market study with operating projections, which concentrates on supply-demand issues and includes financial projections down to the income before debt service. Since this study does not include a full rate of return analysis, the developer is responsible for furnishing the missing financial structure of the deal.

A market study with operating projections usually contains the following six sections:

1. Market area analysis
2. Project site and area analysis
3. Competition analysis
4. Demand analysis
5. Recommended facilities
6. Estimates of operating results

MARKET AREA ANALYSIS

This section of the report is used to analyze important demographic, economic, and other market characteristics of the area surrounding the proposed site. The report includes such areas as census data, area income averages, employment statistics, retail sales figures, industrial and commercial activity, tourism, and transportation. The consultant then determines the positive or negative impact of these facts on the proposed project.

The consultant must use a variety of resources to obtain the information needed to conduct a market area analysis. Intimate knowledge of the area is the most valuable source of information a consultant can possess. If the consultant is not familiar with the area, then personal contacts who live there are the next best source of information.

The consultant should first determine if a feasibility study has ever been conducted in the proposed project area by his or her company. Although existing data may be outdated, it is a good starting point for analyzing and obtaining sources of information about the area. The consultant may be able to save valuable time by updating the report instead of starting from the beginning.

However, many times the consultant is unfamiliar with the area to analyze. In this case, the starting point is usually the local Chamber of Commerce, which has a wealth of information about area businesses. The Chamber can provide information concerning growth and future projects planned for the area.

The consultant will also want to visit local government agencies to obain population census figures and to review construction permits, which can help determine the office and retail developments in the area. Also, the consultant should visit the local library to obtain information about the area's historic, economic, and demographic trends. Another valuable source of data is statistics published by travel-related companies such as American Express or marketing magazines such as *Sales and Marketing Management*. (See Exhibit 4-1 on page 74 for a partial list of possible sources of information.)

Next, the developer must determine if the data collected by the consultant is relevant to the proposed property. The following key determinants will aid the market analysis:

1. Population growth
2. Employment growth
3. Retail sales growth
4. Traffic patterns
5. Commercial and industrial development
6. Tourism
7. Unique area characteristics (theme parks, historical sites, etc.)

Population growth is often a key ingredient to the success of a hotel development. However, the developer will need to know where this growth is occurring. Are the socioeconomic groups that make up the market for the proposed hotel growing? Also, the source of the population figures must be analyzed to make certain that the consultant is using the latest available data.

The developer also must question whether the consultant has adequately examined the impact of other future growth on the proposed hotel. For example, what are the prospects for long-term employment growth in the immediate area? The developer determines this by reviewing what the consultant has used to determine future growth. Also, developers generally are prominent citizens in the community and have a good feel for future economic trends.

The growth of retail sales in the area is another important statistic. Is there a correlation between a geographic shift in area retail sales and traffic patterns around the proposed site? The answer to this and other questions can tell a developer where the consumer dollar is moving.

EXHIBIT 4-1
Sources of Information For
the Market Area Analysis

---

1. Chamber of Commerce
2. Library
3. State Hotel-Motel Association
4. Visitors and Convention Bureau
5. Hospitality Magazines
6. Hotel Directors (Red Book, Mobil
   Travel Guide, etc.)
7. Local Real Estate Offices
8. Sales & Marketing Management
9. State Tourism Departments
10. Local Government Units
11. Travel and Credit Card Companies

Commercial and industrial activity (both current and planned) in the area also must be analyzed. Not only should the report address possible future commercial and industrial growth, but, with so many plants closing, also the probability of future plant closings.

If tourism is a major consideration for the hotel developer, the report should examine the potential for growth in this area. Because tourism is rather loosely defined by many government agencies, the developer should pay close attention to the data the consultant uses. Also, the tourism information the consultant provides should include travelers' income, places of origin, spending patterns, and socioeconomic and age statistics.

This is by no means an exhaustive list of what a market area analysis should contain. For example, information about theme parks, sporting facilities, historical sites, and resorts should be included if they are located in the area.

PROJECT SITE AND AREA ANALYSIS

The consultant should give the developer a detailed site analysis of the proposed property. This begins with a description of where the property will be located. A map is usually included that pinpoints the exact location. This map shows the relation of the site to demand generators and attractions in the area. A general description of the surrounding area and how the hotel will fit into it should also be included.

A map is important to indicate the different types of transportation available in the area. The site's distance from main traffic arteries, airports, and its ingress and egress can easily be shown on the map. Any known future changes to the roadways and streets that provide access to the project site should also be noted on the map.

Although a map is important, the consultant should provide additional data. For example, the consultant should discuss the following eight items:

1. Traffic flow
2. Ingress/egress

3. Visibility
4. Neighborhood
5. Land and improvements
6. Parking
7. Municipal regulations
8. Cost

It should be decided at the time of the initial engagement if the consultant should investigate local zoning, licensing, and building codes.

Traffic Flow

It is vital that a restaurant or hotel developer consider traffic counts (vehicular and pedestrian) before choosing a site. Traffic patterns should be measured during prime operating hours of the proposed hospitality project. The speed of the traffic is another important consideration. Very fast-moving traffic is less likely to stop. Many experts feel that traffic speed between 35 to 40 miles per hour is ideal.

The state highway department should be able to provide fairly accurate traffic counts for most major highways and streets. Highway departments can also provide information about proposed new routes or revisions to existing ones that may affect the project.

Ingress/Egress

Easy ingress to and egress from the proposed hospitality project is a must. This is especially important for hotels that rely on drive-in guests and high-volume establishments such as fast-food restaurants. A restaurant from which guests have difficulty exiting will find it harder to get repeat business because a customer's last experience there was frustrating.

Visibility

A hospitality project should be as easy as possible to see. Visibility factors include the building itself, signs, entryways, and identification from the street or highway. When considering the site and its surroundings, hospitality developers should ask how easily a guest will be able to find the hotel or restaurant.

Most cities have enacted sign ordinances that prevent hospitality firms from erecting large signs to identify the property. Given any sign restrictions, the developer will have to examine other methods of making the site visible. For example, a restaurant may wish to examine a distinctive architectural design that allows the establishment to be easily recognized from the road without a major sign.

Neighborhood

The consultant should analyze the area's demographics for surrounding land use trends. This analysis is important to determine if the site will support the hospitality project. The consultant will analyze the commercial, residential, and industrial development in the immediate area. The analysis should include a statement about the quality of the development and the direction in which the neighborhood appears to be moving (e.g., residential vs. commercial).

The consultant should review such statistics as area population, income, and spending patterns. In addition, the local government's master plan should be reviewed. Area crime statistics and property values should be obtained from the appropriate local government agencies and examined.

Land and Improvements

The feasibility study must analyze the selected location and its relationship to the demand generators discussed above. For example, how does the specific site fit in with the surrounding neighborhood? The consultant will have to determine how the proposed project's physical structure relates to other buildings in the area. It will have to be determined if there are any obstructing buildings that will prevent the site from being easily seen.

It is very important that the land itself be examined by either the consultant or the developer. A soil report is required to show whether the land will support the planned structure. Other concerns are the noise levels in the area and their effect on guests, adequacy and capacity of utilities, the general topography, and the air quality.

Parking

Parking is an important consideration in many urban areas for a hospitality firm. It is important to accurately estimate parking needs during anticipated peak operating hours. Guests enjoy being able to park conveniently to where they are staying or eating. For restaurants, parking may not be a major problem if the traffic patterns indicate that most guests come by foot from adjoining businesses.

Other considerations include whether usage by nonguests (such as restaurant guests who are not staying at the associated hotel) will be allowed and, if so, how much they will be charged and what percentage of parking facilities will be allocated for them. Another related factor is whether guests will be charged for parking. Will valet parking be available? The developer must determine whether the parking spaces will be indoor or outdoor. There are many more parking considerations that have to be addressed for profitability to be determined accurately.

Municipal Regulations

The availability of adequate utilities and other services is an important factor that cannot be overlooked by a hospitality developer. The quality, capacity and cost of electricity, gas, and water must be evaluated. Zoning restrictions should be investigated as well as local health codes, fire safety codes, building regulations, and liquor license requirements. The availability of fire and police protection is also important.

The zoning of surrounding land should be examined closely for indications of direction of community growth. The developer should be familiar with the cost of building permits for new hotels and any unusual building conditions or requirements related to height or space size. The location of any flood plain areas should be noted. What are the permitted uses of any excess land, and how will they affect the hospitality firm's ability to expand?

The developer must understand not only the municipality's rules and regulations but also how they are enforced. For example, a city located near a college may have strict enforcement of its liquor laws, and a developer may want to consider building in the next police jurisdiction as an alternative.

Cost

Although a site may seem perfect after a preliminary investigation, its cost still remains a fundamental consideration. If the landlord demands excessive rent or land costs are prohibitively high, the hospitality project will have difficulty generating a profit even if other factors are ideal.

If the property is to be purchased, not only should the cost of the site be analyzed, but other factors such as clearing and grading, landscaping, and property improvement (driveways, yard lighting, etc.) expenses must be analyzed also.

COMPETITION ANALYSIS

This important section focuses on the competition and its likely impact on the proposed property.

The developer should pay close attention to the total hotel and rooms inventory that currently exists in the market area. It must also be learned if any other properties are scheduled to be built or are likely to be built in the near future.

The competition is analyzed by segments (i.e., those of similar size and class, and those in the same location). The consultant may personally inspect competing properties, review travel rating guides, and interview local hotel managers. The consultant should consider the following factors when analyzing a competing property: location, room rates, market segments, facilities and services, physical condition, chain affiliation, and perception of guests and the surrounding community.

Exhibit 4-2 on page 78 contains a model competitive summary for a hypothetical city. Note how the quality, service facilities, and price/value rankings are rather subjective. The reader of the feasibility study must examine these factors closely to test the consultant's assumptions in arriving at the rankings.

Future projects by competitors may be more important to the economic health of the proposed hotel than the existing properties in the area. The hardest projects to analyze are those in the early planning stages. Although it may be impossible to determine with any certainty whether a proposed hotel will be completed or not, the consultant should provide the developer with as much information about it as possible.

An often overlooked subject is the subsequent retirement of hospitality properties from the market because they are no longer competitive with newer facilities. Also, an analysis should show any properties that may be downgraded in the foreseeable future.

If the developer's proposed hotel includes food and beverage facilities, the report should analyze the supply of and the demand for similar types of eating facilities in the area. This analysis should cover (1) location, especially in relation to competitors that exist or will exist; (2) type of restaurant; (3) menu prices; (4) number of seats; (5) liquor availability; (6) entertainment; (7) perception of guests and the community; and (8) impact of private, social, and fraternal clubs and organizations.

EXHIBIT 4-2

Example of a Competitive Summary

Hotel	Rooms	Year Opened	* Quality Rating	* Service Facility Rating	* Price/Value Rating	Current Quote Rates Single	Double	Guest Occupancy	Current Average Daily Rate (ADR)
1. Holiday Inn	200	1983	5	7	7	$65	$72	68%	$52
2. Ramada Inn	220	1985	6	6	5	$63	$70	66%	$49
3. Hilton Inn	250	1986	7	8	7	$70	$80	69%	$60
4. Howard Johnson's	250	1987	7	7	9	$60	$69	73%	$58

*Rating 1—Worst   10—Best

DEMAND ANALYSIS

Demand analysis is used to determine whether the area of the proposed hotel will support it. Demand analysis attempts to answer the following questions: (1) Is present demand greater than the present supply of rooms? (2) Is the present supply of rooms inferior in quality to the needs of the present market? and (3) Can existing supply meet a new market segment? The sections previously discussed are often considered an introduction to this section of the feasibility report.

There is no hard and fast rule about how detailed the demand analysis should be or how many market segments should be reviewed. Generally, the following markets are analyzed by the consultant: (1) single/commercial; (2) group/convention; and (3) tourist/transient.

The developer must examine closely the data used and the consultant's assumptions in interpreting that data. The data used for demand analysis can be obtained from the U.S. Department of Commerce, local Chamber of Commerce statistics, lodging reports, visitor and convention bureaus, local hotel managers, charge card statistics, and hotel sales tax figures. The developer should ensure that the data used is timely and applicable to the area being studied.

Based on the data, the consultant will determine the compound growth rate. He or she will also determine the estimated average daily room demand and the percent of the total it represents among the various segments. Exhibit 4-3 below is an example of a typical hotel market with estimated average daily room demand and the portions of the total controlled by each segment.

In most markets, the commercial demand represents the largest segment of demand. However, commercial and convention demand will occur Sunday through Thursday in many markets, limiting the potential-room night demand and the occupancy rate a typical hotel can hope to achieve. Depending on the market, the tourist/transient demand will more likely occur on the weekends and during the week in peak vacation months.

The next step is to analyze the market demand growth in terms of daily supply and demand for all lodging properties within the market being studied. The growth rates determined in Exhibit 4-3 are applied to the supply of rooms for the next three to five years. Exhibit 4-4 on page 80 shows growth rate in room supply over the next five years for a hypothetical hotel. Notice how the additional planned rooms in the market change the room occupancy percentage over the years.

The market demand is more complicated than just a plot of the anticipated growth rate of each segment. The consultant must consider the impact of other hotels coming into the market as well as

EXHIBIT 4-3
Example of Daily Room Demand By Market Segment

Market Segment	19xx Estimated Average Daily Rooms Demand	Portion of Total
Single/Commercial	586	53%
Group/Convention	340	31
Tourist/Transient	185	16
	1,111	100%

EXHIBIT 4-4

Example of Projected Growth Rates by Market Segment

Market Segment	19xx	19xx	19xx	19xx	19xx
Single/Commercial	3%	2%	2%	3%	3%
Group/Convention	1	2	2	2	3
Tourist/Transient	2	3	4	4	4

EXHIBIT 4-5

Example of Addition and Deletion of Rooms

	19xx	19xx	19xx	19xx
Beginning Average Daily Room Supply	1,803	1,603	1,758	2,258
Holiday Inn	(200)			
Stratford Inn		150		
Mariott			250	
Hyatt			250	
End of Year Average Room Supply	1,603	1,758	2,258	2,258

the deletion of competing properties. Also, the report must take into account average daily additions and deletions to the supply of rooms when properties in the area close all or a portion of their facilities for major renovations. Exhibit 4-5 above shows additions and deletions that are available to the consultant. A major assumption in this exhibit is that the consultant has incomplete information about all hotel additions and deletions. After all, hotel companies do not share development plans with each other.

The next logical step is to determine the proposed hotel's market penetration. Generally, a new hotel will take occupancy away from older properties. The property usually operates at a higher occupancy rate than the competition and thus captures a greater market share. This anticipated demand is reflected in the projected occupancy rate shown in Exhibit 4-6 on page 81. Note that for the first year, the projected occupancy rate will be lower than those for surrounding properties. This is usual for properties just coming into the market as they establish themselves.

Once the demand has been reasonably determined, the consultant then will be able to determine the projected average room rate amounts for the various segments. These must be analyzed carefully, because increased room supply could raise the competition and thus reduce the average room rates. However, the consultant should present what he or she determines to be the most likely obtainable room rates under the facts. Exhibit 4-7 on page 81 shows how the recommended room rates for a property might be presented to a developer.

The more logical the consultant's presentation of the data, the easier it will be for the developer to analyze it and the consultant's underlying assumptions. The developer should conclude whether the consultant's assumptions are reasonable. The project's risk is more easily analyzed when the consultant's assumptions are known.

EXHIBIT 4-6

Example of Projected Annual Occupancy
of Proposed 200 Room Hotel

Year	Average Annual Room Occupancy
19xx	60%
19xx	65
19xx	68
19xx	72
19xx	73

Based on the Above Average Occupancy
The Proposed Hotel's Room
Sales By Segment

Market Segment	Proposed Hotels Portion of Total
Single/Commercial	75%
Group/Convention	5
Tourist/Transient	20
	100%

EXHIBIT 4-7

Example of Average Daily Room Rates by Segment

Segment	Average Daily Rate
Single/Commercial	$48
Group/Convention	$46
Tourist/Transient	$54

Average Daily Rate in Proportion to Segment Sales

Segment	Average Daily Rate	Proposed Hotel's Portion of Total	Weighted Daily Room Rate $(1) \times (2)$
Single/Commercial	$48	75%	$36.00
Group/Convention	$46	5	2.30
Tourist/Transient	$54	20	10.80
		100%	$48.10
		Round	
		To	$48.00

As noted, usually the consultant projects the estimated annual growth rates for the different market segments studied for the next two to five years. Developers should realize that the further the estimates are made into the future, the less accurate they are likely to be. It is very important for the developer to realize that the estimates are based on assumptions that may not materialize in the future.

RECOMMENDED FACILITIES

Many times, the consultant is asked to recommend the type of hotel that would best fit the proposed location, given the feasibility study's overall analysis. Although this service is optional, such a recommendation might save a project in which the current concept proves to be inappropriate for the area. The starting point for such a recommendation is to critique the existing design plans for the proposed hotel. Unless it is absolutely necessary to recommend a totally different type of hotel, the feasibility report should recommend modifications to the existing plans based on market needs.

Often, the developer is franchising or building a chain-affiliated entity for which a certain design is required. The consultant should be informed of this so that he or she does not waste time or money redesigning a fixed plan.

Generally, the consultant will recommend an overall design concept to which he feels the planned hotel's market is most receptive. The recommended design should fit into the community, and the hotel's decor should be planned with the hotel's typical guest in mind.

It is very important that the consultant consider the everchanging guest preferences in design and amenities when reviewing a hotel's design. Such design considerations as room size, carpeting, air conditioning, layout and design, heating fixtures, and room supplies are all important when trying to please the increasingly sophisticated traveler.

This section of the report should also discuss guestrooms. The number of guestrooms supplied should closely match the number of rooms demanded. The developer should ensure that the projected occupancy levels are reasonable, not based solely on the consultant's most optimistic projections. Also, the mix of single- and multiple-occupancy rooms should match projected demand. Finally, the consultant should address any special room considerations such as suites, whirlpools, and wetbars.

Often in the past, a hotel paid less attention to food and beverage operations than to the room operations. However, with increased competition in the industry, hotels are beginning to see food and beverage operations as profit centers. The consultant should review the capacity and size of food and beverage facilities to ensure that the expected hotel demand will support these facilities. It is also important for the consultant to review the demand for the food and beverage facility from nonguests because they can represent a significant market.

ESTIMATES OF OPERATING RESULTS

The Estimate of Operating Results is the final section of a market study that includes operating projections. This section is based on the results of the demand analysis and presents estimated revenue and expenses and/or cash projections before debt service and return on investment. The consultant will generally use the *Uniform System of Accounts for Hotels* developed by the American Hotel and Motel Association in presenting the information. Exhibit 4-8 below shows a projected statement of cash flow before management fees, property taxes, debt service, and income taxes. Amortization and depreciation expense are not included because they are noncash items.

The developer usually takes these numbers and applies to them the cost of building, financing costs, real estate taxes, management fees, and income tax to calculate the after-tax return on the project. (See Chapter 5 on methods for calculating the rate of return.) However, many times the consultant is asked to complete the projected income and loss projections and to supply the relevant rate of return calculations for the developer. Since the information for such calculations is present in other sections of this book, this chapter will focus on the cash flow before the fixed expenses listed above.

The developer should begin with the estimated room occupancy and average room rate developed in the demand analysis section. It is very important for the developer to analyze the average room rate expected in relation to the demand analysis to ensure a reasonable number. This number is very important because all the variable cost factors will be related to the total revenue developed. Exhibit 4-9 on page 84 shows the projected room revenue developed for the hypothetical hotel shown in Exhibit 4-8 below.

Many times, the consultant will base the data for future years on a projected inflation rate. This must be taken into account by the reader and adjusted if necessary; otherwise operations could

EXHIBIT 4-8
Example of Projected Cash Flow Before Management Fees,
Property Taxes, Debt Service, and Income Taxes (000's omitted)

Revenues	19xx	19xx	19xx	19xx	19xx
Guestrooms	$2,102	$2,277	$2,432	$2,575	$2,664
Telephone	38	45	49	51	53
Other	32	34	36	39	40
Total Revenue	$2,172	$2,356	$2,517	$2,665	$2,757
Department Expenses					
Rooms					
Payroll	$ 543	$ 565	$ 579	$ 560	$ 579
Other	239	259	252	267	276
Total Rooms Expense	$ 782	$ 824	$ 831	$ 827	$ 855
Telephone	40	46	47	46	46
Total Departmental Expense	$ 822	$ 870	$ 878	$ 873	$ 901
Gross Operating Income	$1,350	$1,486	$1,639	$1,792	$1,856

continued

EXHIBIT 4-8 (continued)

Unallocated Operating Expenses	19xx	19xx	19xx	19xx	19xx
Administrative and General	$ 174	$ 188	$ 176	$ 187	$ 165
Marketing	43	47	50	40	41
Advertising	42	47	48	42	42
Franchise Fee	87	94	101	107	110
Energy Costs	141	141	151	160	165
Property Operation and Maintenance	141	142	153	162	169
	$ 628	$ 659	$ 679	$ 698	$ 692
Income Before Management Fees, Fixed Charges, and Reserve	$ 722	$ 827	$ 960	$1,094	$1,164
Fixed Charges and Reserves:					
Insurance	$ 9	$ 9	$ 10	$ 11	$ 11
Reserve for Replacement of Fixed Assets	87	89	76	77	72
	$ 96	$ 98	$ 86	$ 88	$ 83
Cash Flow Before Management Fees, Property Taxes, Debt Service, and Income Taxes	$ 626	$ 729	$ 874	$1,006	$1,081

EXHIBIT 4-9

Example of Projected Room Revenue by Segment For Proposed 200 Room Hotel

Year	(1) Average Annual Room Occupancy	(2) Number of Rooms	(3) Average Daily Rate*	Room Revenue (1) × (2) × (3) × 365 days
19xx	60%	200	$48	$2,102,400
19xx	65	200	48	2,277,600
19xx	68	200	49	2,432,360
19xx	72	200	49	2,575,440
19xx	73	200	50	2,664,500

*Stated in Constant Dollars

appear to be better (or worse) than they actually are. A better method would be to show the forecasted revenue and expenses in current year constant dollar amounts or to show the constant dollar and inflated dollar amounts separately.

The food and beverage department is another revenue generator. The consultant determines the gross revenue from this department from the demand analysis. To do this, the consultant calculates the anticipated number of hotel guests who will be served breakfast, lunch, and dinner segments. In addition, the consultant estimates the number of nonguests who will choose to eat in the establishment. The hotel then calculates the total covers by meal period for each year. Total food revenue is then calculated by taking the total number of covers for the various meal segments and multiplying them by the average check for each meal. (See Exhibit 4-10 below for an example of projected food revenue.)

Other income sources include meeting room income, telephone calls, rental income, and vending machines income. These are based on the occupancy of the hotel and are stated as a percent of total room revenue.

It is just as important for the developer to analyze operating expenses as well. The consultant should state in the report the assumptions used in deriving the various operating expenses of the project. Frequently, these expenses are obtained from industry statistics in studies conducted by Laventhol & Horwath or Pannell, Kerr, Foster for similar properties. The consultant then adjusts these statistics for local market conditions. These adjustments should be stated in the report. For example, marketing expenses may be stated as a percentage of guestroom revenue. However, marketing expenses should also have been computed on the basis of a fixed and a variable cost relationship. Also, the consultant should include a breakdown as to what marketing activities generated the expenses incurred.

The biggest category of expense for most hotels is "rooms expense." And the largest single component of rooms expense is salaries paid to maintain guestrooms, including housekeeping, bellmen, laundry, and front desk personnel. The consultant should be able to determine the hours worked from the property's anticipated work schedules. Some of the salaries paid in the rooms division vary as room occupancy varies, but a fixed portion is based on the minimum staff required to service guests.

EXHIBIT 4-10
Example of Projected Food Revenue

Outlet	(1) Average Check	(2) Average Daily Cover	Total Yearly Revenue $(1) \times (2) \times 365$
Coffee Shop	$6.50	63	$149,468
Restaurant	9.00	79	259,515
Banquets	7.00	67	171,185
Room Service	7.50	27	73,913
		Total Food Revenue	$654,081

Other expenses for the rooms division include lines, uniforms, toiletries, reservations expenses, and complimentary services such as newspapers, continental breakfasts, and laundry supplies. Again, many of these expenses contain a fixed and variable portion, which varies from hotel to hotel. These expenses should decline as the property becomes more efficient.

The two biggest expenses associated with any food and beverage operation are sales and labor. The food and beverage costs are directly related to the amount of food and beverage sold. To obtain reasonable cost figures, the consultant projects sales and, comparing similar food and beverage operations, arrives at a percentage to total sales. Labor costs can be calculated from the work schedules developed for staffing the food and beverage operation.

Other expenses generally included in the food and beverage section include china, silverware, linens, cleaning, supplies, entertainment, licenses, laundry, and uniforms. Again, the consultant analyzes the expenses in light of what similar properties pay for these items.

The single biggest item associated with telephone usage is the cost of local and long-distance calls. Other costs include equipment and payroll. Generally, if a hotel breaks even for telephone service, it is considered to be doing well.

The next major expense category is unallocated operating expenses. Administrative and general expenses make up the largest dollar total for this category. The largest component in this category is the payroll expenses for all administrative personnel not directly connected with a department. This includes the general manager, accounting staff, and other support personnel.

Other expenses in the administrative and general category include commissions on credit cards, auditing and data processing, stationery, dues, publications, donations, postage, bad debts, security, and professional fees. The expenses in the administrative and general expense category tend to remain fixed.

If the company has hired an outside management firm to run the hotel, expense projections should include the fixed portion of the management fee (sometimes known as the basic management fee arrangement) under the undistributed operating expenses.

Because management will establish the annual budget for the marketing department, marketing expenses are usually the most discretionary aspect of the undistributed operating expenses. Since it takes some time before the results of any marketing efforts are realized, these expenditures are usually highest in relation to total sales during the first years. As time goes by, the ratio to total sales should decline. The consultant should be able to derive the marketing expenses for the proposed property from the operational marketing budget.

Franchise fees for franchised properties are usually stated as a percentage of gross room revenue. This is spelled out in the franchise agreement. The advertising assessment that many franchise agreements require may be shown as a separate expense category and is usually assessed on a percentage of gross room revenue also.

Energy costs for a hotel include electricity, heating fuel, water, and sewer service. Energy costs have received a great deal of attention in recent years as fuel costs have increased significantly. These are relatively fixed, although there is some variation in energy used by guests. The consultant must be particularly sensitive to possible changes in energy costs when making assumptions about overall future costs.

The property operation and maintenance expense section includes the salaries of the maintenance engineering staff. Other related expenses include supplies, painting, removal of waste material, landscaping, and electrical, building, furniture, and mechanical repairs. Except for repairs necessary to keep the property running, many maintenance expenses can be deferred for a number of years. Thus, they are variable to the extent to which management places a priority on maintenance. One expects fewer maintenance requirements for a newer property than for an older property over the same time. The consultant should anticipate that maintenance expenses will increase as the property ages.

The last category is the fixed charges. Here, the consultant focuses on the facility's property taxes, property insurance, and reserve for replacement. Real property taxes are assessed by the local governing unit and are based on the fair market value of the hotel. The consultant analyzes the local tax rates and applies them to the anticipated fair market value of the property.

The consultant will need to forecast the insurance needs of the property. An insurance agent or broker can be most helpful in analyzing the property to determine adequate insurance requirements.

Because a hotel is used heavily by the public, there is considerable wear and tear on furniture, fixtures, and equipment. These items will have to be replaced regularly and the hotel must set aside a certain percent of annual income for this. A consultant normally designates the replacement reserve as a percentage of anticipated room sales. This is derived from the experience of similar properties in replacing their furniture, fixtures, and equipment.

As with other sections of the feasibility study, the consultant must make assumptions about the proposed operation of the project. Especially important are the expected occupancy and projected room rates. If projections are overly optimistic, the chances for a successful project dim significantly. The developer should examine the consultant's report for probable estimates rather than estimates that will hold up only if everything goes exactly as hoped for.

SUMMARY

Financial institutions, developers, and investors all have used the feasibility study to help them determine whether a proposed hospitality project has a chance to succeed. With the enactment of the TRA 1986, the feasibility study is even more important because the deductibility of tax shelter losses are limited for most investors in hospitality projects.

The feasibility study should be realistic and major assumptions completely defined. The reader should not have to guess how the consultant arrived at his or her conclusions. There should be a frank discussion of the material factors that go into a successful hospitality operation. The material factors include:

- Market area analysis
- Project site and area analysis
- Competition analysis
- Demand analysis
- Recommended facilities
- Estimates of operating results

The market area analysis is the macro view of the area where the proposed property will be located. Area characteristics such as demographic trends and economic development are critical to the future success of any hospitality project. Retail sales are one of the best indicators of economic growth in the area.

The consultant relies on many resources for obtaining the most current and complete information possible for the area being studied. The local Chamber of Commerce is the best starting point, but other resources, such as the local library, local government units, and key individuals in the community, should also be consulted.

The project site and area analysis provide the micro view of the proposed hospitality project. The consultant should show on a map the exact location of the project and its relationship to the main demand generators and competition. The map should also show the property in relation to main transportation arteries and transportation centers, such as airports.

The consultant analyzes the specific site and considers such factors as traffic flow, ingress/egress, visibility, neighborhood, land and improvements, parking, municipal regulations, and cost of the site. Specific examples should be provided for each factor.

One of the most important factors affecting the profitability of a hotel property is competition from both new existing and proposed properties. Not only should the other properties be reviewed and rated in comparison to the proposed hotel, but area food and beverage operations should also be analyzed for their impact (assuming food and beverage services will be provided at the proposed project).

To justify building a hospitality project, there must be growth in the market. If the market is stagnant, the project can only be justified if there is a reasonable expectation that it can take business away from the other hotels and/or restaurants in the area. The market is usually divided into three segments for a hotel: single/commercial, group/convention, and tourist/transient.

The consultant will determine the growth rate (if any) for these three segments and then compare them to the market the project is trying to attract. The consultant will also show the share of demand that the property should be able to obtain under the assumptions presented in the study. The developer must completely understand the consultant's assumptions to determine if they are reasonable.

The consultant is often asked to review and offer suggestions on the design of the proposed hotel project. Although many properties are franchised and thus limited in the number of changes that can be made to their design, the consultant can still comment on whether the facility can accomplish the developer's goals. After studying the area's market conditions, the consultant is in an excellent position to recommend how the project's overall design can maximize current market needs. The consultant should ensure that guestrooms are sufficient for the demand expected and that banquet and eating facilities will be adequate to service the anticipated number of guests.

The final section of the feasibility study is the estimate of operating results. The developer must analyze this part of the report carefully and make certain it is consistent with the financial data presented in previous sections of the study. Also, the assumptions used in developing the operating expenses must be examined carefully to ensure their reasonableness. Finally, the developer should remember that the study is based on major assumptions.

GLOSSARY

Competition analysis A review and study of existing and future hospitality projects that will compete with the hospitality project being considered.

Consultant   In the hospitality context, someone who specializes in the hospitality industry and who uses that expertise to advise interested parties.

Demand analysis   The study of who will be most likely to be served by the hospitality project and whether there is demand for the proposed hospitality project.

Developer   A person or company that builds hospitality projects on vacant land either to be owned by the developer or to be sold to a third party.

Feasibility study   A report for a hospitality project in a given location, undertaken to ascertain the probable financial success of the project.

Laventhol & Horwath   A consulting firm that specializes in the hospitality industry.

Market analysis   An analysis of the area in which the hospitality property will be located. Market analysis takes into account the factors that will influence the construction of a new project.

Pannell, Kerr, Foster   A consulting firm that specializes in the hospitality industry.

Project site and area analysis   The specific location where the hospitality project will be located. The suitability of the specific location and immediate area for use as a hospitality business.

Uniform system of accounts for hotels   A uniform accounting system for hotels developed by the American Hotel and Motel Association to assist preparers present financial reports for hotel operations.

Zoning ordinance   A legal division of a locality into areas (zones) that define what is permissible land use within those areas.

References

Beal, Paul and David A. Troy. "Hotel Feasibility Analysis. Part 2." *The Cornell HRA Quarterly,* May 1982, pp. 21-27.

Martin, Richard. "Site Selection: Fundamentals for Success Still Location, Location, and Location." *Nation's Restaurant News,* Nov. 24, 1986, p. F7.

Nelson, Richard L. "Checklist: Site Evaluation." *Fast Food,* May 1969, pp. 118-126.

Rushmore, Stephen and Thomas Arasi, "Stretching Feasibility." *Lodging Hospitality,* April, 1986, p. 41.

Rushmore, Stephen. *How to Perform an Economic Feasibility Study of a Proposed Hotel/Motel,* 1st ed., American Society of Real Estate Counselors, 1986.

Tarras, John. "Planning a New Property? Study Feasibility." *Hotel and Resort Industry,* Sept. 1987, pp. 66-71.

Recommended Reading

Cahill, George. "Cahill on Hotel Feasibility." *Hospitality Valuation Services Bulletin,* Summer 1987.

Rushmore, Stephen. *How to Perform an Economic Feasibility Study of a Proposed Hotel/Motel,* 1st ed., American Society of Real Estate Counselors, 1986.

Tarras, John. "Planning a New Property? Study Feasibility." *Hotel and Resort Industry,* Sept. 1987, pp. 66-71.

Chapter 5

Measuring Rate of Return

INTRODUCTION

Regardless of whether one owns or invests in hospitality development, profit making is the major objective. More importantly, when faced with risk and other project opportunities, owners and investors must measure the rate of return to get a better idea of which hospitality projects should be pursued and which should be discarded.

Return is defined as a cash yield on the investment. The other important consideration for the hospitality owner or investor is how quickly he or she receives cash from the investment. The measurement of return often hinges on when money is received. This chapter will consider this form of analysis under various discount methods presented later in the chapter.

Despite the importance of maximizing profits, it should be noted that many individuals invest in a hospitality property (especially a hotel) because of the glamor associated with owning such a property. This type of investor is likely to accept a lower return on his or her investment because the psychological aspects of owning a hospitality firm make up for the smaller return. Also, in recent years, foreign buyers have purchased hotels in the United States and accepting a lower rate of return than would most U.S. buyers. Several factors contribute to this increased foreign investment:

- Many foreign buyers are attracted to the political stability of the United States.
- Many foreign investors look at the long run and feel that in the future, the underlying value of the properties will increase substantially.
- For many foreign investors, the rate of return is higher in the United States than in their own countries.

KEY CONCEPTS

To properly measure the rate of return on a hospitality project, it is important to understand some key concepts. The following items are important for an understanding of the various return on investment techniques that will be discussed later in this chapter:

- Cash flow
- Present value theory

- Leverage
- Appreciation and equity build-up

Cash Flow

Cash flow is the amount of money generated by a hospitality project after payments have been made (1) on all operating expenses, (2) for replacement reserves, and (3) for debt service (principal plus interest). Cash flow determines which of the various discounted measurements to use that are discussed later in the chapter.

Cash flow statements differ significantly from income statements. The income statement is an accounting statement that matches income and expenses for a given period regardless of whether the cash is actually paid out at that time or not. Thus, a hospitality operation can show large operating losses due to noncash deductions, such as depreciation, and still generate positive cash flow. In another sense, cash flow can be defined as the difference between the inflows and outflows of cash during the year.

The biggest difference between the income statement and a cash flow statement is usually depreciation. Depreciation is a deductible and noncash expense allowable for income tax purposes. It does not affect cash and must be added back to net income in order to arrive at cash flow. Also, any accrued expenses, such as accounts payable, must be added back to net income because they have not yet been paid out. Items that would be subtracted from net income are any accrued income items, such as accounts receivable. The income statement also must be adjusted for cash items paid that do not appear on the income statement. The most common example is principal repayments of loans and dividends made during the year. (See Exhibit 5-1 below for a simplified income statement and cash flow statement comparison.)

EXHIBIT 5-1
Comparison of Income Statement to a Cash Flow Statement

Income Statement		Cash Flow Statement	
Gross Revenues	$3,168,200	Sources	
Less: Hotel Operating Expenses	1,900,900	Net Profit (Loss)	$(81,722)
		Depreciation	317,500
Gross Operating Profit	1,267,300	Loan Proceeds	60,000
Less: Fixed Charges			
Mortgage Interest	854,100	Total Sources	295,778
Depreciation	317,500	Applications	
Management Fee	177,422	Accounts Receivable	$126,000
	1,349,022	Principal Repayment on	
		Mortgage Debt	28,600
		Distributions to Owners	100,000
		Total Applications	254,600
Net Profit (Loss)	($81,722)	Net Cash Flow for the Year	$ 41,178

When the hospitality operation's expenses exceed cash inflows, the operation is said to be operating in a "negative cash flow" position. This means that the hospitality firm has to draw upon cash reserves, borrow additional funds, or raise more equity from investors in order to stay solvent. A hospitality operation can show a profitable net income statement and still operate with a negative cash flow.

Present Value Theory

Present value theory is the key for understanding any of the more complex rate of return methods. An investor in a hospitality project is concerned not only with how much cash he or she receives from the project but also with the timing of those cash flows. In this light, sooner is better, and there are several reasons why a dollar received today is more valuable than a dollar received in the future. Inflation is the most obvious reason.

The history of the United States is marked by steadily rising prices (except for a brief period during the Great Depression of the 1930s). This means that a greater number of dollars are required to pay for a particular item or service today than in the past. For example, if the inflation rate is expected to be 8 percent during the upcoming year and a hotel is owed $1,000 that will be paid to it at the end of the year, the payment when received will only be worth $925.93 in today's dollars. (See Appendix 1 under the present value table for 8 percent for one period of time.)

By way of another example, assume that a hospitality firm receives the aforementioned $1,000 today and invests the sum in an interest-bearing account that pays 8 percent simple interest. The firm would have $1,008 at the end of the year. This is commonly known as the "opportunity cost" of receiving a dollar in the future instead of today.

Unfortunately, no matter how hopeful we are of receiving payment in the future, there always is some risk that the payment will not be made. Obviously, the greater the risk perceived, the more likely the investor is to demand a higher return on his or her investment to assume that risk. This is one reason why so many businesspeople are willing to offer cash discounts from the sale of goods and services. The longer before payment is received, the greater is the possibility that the hospitality firm will not receive its money.

As will be shown later in this chapter, the more accurately one can measure any of the above variables of present value, the more accurately one can obtain the appropriate discount rate in analyzing a hospitality project. To get a more accurate representation of how well a hospitality project will perform, it makes sense to discount the future cash flows to their present value.

Leverage

Most hospitality projects are built with borrowed funds. It is extremely important to understand how leverage can work for a hospitality project (positive leverage) and against a hospitality project (negative leverage). Generally, the more debt there is in a hospitality project, the greater the leverage but also the greater the need for reliable cash flow to service the debt. Thus, most hospitality firms in which the seasonality of business can cause wide swings in cash flow from year to year may wish to consider leveraging the property to a lesser degree.

Positive financial leverage operates when the hospitality investor or owner can borrow funds at a lower rate in interest than the rate of return the project earns. Under positive leverage, the more the investor or owner can borrow, the more the return on the investment increases.

The following example shows how leverage works in the hospitality industry. A group of investors have $300,000 to invest in a hotel project. They can purchase a small hotel for the $300,000 cash or use the money to make a 30 percent down payment on a $1 million hotel, borrowing the remaining $700,000 at 12 percent for 20 years. Assuming that each project can generate a 15 percent return before debt service and income taxes, the hotel property leveraged with 12 percent debt would generate the higher return to the investors or owners. The result is that in the first year, the all-cash deal would return $45,000 at a 15 percent return on the investors' investment, and the leveraged project would return $57,509 at a 19.17 percent return on the investors' investment. (See Exhibit 5-2 on page 95 for the detailed calculation of these rates of return.)

As this simplified example demonstrates, by borrowing to help finance the project, the investor or owner increases the return on the equity actually invested. What happens if the estimate on earnings was overly optimistic? For example, instead of a 15 percent return on the total investment, the project returns only 10 percent. Then, the return on total investment on the borrowed funds decreases significantly when compared to the all-cash investment hotel project. The total return on the all-cash deal will be $30,000, or 10 percent, on the investors' investment, while the total return on the leveraged hotel project would be $7,509, or 2.51 percent, on the investment. This is an example of how negative leverage operates. (See Exhibit 5-2 on page 95 for calculations and assumptions.)

On the other hand, any incremental increase in the rate of return above what is expected will significantly increase the return on investment for the leveraged investor or owner. For example, if earnings on the hotel investment increased to 20 percent of the total investment, the all-cash project return would be $60,000, or 20 percent, on the investors' investment, while the return on the leveraged project would be $107,509, or 35.84 percent, on the investment. (See Exhibit 5-2 on page 95.)

The above examples show how leverage would operate for one year. The same concept would apply over a number of years and would include consideration of any appreciation in value of the hospitality property over time. Thus, understanding how leverage operates in the hospitality industry is important to realize how many great fortunes in this country were made in hospitality development. This knowledge also explains why so many investors and owners have lost fortunes in hotel development when the financial leverage operates in a negative fashion.

Appreciation and Equity Build-Up

Predicting the future appreciation of a hospitality property is one of the most difficult financial forecasts. Appreciation is simply the value of the property increasing over time. A real increase in the value of a hospitality property can be due to the improvement of the surrounding area, thus increasing demand for the hospitality property. This is different from property values increasing solely because of inflation.

One main reason why appreciation is so speculative in planning a hospitality project is that so much of a hospitality firm's value depends on providing satisfactory service. Because the quality of this service is important to persuading a guest to return to a property, the property's management can

EXHIBIT 5-2
Examples of Financial Leverage

Investor Return at 15%

All Cash	Leveraged
$300,000 Purchase Price	$ 300,000 Down Payment
————	700,000 Mortgage
	$1,000,000 Purchase Price
	————
$300,000	$1,000,000
× 15% (Rate of Return)	× 15% (Rate of Return)
————	————
$ 45,000 Profit Before Taxes	$ 150,000
	92,491* Less Debt Service
	————
	57,509 (Profit Before Taxes)

Rate of Return in the Above Example

All Cash	Leveraged
$ 45,000 ÷ 300,000 = 15%	57,509 ÷ 300,000 = 19.17%

Investor Return at 10%

All Cash	Leveraged
$300,000	$ 300,000 Downpayment
× 10% (Rate of Return)	700,000 Mortgage
————	————
$ 30,000 Profit Before Taxes	$1,000,000
	————
	1,000,000
	× 10%
	————
	100,000
	92,491* Less: Debt Service
	————
	$7,509 (Profit Before Taxes)

Rate of Return in the Above Example

All Cash	Leveraged
$ 30,000 ÷ 300,000 = 10%	7,509 ÷ 300,000 = 2.51%

Investor Return at 20%

All Cash	Leveraged
$300,000	$1,000,000
× 20% (Rate of Return)	× 20% (Rate of Return)
————	————
$ 60,000 Profit Before Taxes	$ 200,000
	92,491* Less: Debt Service
	————
	$ 107,509 Profit Before Taxes

Rate of Return in the Above Example

All Cash	Leveraged
$ 60,000 ÷ 300,000 = 20%	$107,509 ÷ 300,000 = 35.84%

---

*Payments include both principal and interest.

95

influence the value of the underlying real estate either positively or negatively to a much greater extent than other real estate ventures that merely provide just space for rent.

Contrary to what many people believe, inflation alone does not cause the underlying value of hospitality properties to increase. As demand increases for hospitality properties, so do the prices for the properties, regardless of the inflationary influences (although there is no question that inflation can influence the acceleration of values). For instance, in Texas during the past few years, hotels have not increased in value, but have actually decreased as the market remains depressed from the collapse of oil prices and previous overbuilding of hotel properties. Therefore, the underlying value of a hospitality property will either increase or decrease based on the supply and demand for that property, which are influenced by many factors, both local and national.

Historically, the underlying value of hospitality firms has exceeded the inflation rate. Certainly, an owner or investor desires that the value of the hospitality project exceed the inflation rate. Many investors accept a smaller cash flow return from a hospitality firm if they expect the future demand for the property to increase significantly over time. Presently, many foreign investors are investing in hotels in the United States and are willing to accept a lower rate of return from operations than U.S. buyers because they expect appreciation over time to more than offset the current lower return on investment.

Therefore, when projecting a total return from an investment in a hospitality project, it is important to analyze not only the return from operations but also the projected return the investor will receive from the sale of the property. In fact, many hotel projects have been syndicated to investors where the entire rate of return was based on the projected sale of the property influenced by the increase in value of the land and building.

"Equity buildup" is another indirect form of appreciation. Because a hospitality property is typically financed by some type of mortgage, the loan is reduced over the years from the cash flow generated by the property's operations. (See Appendix 3 for mortgage amortization schedule.) Therefore, even if the property is eventually sold for its original cost and the cash flow from operations was just sufficient to service the property, the investors would receive cash payments exceeding their original investment from the sale of the property based on the mortgage loan having been paid down.

But what happens if the hospitality property cannot be sold at its original price but instead can only be sold for the balance remaining on the mortgage? In this case, taxable gain may result because the depreciation taken on the hospitality property will cause the basis to the investor to be less than the redeeming value of the mortgage. This creates a taxable gain without generating any cash to pay the taxes owed.

MEASURING RETURNS ON HOSPITALITY PROJECTS

Cash-On-Cash Return

Perhaps the most common method for measuring an investment's rate of return is the simple cash-on-cash method. This is popular because it shows investors the amount of money they will make on the property in relation to their investments each year. Although the time value of money is ignored and oversimplified, the investor is given a quick method of weeding out undesirable hospitality projects.

The formula for a cash-on-cash return is determined by dividing the cash flow from a project by the equity investment. (See Exhibit 5-3 below.) The cash-on-cash return can be calculated for the cash flow before taxes or, preferably, for cash flow after income taxes.

The equity investment represents the actual money put up by the owners or investors. The example in Exhibit 5-4 below shows how a hypothetical hotel project's operational cash flows. It also shows the subsequent sale of the property as a return on the investors' original investment. Note how the rate of return increases substantially after a few years. This could be the effect of inflationary pressures as well as increased operational efficiencies. Although the return looks rather impressive, it is difficult to know how well the investors or owners are actually doing without applying a discount rate.

Also, the cash-on-cash method makes comparing two projects for the best return difficult. For example, suppose an investor is considering another hotel project. This project may show no cash flow from operations during the first five years, but upon the property's sale at the end of five years, the investor receives an after-tax cash flow from the sale of the property equal to that obtained in

EXHIBIT 5-3
Cash-on-Cash Calculation

$$\frac{*Cash\ Flow}{Equity\ Investment} = Cash\text{-}on\text{-}Cash\ Return$$

*Cash flow is determined in the same manner as in Exhibit 5-1.

EXHIBIT 5-4
Example of a Cash-on-Cash Calculation

Year	Equity Investment	Cash Flow Project Including Sales Proceeds in Years
1	$120,000	0
2		$ 8,000
3		15,000
4		24,000
5		28,000
5 (Sale of Project)		216,000
	$120,000	$291,000

$$Cash\text{-}on\text{-}Cash\ Return\ \frac{291,000}{120,000} = 242.50\%$$

EXHIBIT 5-5
Example of the Weighted Cost of Capital

	Return Percentage		Percentage of Total		
Debt Service	11.76%	×	70%	=	8.23
Equity	13.	×	30%	=	3.90
			100%		12.13%

Exhibit 5-4 ($291,000). The return, 242.5 percent, will be the same, but the example in Exhibit 5-6 on page 101 shows a better investment because the investor would receive cash earlier from the project than in the second example.

As noted earlier, the weakness of the cash-on-cash method is that it does not take into account the time value of money. This is why for a more sophisticated measure of return an investor or owner would use a method such as the internal rate of return that considers the time value of money.

Payback Method

Another simplified way of calculating a return is the payback method. This simple method merely calculates the time it takes to recover an investor's equity contribution. It is shown in the following formula:

$$\text{Payback Period} = \frac{\text{Total Investment Cost}}{\text{Cash}}$$

For example, an investor has $10,000 to invest in a restaurant venture. Assume that the investor's share of projected cash flows for each of the first five years of operation are as follows: $2,000, $3,000, $3,000, $4,000, and $5,000. The investor will be paid back his or her investment after 3½ years. Notice that the cash flow and not the income statement is the important measurement used in the payback analysis.

The only purpose of the payback analysis is to measure the time period when one may expect a payback on investment. The thinking is that the longer the investment takes to pay back the original investment, the riskier the hospitality project. However, the payback method has the same weakness as the cash-on-cash method in that it does not consider the time value of money. Therefore, the payback analysis is generally used only to gain a rough idea of how fast different projects will return the investor's investments for ranking purposes.

Discounting

As previously discussed, the timing of cash flows is as important as the amount of the cash flows. In other words, the time when owners and investors receive their cash is of the utmost importance to them. Therefore, it is important to understand the discount process clearly.

The first factor in understanding the discount process is learning how compound interest operates. When interest is compounded, it is added to the principal, and interest is then calculated on that amount. This simple method is simply reversed for discounting purposes. Thus, if the investor or owner wishes to know what the present value of a future payment will be, he or she selects a discount rate and applies the following formula to arrive at the present value:

$$PV = FV \div (1 + r)\, n$$

The user is likely to use a compounding table or a financial calculator to find the interest rate to be used. (See Appendix 1.) To know the present value of $100,000 received 10 years from now using a 10 percent interest factor, apply the formula and arrive at $38,554 ($100,000 ÷ (1 + 10%) 10). Appendix 1 reveals that the discount factor under 10 percent at 10 periods of time is .385543. Multiply that by the $100,000 to arrive at $38,554.

Because income is received or payments are made over a period of time and not at one time, the investor or owner will have to calculate the future annuity value. The reverse also holds true for discounting a stream of cash flow statements or payments back to the present. The present value of an annuity stream can be derived using the following formula:

$$PAV = 1 \div v)\, n \div i$$

Or we could again look up the value in an annuity table under the interest rate and number of periods covered to obtain the value.

For example, if an investor received $10,000 per year over 10 years, what would be the present value of the income stream, assuming a 10 percent discount rate? The amount could be calculated using the above formula or by looking up the amount in the present value annuity table in Appendix 1, which shows the present value to be 6.144567 for Year 10 at 10 percent, which, multiplied by $10,000, gives $61,446.

Although the mathematics of arriving at an appropriate discount rate are easy to calculate using the tables, calculators, or personal computers, the investor or owner still must determine the appropriate acceptable discount rate. The owner or investor must consider many factors in selecting a discount rate. Some of the more common factors are discussed in the remainder of this section.

Risk Factors

The investor or owner will have a wide range of investment opportunities to select from at varying risk levels when determining which projects will provide the greatest return. For instance, it may make very little sense to invest in a hospitality project where the total return over the next 30 years may be calculated at 9 percent when treasury securities yield 9 percent with very little risk. Therefore, the hospitality owners or investors must determine how much risk they are willing to assume on a project and what is a fair return on the risk assumed.

Although there are numerous types of risk to be considered by hospitality investors or owners, the most important considerations are risk of future inflation, risk of failure, financial risk, and liquidity risk.

Risk of future inflation. It is very difficult to predict what the future inflation rate will be. Ever since the Great Depression, the United States has experienced various levels of inflation. However, during the past 10 years, the inflation rate has fluctuated the greatest, making it increasingly difficult to predict future rates.

The risk to the investor or owner is to underestimate the inflation rate and its effect on the ability of the hospitality operation to raise room rates or menu prices fast enough to keep pace with inflation. Failure to do so could result in a decline in cash flow. Although inflation itself does not cause a hospitality property to increase in value, real estate values have tended to keep pace with inflation. Also, because they can change their room rates and meal prices quickly, hospitality properties are in a better position to pass along rising prices to guests than other forms of real estate investment.

In recent years, high inflation accompanied by an economic recession has been another problem. This has resulted in not only higher prices for financing, building materials, and supplies, but also in lower room occupancies and restaurant sales.

Risk of failure. Risk of failure is the hospitality property's inability to perform as expected. Hospitality businesses rely on good management; therefore, they are more susceptible to losses due to poor management than other types of real estate investments. Thus, it is generally true that a well-known project will lower the risk of failure as opposed to an independent management company.

Another business risk common to the hospitality industry is that if in the future competitors build in the vicinity of the property, there is a risk that the projected cash flow for the property will not be sufficient to generate the projected rate of return. Other factors that increase business risk in the hospitality industry are changing customer tastes, demographic changes in the area where a property is located, local or regional economic disruptions, and changes in transportation routes.

Financial Risk. Financial risk is only the inability of the hospitality project to generate enough cash to support the debt service. Again, due to the riskiness of certain hotel projects, many syndications may guarantee payment of debt service for a number of years to make a hotel project more attractive to investors.

Liquidity Risk. Many investors and owners have experienced liquidity risk when they have had to sell their interest in a hospitality project quickly and could find no buyers or only buyers who were willing to pay a small fraction of the real worth of the project's value.

Hospitality projects generally are not liquid assets. Therefore, the investor or owner in a hospitality project will want to maintain sufficient liquid assets such as money market accounts or bank lines of credit to see him or her through cash shortages. Many hospitality investors and owners have lost valuable property because they have been forced to sell their properties at below market value to meet loan obligations.

Weighted Cost of Capital

A popular method of deriving the discount rate to use in a hospitality project is the weighted cost of capital approach. This method combines the debt service factor along with the investor's desired rate of return in proportion to the total project cost. This method is most effective when dealing with hospitality projects where equity contributions are from limited partners.

Exhibit 5-5 on page 98 shows how the percentage weight given to debt service is 70 percent of the total project cost. The remaining 30 percent is derived from outside investors. The return on equity to the equity investors should be higher than the cost of capital because the investors are usually more at risk than the mortgage lender. In this example, the desired rate of return for the equity investors is 13 percent, while the debt service constant for the mortgage is 11.76 percent. In light of each of the two components, the hospitality project must generate a return of 12.13 percent to be attractive to investors under the assumptions presented. Or put another way, this is the so-called "hurdle rate" in which various alternative investments are weighed against the first to determine their desirability as an investment.

Net Present Value (NPV)

The easiest discounting method is the net present value method (NPV). The hospitality owner or investor selects a rate of return acceptable to him or her. The NPV is most useful in comparing alternative investments in which the cash flows and the timing of the cash flows vary significantly from project to project.

A common way to apply the internal rate of return method in the hospitality industry is for the owners or investors to select satisfactory rate of return to their needs. They then apply that discount rate to the hospitality project's cash flow projections and derive a present value dollar figure. This present value of the future income is then compared with the initial investment. If the present value is larger than the actual required investment, the project is considered sufficiently attractive to justify the investment.

The best way to examine the NPV method is with the following example. An investor wants a rate of return for a hotel project to return at least 14 percent annual average return. Assume that the investor wishes to invest $10,000 in the project. This initial investment is made at Time 0, since the investment takes in the present. The initial investment is then compared against the after-tax cash flow for each year discounted by 14 percent. (See Exhibit 5-6 below.)

Because the present value of discounted cash flow equals $11,093, which is more than the initial investment of $10,000, the investment meets the acceptability criteria. This assumes that all the underlying assumptions relating to the project are realistic. For instance, one major assumption in

EXHIBIT 5-6
Example of Net Present Value (NPV)
14% Rate of Return Desired

Year	Investment	Cash Flow	From Tables Present Value at 14%	Discounted Cash Flow
0	$10,000	0	1.0	
1		0	.877	—0—
2		$ 3,000	.769	$2,307
3		6,000	.675	4,050
4		8,000	.592	4,736
	Totals	$17,000		$11,093

the example above was that the cash flows in a year occur at the end of the year in question. If this is inaccurate, the assumption could result in an error in discounting the cash flows.

Although the above project example meets the investment criteria of 14 percent, the investor or owner does not know the exact yield rate. For that we must use a slightly more sophisticated method, known as the internal rate of return (IRR).

Internal Rate of Return (IRR)

The internal rate of return (IRR) is a very popular method of measuring the investment analysis of hospitality property. Its main advantage is that it gives weight to the time value of money devoted to one project as opposed to alternative projects.

Simply defined, the rate of discount, when applied to projected cash flows, will produce a total "present value" equal to the initial investment outlay. Put another way, the IRR is the discount rate that equates all the hospitality project's cash inflows to the outflows. Cash flows consist of income from operations plus the sales price at the end of the analysis period.

Using the data in Exhibit 5-6 on page 101, we see that the 14-percent discount rate, the present value of projected cash flows, equals $11,093. A 17-percent discount rate with the same data yields $10,209. (See Exhibit 5-7 below.) This exceeds the initial investment of $10,000; therefore, the IRR must be greater than 17 percent.

If a discount rate of 18 percent is used (see Exhibit 5-7 below), the present value of the projected

EXHIBIT 5-7
Calculation of NPV of an Income Stream at 17%

Year	Investment	Cash Flow	From Tables P. V. at 17%	Discounted Cash Flow
0	$10,000	0	1	
1		0	.855	0
2		$ 3,000	.731	$2,193
3		6,000	.624	3,744
4		8,000	.534	4,272
	Total	$17,000		$10,209

Calculation of NPV of an Income Stream at 18%

Year	Investment	Cash Flow	From Tables P. V. at 18%	Discounted Cash Flow
0	$10,000	0	1	
1		0	.847	0
2		$ 3,000	.718	$2,154
3		6,000	.609	3,654
4		8,000	.516	4,128
	Total	$17,000		$9,936

cash flows equals $9,936. This value is less than the initial investment of $10,000; therefore, the IRR is between 17 percent and 18 percent. The actual IRR is 17.75 percent.

Although one can determine the exact IRR for a project through discount tables and interpolation, there is no need to work out the calculations by hand because of the availability of sophisticated calculators and personal computers. This allows the owner or investor more time to actually analyze the project instead of grinding out numbers.

Although the IRR is useful for analyzing hospitality investments, it is not perfect. One major assumption of the IRR is that the owner or investor can earn the same rate of return by reinvesting revenues while the project operates. Obviously, this assumption may not hold up in every project considered.

SUMMARY

For owners or investors to make any type of intelligent investments in hospitality projects, they need some way to measure rates of return. The importance of measuring the rate of return takes into consideration not only the return on one project but also how that project compares with other projects investors may be interested in.

Cash flow from the hospitality project is a very important component in measuring return on investment. The investor or owner judges the success of the project by how much money is returned over the course of operations and the subsequent sale of the project. The investor or owner may use the simple payback analysis or cash-on-cash method of analyzing the rate of return. These methods provide a quick and easy way to measure return on a hospitality project. The biggest disadvantage of these methods is that they fail to consider the time value of money.

"Present value" is simply the premise that a dollar today is worth more than a dollar tomorrow. This concept is easy to apply, but its main application is to determine just how much more that dollar is worth today than tomorrow. For this, the investor or owner must know the projected inflation rate, the likelihood of generating income in the future, and the subsequent collection of funds. The longer in time that one waits for income, the greater the risk that money will not be available for collection.

Leverage is a way to use other people's money in such a way that the investor or owner is able to earn a greater rate of return on that money than he or she pays out. If the investor or owner calculates incorrectly or events turn out differently than projected, the borrowed funds could cost the hospitality project more than the project is earning, thus creating a situation of negative financial leverage.

Appreciation is the most speculative of the various methods used to calculate rates of return. Many successful hotel projects owe their success almost entirely to the appreciation of the property on which the project was located. Also, since the operation of a hospitality project is so service oriented, its value often is determined by how well the property is managed.

Before utilizing the time value of money method, the owner or investor must select the appropriate discount rate to use in analyzing the hospitality project. "Discounting" consists of assigning the discount rate to the future income projections to arrive at the present value of those income streams. However, arriving at the appropriate discount rate can be rather involved because of the many variables involved. The discount rate is the calculation of what the owner or investor has determined to be an acceptable rate of return, taking into consideration such risk factors as future inflation, failure of the project, not meeting debt service, and liquidity risk. Also, individuals may differ about what is an appropriate discount rate to use. For instance, many foreign buyers of U.S. lodging properties have been accepting a smaller return on their investments and thus are paying more for properties than many U.S. firms. This is due to the foreign investors' belief that these investments are safer and will yield a greater return in the long run than the U.S. firms believe.

The "internal rate of return" offers the advantage of taking into consideration the time value of money. The IRR is the rate of discount applied to projected cash flows that produces a total present value equal to the initial investment outlay. The major assumption used in the IRR is that each year's cash flow can be reinvested at the same rate of return, which may not be realistic in every circumstance.

GLOSSARY

Amortization   Reducing debt by the series of periodic payments that make up both an interest and principal component.

Annual percentage rate (APR)   The real rate of interest paid by a borrower on a loan. Often there are additional charges or fees charged by the lender that raise the effective rate of interest on a loan.

Appreciation   The increase in value of property because of increased desirability of the area.

Balloon note   A note that will not be fully paid off over the life of the note but instead will show a large balance at the end of the loan term (balloon).

Capitalization   The conversion of future cash flow into present value.

Cash flow   The actual cash flow from a hospitality project after deducting all the operating expenses and debt service.

Discount rate   The percentage by which future cash flows are reduced to calculate a present value.

Equity   That part of the investment that represents the owner's or investor's own money.

Financing costs   The total charges involved in the loan process including interest cost.

Financial risk   The risk that the property will not generate sufficient income to service the debt.

Internal rate of return   A finance method that discounts the present worth of future cash flows so that they equal the initial cash investment.

Leverage   The use of borrowed funds to attempt to increase the rate of return on a property.

Liquidity risk   The risk that property will not be readily convertable to cash when needed.

Loan constant   The repayment of the loan with principal and interest repayment is stated as a yearly percentage rate. The percentage rate is based on the monthly payment in relation to the principal originally loaned.

Loan-to-value ratio   The percentage of the total cost of the property that a lender will loan upon.

Mortgage   A lien on real estate securing a loan.

Negative cash flow   A situation that occurs when cash flow from operations does not exceed expenses.

Net present value   The current value of cash proceeds to be received sometime in the future.

Risk of inflation   The risk that a hospitality project will not be able to adjust prices to raising prices due to inflation.

Risk of failure   The risk that a property will not be profitable due to any number of reasons from poor management to a weak economy.

Time value of money   The concept that a dollar today is worth more than a dollar at some point in the future. The dollar is worth more today because the holder can invest it to generate a return and there is a risk that the money may not be collected in the future.

References

Arnold, Alvin L. *Real Estate Investor's Deskbook.* New York: Warren, Gorham & Lamont, 1987.

Floyd, Charles F. *Real Estate Principles.* Chicago: Longman Financial Services Publishing, 1987.

Kahn, Sanders A., and Case, Frederick E. *Real Estate Appraisal and Investment.* New York: Ronald Press, 1977.

Maisel, Sherman J., and Roulac, Stephen E. *Real Estate Investment and Finance.* New York: McGraw-Hill, 1976.

Selden, Maury, and Swesnik, Richard H. *Real Estate Investment Strategy.* New York: John Wiley & Sons, 1970.

Seldin, Maury. *The Real Estate Handbook.* Homewood, Illinois: Dow Jones-Irwin, 1979.

Recommended Reading

Lusht, Kenneth M. *Real Estate Mathematics; Fundamentals and Applications.* Cincinnati: South-Western Publishing Co., 1982.

Seldin, Maury. *The Real Estate Handbook.* Homewood, Illinois: Dow Jones-Irwin, 1979.

Maisel, Sherman J., and Roulac, Stephen E. *Real Estate Investment and Finance.* New York: McGraw-Hill, 1976.

Chapter 6

Financing Procedures and Costs

INTRODUCTION

As mentioned in Chapter 1, the hospitality industry is very management-intensive. Subsequently, there is greater dependence on management for generating a profit for a hospitality project. This is especially true in the hotel business, where the lender not only issues loans on the real estate value of the property but also on management's ability to run the property profitably. The role of financing in the hospitality industry is pervasive, and it is not uncommon for a hospitality project to carry a loan amount up to 75 percent of the value of the property.

As in other chapters, "hospitality project" in this chapter refers to hotels, restaurants, clubs, etc., but lender financing plays such an important part in the hotel industry that this chapter emphasizes the hotel industry. Also, many restaurants are leased, and when real estate ownership is involved, borrowing from the lender usually involves shorter-term loans than those for larger hotel projects.

Hospitality financing usually involves two different scenarios: a new property or the purchase of an existing property. The financing for an existing property is easier because the major requirement is to obtain financing for part of the purchase price. The financial considerations in building a new building are more complex than those for the purchase of an existing building and will be taken up first in this chapter.

DEVELOPMENT OF A NEW PROPERTY

Financing a new hospitality project involves the detailed preparation of a budget to anticipate the total cost of the project. Exhibit 6-1 on page 108 illustrates how a typical hotel budget is prepared. This section will focus on the different aspects of obtaining financing for the particular steps in the building process: (1) land acquisition, (2) construction financing, and (3) permanent financing.

Land Acquisition

The developer will first want to secure the land for the hospitality development. The developer usually takes out an option to purchase the property over a specified period of time (usually a few months). This allows the developer to inspect the property for building suitability and meet or have

EXHIBIT 6-1

Example of a Construction Budget for a New Mid-Priced
250-Room Hotel Project Cost (000) Omitted

Description	Budget Amount
Land	$ 900
Building	5,000
Furniture, Fixtures & Equipment	1,500
Total Fixed Assets	$7,400
Pre-Opening	220
Property Taxes During Construction	33
Construction Interest	275
Developer's Fee (5% of Hard Cost)	370
Franchise Commitment Fee	40
Legal & Other	35
Working Capital/Operating Reserve	300
Total Project Cost	$8,673

changed zoning and government requirements in order to proceed with the project. Once the land has been approved for building, the developer will exercise the right to purchase the property.

Although many factors are taken into consideration at this point about the type of financing available, usually the purchase and financing of raw land are more difficult to obtain then if there was an operating property already on the site. This is because there is a greater risk that the proposed property may never be constructed. If the hospitality firm has sufficient assets of its own, it may be able to borrow the money on its own name. On the other hand, the hospitality firm may purchase the land by means of a land contract. In this form of financing, the seller of the property finances part of the acquisition price. The developer generally finances the land acquisition over a relatively short period of time, fewer than five years in many cases.

Also, it is not uncommon for the developer to share an interest in the hospitality project if the seller has a very desirable site that he will sell only on condition that he be given an interest in it. Generally, the developer would rather purchase the land outright and avoid sharing profits with an outside party.

Construction Financing

Once the property has been acquired, the developer secures the necessary construction loan financing to develop the property. Although the land acquisition financing is sometimes included in the construction financing, for the purposes of this chapter the items will be considered separately.

The construction loan is a specialized loan for preparing land for construction, building, and any pre-opening expenses necessary to operate the hospitality property. Generally, the developer draws the loan amount in increments from the financial institution as certain parts of the project are completed. This is done to prevent the developer from using the funds for other purposes and to

EXHIBIT 6-2
Types of Construction Categories

1. Architect & Engineering Fees
2. Construction Contract
3. Project Management
4. Elevator
5. Pool
6. Contingency Costs
7. Legal Fees
8. Guest Room Furnishings
9. Operating Equipment
10. Signs
11. Front Office System
12. Telephone System
13. Energy Management System
14. Pre-Opening Operations
15. Pre-Opening Hotel Services

reduce the risk to the lender by matching the funds released to the value of the property. The developer uses the loan proceeds to pay subcontractors working on the project. (See Exhibit 6-2 above for the types of categories included in the construction of the property.)

Although many lenders issue construction loans, traditionally the commercial banks, and more recently life insurance companies, were the main lenders for construction projects. Savings and loan institutions were involved in construction financing until the recent savings and loan crisis put an end to most of these types of loans.

Construction loans are considered very risky by lenders. At some point, the project may not be completed, and the lender's only recourse is to foreclose on an incomplete building that may be difficult to sell without considerable additional investment in the property. Therefore, the interest rate demanded by the lender is usually higher than that for the permanent financing. The lender may also look for the developer to provide personal guarantees that the loan will be repaid. Interest is usually added to the principal balance, and the total is repaid when the permanent financing is utilized.

As mentioned earlier, construction financing is riskier than other types of financing. As a result, construction lenders may insist that the developer have a commitment from a reputable lender for the permanent financing. This commitment is a promise by the lender that funds will be made available if the developer adheres to the plan and specifications for the building of the hospitality project. The construction lender is often the same as the permanent lender for the project.

Permanent Financing

The developer of a new property wants to secure the permanent financing at the lowest possible cost. Often, this involves checking with many different lenders and comparing total costs of all types of financing. Frequently, the availability of financing will dictate how much shopping the developer will realistically be able to do. There are many creative forms of permanent financing available, and this section discusses some of the more common financing instruments.

The permanent financing or mortgage is activated when all the conditions have been met to operate the hospitality project as a going concern. This usually occurs when the hospitality project receives its "certificate of occupancy" to do business.

As mentioned, permanent financing is usually obtained by the developer through a mortgage loan commitment. The lender and developer enter into a contract whereby the lender supplies the mortgage for the property if the hospitality project is completed as specified in the commitment contract.

The commitment agreement is a very detailed document that spells out such important items as the amount of the loan, interest rate, terms, full description of the property, and other relevant items.

The lender must investigate the developer and obtain an appraisal and other important, time-consuming items. They will want to recoup these costs by charging a fee for the loan commitment.

Financing Existing Hospitality Properties

Every year, many existing hospitality properties are sold to individuals and corporations. For example, several hospitality firms have sold an entire group of hotels or have restructured and sold most of their operating hotels. If the individual or corporation sells an existing property, the new owners will more likely finance part of the purchase price.

The real estate aspect of hospitality property is very important in today's sales. Historically, demand for real estate in this country has risen. The buyer generally contributes equity in the amount of 25–30 percent of the total purchase price, with the balance coming from lenders or the seller or from some combination of the two. One of the often-quoted advantages of hotels has been their ability to raise room rates quickly in response to inflation. This is not the case with office buildings that often have long-term leases. However, this advantage has been offset by the continued oversupply of hotel rooms. In recent years there has been a substantial growth in the number of hotel rooms, to the point that in many markets occupancy rates have been in the 40–50 percent range.

The buyer of an existing property, however, has one major advantage: knowing the operating history of the property, which can be an indication of future income streams. (See Chapter 10 on buying and selling hospitality properties for more details.) The seller may carry part or all of the financing of the property if a qualified buyer is unable to secure financing at reasonable rates. Creativity is the key element for financing a hospitality project. Often, the hospitality manager has the expertise to run a hospitality operation but lacks the financial means to purchase the property. At times likes this, it is very important to be creative in locating sources of capital. (See Chapter 7 on raising capital.)

TYPES OF LOANS AND MORTGAGES

A mortgage is defined by *Blacks Law Dictionary* as "an interest in land created by a written instrument providing security for the performance of a duty or the payment of a debt." The mortgage is the pledge that if the loan is not repaid, the lender is entitled to the property in question. The person who borrows the money is called the mortgagor, and the lender is called the mortgagee. Although there are many types of mortgages that may be placed on a property, the ones listed below are the more common types in the hospitality industry.

Instead of mortgages, some states have what is called deed of trust. They operate very similarly to mortgages except that they simplify the foreclosure procedures. Under a deed of trust, title is conveyed to third party, known as a trustee, who holds the title as security for the loan. When the debt is paid off, the trustee conveys title to the borrower. However, if the borrower defaults in paying the debt, the trustee sells the property to pay off the debt.

Mortgages also have foreclosure procedures, but they usually require that the lender go through formal foreclosure proceedings. In most states, the borrower has the right of equity of redemption that usually allows the borrower a certain amount of time to redeem any property foreclosed. However, the usual practice is for the hospitality firm to offer a deed in lieu of foreclosure. This saves the lender from having to go through the long and involved formal foreclosure proceedings.

After foreclosure, the hospitality property is sold at auction, and the proceeds are applied to the outstanding debt. Since a hospitality firm would be unlikely to allow foreclosure if the property were worth more than mortgage, the property owner may be liable for any deficiency from the sale of the property unless the loan was nonrecourse. If the loan was recourse, the lender can obtain a deficiency judgment against the borrower for the difference in sale price and the outstanding mortgage.

Conventional Mortgages

In this type of arrangement, the borrower usually signs a promissory note agreeing to pay back the principal sum of the loan plus interest on the outstanding balance. The loan is secured by the borrower, who agrees to mortgage the hospitality property. This gives the lender additional security that the loan will be repaid.

The interest rate on a conventional mortgage is usually fixed, and the loan is amortized from 10–20 years with a constant payment schedule for the life of the loan. An amortized loan with constant loan payments is shown in Exhibit 6-3 on page 112. Note that the principal payments change over time, but the total payment remains constant. As the loan is paid off, each payment goes toward repaying the principal. Under this type of loan, the lender receives interest up front. It is seldom beneficial for the borrower to pay off an older loan, because the interest savings will be less then if the payoff had been accomplished earlier.

Variable Interest Rate Mortgages

With the onset of inflation in the early 1980s, lenders were more reluctant to issue fixed rate mortgages and therefore sought to issue either very high fixed interest rate loans or issue all future loans on a variable interest rate method. Under a variable interest rate method, the loan is adjusted periodically to reflect the lender's increased cost of capital. Usually, the rate is two to four percentage points above the prime rate at a given time. The loan principal can still be amortized over the life of the loan, but interest will be changed periodically to reflect the different interest rate.

Other indexes can be used by the lender in setting the interest rate adjustment. For instance, the

EXHIBIT 6-3
Loan Amortization Schedule
$15,000,000 Loan 20 Years 10% Interest Rate

Year	Total Payment	Interest	Principal Repayment	Remaining Balance
1	$ 1,761,894	$ 1,500,000	$ 261,894	$14,738,106
2	1,761,894	1,473,811	288,083	14,450,023
3	1,761,894	1,445,002	316,892	14,133,131
4	1,761,894	1,413,313	348,581	13,784,550
5	1,761,894	1,378,455	383,439	13,401,111
6	1,761,894	1,340,111	421,783	12,979,328
7	1,761,894	1,297,933	463,961	12,515,367
8	1,761,894	1,251,537	510,357	12,005,010
9	1,761,894	1,200,501	561,393	11,443,617
10	1,761,894	1,144,362	617,532	10,826,085
11	1,761,894	1,082,609	679,285	10,146,800
12	1,761,894	1,014,680	747,214	9,399,586
13	1,761,894	939,959	821,935	8,577,651
14	1,761,894	857,765	904,129	7,673,522
15	1,761,894	767,352	994,542	6,678,980
16	1,761,894	667,898	1,093,996	5,584,988
17	1,761,894	558,498	1,203,396	4,381,588
18	1,761,894	438,159	1,323,735	3,057,853
19	1,761,894	305,785	1,456,109	1,601,744
20	1,761,894	160,174	1,601,220	24
Total	$35,237,880	$20,237,904	$14,999,976	
			24*	
			$15,000,000	

*Difference due to rounding.

lender could tie the interest rate to some percentage point above the lender's prime loaning rate, U.S. Treasury bond yields, cost-of-money index used by the Federal Home Loan Bank, Federal Reserve discount rate, or some other agreed-upon index. There may be a cap to which the rates may rise in a given year (e.g., two percentage points up or down). There may also be a cap over the life of the loan (e.g., the interest rate cannot rise above six percentage points from the initial loan rate).

If the hospitality firm expects interest rates to drop, the adjustable rate mortgage may be appropriate because the initial interest rate is usually lower than the prevailing fixed rate mortgage. On the other hand, if interest rates are expected to drop and are currently favorable, the hospitality firm may be better off with a fixed-rate loan. Either way, the days of signing a mortgage document and forgetting about it until the payoff are long gone.

Care must also be exercised in determining the index to be used. Some indexes are more volatile over the short run than others. Also, certain indexes may react slower to a decline in the cost of funds to the lender. Thus, the borrower may pay a higher rate of interest than under another index.

Balloon Mortgages

A balloon mortgage is characterized by the deferral of payment of the principal until the maturity of the loan. The balloon mortgage can provide that the loan be amortized for a number of years, but the loan is due and payable in a shorter period of time. For instance, a hospitality owner may borrow money from a lending institution at x percent rate. The loan is amortized over 25 years, but the loan is due and payable in five years. Thus, at the end of five years, the loan will have to be repaid. More likely, the loan will be refinanced for an additional period of time at the then-prevailing interest rate.

Another version of the balloon mortgage is when the loan provisions provide interest-only payments over a number of years. Then, the principal balance would be due and payable. Many financing deals such as this kind are structured whereby investors hope to repay the loan out of the proceeds from the sale of the hospitality project. This method works best under rapidly escalating real estate values.

The lender can avoid the problem of rising interest rates by having the borrower share the risk by shortening the due date of the loan. Also, if the lender does not wish to loan any future amounts to the hospitality firm because of stagnating or declining earnings of the firm, he or she can require the loan to be repaid at the earlier maturity date or have the hospitality firm refinance with another lender.

Participation Mortgages

Participation mortgages became popular in the early 1980s when interest rates were very high. In order to make a loan attractive to a lender, the borrower often had to share an interest in the profits with the lender. This type of loan became popularly known as a "mortgage equity participation" or "mortgage equity with an equity kicker." Usually, the lender provides funds at below-current interest rates with the understanding that the lender will participate in the profits of the enterprise. The lender does not normally assume the risk of business loss; he or she will only share in the profits of the hospitality project if and when they occur. Because interest rates have declined since those earlier rates, this type of loan is not as popular as it was during the early 1980s.

The borrower's main advantage is that he or she can receive financing for the hospitality project at an initial lending rate that is below the current rate. This allows the project's breakeven point to be lower than it would if the borrower had to pay the going interest rate. Thus, many projects that could not be built because of cash flow projections could now be considered. The main advantage to the borrower is that he or she has the chance to increase the return by participating in the gross income or in the profits of the hospitality project.

There are many different types of participation mortgages in which the lender can participate in the hospitality firm's business. Some of the more common ways include the following:

- Percentage of gross income.
- Percentage of gross income above a stated gross income level.
- Percentage of net income.
- Percentage of net income above a stated net income level.

Convertible Mortgages

Convertible mortgages were also popular during the early 1980s. This type of mortgage allows the lender to offer the borrower a lower rate mortgage with the right at some future date to convert the loan into an equity ownership. If the lender does not exercise the convertible feature, the borrower simply repays the loan principal plus interest.

The lender has the advantage of obtaining a current return of funds loaned plus protection against future increases in inflation. The lender can choose the best opportunity for seeking the conversion.

The borrower has the advantage of obtaining funding for the hospitality project at rates below the prevailing interest rates. The down side for the borrower is that if the project does extremely well, the financial institution will become partners with the hospitality developer. If the project does not perform well, the hospitality project will stay with the developer.

Zero Coupon Mortgages

Zero coupon mortgages are yet another form of mortgage financing. This type of mortgage loan defers the payment of interest until the loan matures, at which time the entire debt of principal and deferred interest are due. The hospitality firm is the borrower by virtue of issuing a zero coupon mortgage note to a lender or noteholder. The lender then transfers the net amount shown on the mortgage note to the borrower. The borrower agrees to pay at some future date both the principal and interest compounded during the period the note is outstanding.

Under the Internal Revenue Code, interest must be accrued to the mortgageholder and included in his or her taxable income, as if he or she had actually received that amount. Similarly, the borrower may deduct the interest payments even though he or she is not obliged to pay the interest until the note's maturity.

The most obvious advantage for the borrower is that there are no debt service payments until the note is due at its maturity. However, because the debt is accumulating from the addition of unpaid interest, the property must appreciate in value equal to the note accumulation. Otherwise, the property will have to set up an account to accumulate cash to pay the note when it comes due.

The obvious disadvantage to the lender is that the interest income is due each year although there has been no cash received. However, the greater return that may be realized by the lender may be worth the risk of accepting a zero coupon mortgage. Also, many lenders such as pension funds are tax exempt entities, and reporting additional income would not result in any additional cost to them. There is a risk that the hospitality fund may not be able to repay the note at its maturity and therefore must be cautious that the property being given the money is valued fairly. Speculative properties may increase the risk that the note will not be repaid at maturity.

Junior or Second Mortgages

First mortgages have superior standing to other mortgages. All other mortgages on the property are known as junior mortgage instruments. They can be the second, third, or fourth mortgage on the property.

Most people are familiar with second mortgages; they are the most popular of junior mortgages. The second mortgage can be very similar to the first mortgage in its terms, but it usually carries a higher interest rate than the original mortgage because the risk is higher in that if there are insufficient funds from the sale of the property to satisfy both loans, the first mortgage will have the higher claim.

A second mortgage is frequently assumed because the hospitality firm does not wish to refinance a property in light of heavy prepayment penalties. Another reason for taking a second mortgage is when the hospitality firm needs cash immediately but feels that interest rates will be lower in the future and thus wishes to delay refinancing the property until a later time.

The second mortgage often comes into play when the owner of the hospitality property wishes to sell the property and is willing to help finance the purchaser of the property by agreeing to accept a second mortgage for the difference between the assumption of the old and the remaining balance owed. (See purchase-money financing on page xx for details.)

Wraparound Mortgage

The wraparound mortgage is another form of the second mortgage. Instead of being subordinate to the primary mortgage, this mortgage actually "wraps itself around" the total mortgage. That is, the borrower pays one loan payment to the lender and the lender in turns pays the primary mortgage lender. This is common when the buyer is unable to "assume" or take "subject to" the original mortgage.

The following example illustrates how a wraparound mortgage works.

> Smith owns the Blue Motel and has a mortgage balance of $100,000 at 8 percent. Jones wishes to purchase the motel for $400,000, with a $100,000 downpayment and a $300,000 land contract carried by Smith at 11 percent interest. To reduce the total mortgage cost and make the property more attractive to a seller, Smith may sell the property for $400,000 and take a $300,000 land contract at 10 percent (11 percent on $200,000 and 8 percent on $100,000). Smith would then pay on the original mortgage. This lowers the interest cost to Jones and thus makes the Blue Motel more attractive to the purchaser without changing the selling price of the property.

SELLER FINANCE INSTRUMENTS

Purchase-Money Mortgages

In purchase-money mortgages, the seller of a hospitality property makes the mortgage himself for the property. The seller signs a note for the unpaid portion of the amount owed, and the mortgage will be on the property to secure payment of the note, much like a regular mortgage.

Some properties are difficult to finance through regular financing channels, and the purchase-money mortgage may be the only way to sell the property. Also, many times the seller of the property helps finance part of the selling price because the rate of return may be higher than he or she could receive in other investments.

Land Contracts

The land contract, or conditional sales contract, is the primary method for selling property for many smaller hospitality operations. The land contract is similar to the money-purchase mortgage in that the seller provides financing to the buyer of the property. However, under the land contract, title does not pass until the loan is paid off. The buyer has what "equitable title," while the seller retains the legal title. If the buyer defaults on a loan payment under common law, regardless of the amount paid in, he or she forfeits the property, which reverts back to the seller. Most jurisdictions have mitigated this harsh common-law rule, but the buyer still must understand fully his or her state's particular legal requirements when using the land contract.

Many times, the buyer is unable to find outside financing for the purchase of the hospitality property. In these cases, the land contract is the only method of financing the transaction. However, the land contract is most useful when the buyer can make a small downpayment on the property. Often, the seller is willing to carry the financing of the property because the property is difficult to sell or the seller may be able to obtain a higher selling price in exchange for taking on the risk of financing the buyer's acquisition. Because the seller is in effect the mortgagee under this type of transaction, he or she should ascertain whether the seller will be able to meet the debt obligations after the sale.

Syndicators will often purchase hospitality property on a land contract basis either with very little down or no down payment at all in exchange for a higher selling price. The syndicator can then obtain the funds necessary for acquisition of the property using the operations of the hospitality property to service the debt. The limited partners have the advantage of higher depreciation writeoffs then if the property were purchased through conventional lending institutions. Usually, the interest rate can be lower on the debt service than from the lending institutions. This assumes the property is at fair market value and the IRS-imputed interest rules do not apply.

SHORT TERM FINANCING/OPERATIONAL BORROWING

The mortgage and seller financing the loans discussed above usually have in mind either long-term financing (10 years or longer) or intermediate-term financing (five to seven years). These types of loans are usually amortized over the length of the loan period or are treated as balloon payments with the principal due at the end of the year. The following are descriptions of short-term loans that are used in hospitality operations to cover periodic shortfalls in cash flow or to cover other unexpected short-term problems.

Line of Credit

A line of credit is an unsecured loan made available to a hospitality operation for a limited period of time (such as 30, 60, 90 days). Under a line of credit, the hospitality operation normally must qualify for the loan amount. The notes can be rolled over at the end of the time period if such an arrangement is provided for.

A bank can deny the line of credit any time up to the actual disbursements of the funds . Also, the notes are for a short period and may have to be paid back at the end of that period if the lending institution does not wish to roll the notes over. Because so many hospitality operations are seasonal, the line of credit may be a excellent way of securing funds for short periods when business is slow.

Revolving Line of Credit

A revolving line of credit is generally a more attractive device for a hospitality firm. In this arrangement, the hospitality firm and the lending institution agree ahead of time about how much money will be available for the firm to draw down upon during a specified period (usually three years) before the revolving line of credit must be renegotiated. This agreement allows the hospitality firm to draw down on funds as needed, and interest is paid only on the actual amount borrowed. However, the hospitality firm normally must pay a commitment fee in addition to any interest due on amounts borrowed for the right to this service.

The interest rate is usually tied to some premium over the current prime interest rate. A very seasonal hospitality firm that often runs into temporary cash shortages due to payroll requirements may find the revolving line of credit indispensable. However, the right to this liquidity is expensive, and the hospitality firm should analyze its operations closely to determine how much protection is needed.

NEGOTIATING A LOAN

Generally, almost everyone involved in the hospitality industry uses debt financing at some point. When the need arises, the hospitality executive must focus his or her attention on convincing the lender why money should be loaned to the company. Therefore, it is imperative for the hospitality executive to understand the lender's position before granting a loan. Many independent hospitality firms have difficulty obtaining financing because of the high failure rate of many independent hospitality firms, which results in bad debt for the lending institution. There are many important strategies one should pursue before applying for a loan. This section focuses on how to organize and properly follow the steps for obtaining a loan.

Before entering into negotiations with any financial institution, the executive must understand that a lender makes money from the interest charged on the loan. Unlike the borrower, the lender does not want to be in the hospitality business and quite often does not really understand it. Therefore, it is up to the hospitality executive to convince the lender not only why this hospitality property is so important but also how this property differs from the ones that have failed. Selecting an appropriate lending institution is the first step towards beginning the loan process. The starting point should be contacting those institutions with whom the firm and/or the principal owners of the hospitality firm maintain their accounts. However, the executive must be careful where he or she first establishes a banking relationship because lending institutions may differ significantly from one another. Many restaurateurs have been extremely disappointed and frustrated to find out that a financial institution with which they have previously done business now refuses to loan funds due to a very conservative lending policy concerning restaurants. On the other hand, many financial institutions are quite willing to loan money to a new restaurant. Some financial institutions may want to loan to a new or expanding hospitality venture. For example, a lender may have money available for the particular loan or the hospitality industry may be targeted by the lending institution for loans.

A hospitality executive should shop for the best loan on the best possible terms. One way of doing this is a referral to a lender by someone whose opinion is respected by the lender. These referrals may be made by the hospitality firm's accountant, attorney, or friends who are running successful hospitality firms.

Once a lender is approached, he or she will need to know in detail why the hospitality executive needs the loan. A hospitality firm that approaches a lender with vague needs and dollar amounts is asking to be rejected. The executive must first carefully think through his or her need, because advance preparation is critical to obtaining the loan. The hospitality executive should know and ask for the exact amount needed. Although this step requires a detailed analysis, it will save the borrower a great deal of grief in both the short and long run. For example, if the hospitality executive asks for too little, either he or she have to approach the lender later to reapply for more money or the lender might notice the inadequate amount and realize the borrower is not fully prepared. Asking for too much in the hopes of "bargaining" for a lesser amount is also a common mistake because this strategy shows a lack of professionalism and accuracy.

The financial plan or loan proposal is the hospitality executive's primary selling point for obtaining a loan. Many hospitality executives who lack financial sophistication tend to shy away from this very important aspect. If this is the case, the executive should seek the advice of his or her accountant or CPA, who has the proper training and experience in preparing loan requests. Lending officers take financial statements very seriously, and the hospitality executive should take the time to prepare them properly and accurately from the beginning.

As previously noted, the lender looks at many criteria when determining whether a loan should be granted. However, the most important factors analyzed are often described as the "four C's" of credit:

1. Character
2. Capacity
3. Capital
4. Collateral

The borrower's *character* includes hospitality experience, honesty, integrity, and willingness to pay. The hospitality executive should outline for the lender the experiences and special skills of the firm's top management. In many instances, the borrower's track record will be a major factor on how large a loan the hospitality firm will be able to obtain.

Furthermore, the hospitality executive should describe and identify the hospitality firm's product, market, customers, and competitors. This process enables the lender to obtain a more accurate picture of the hospitality project that the executive will introduce to the public. This description also helps the lender understand how the hospitality executive's prior experience fits into the plans.

The hospitality executive should never underestimate personal attributes including self-confidence, manner of presentation, and personal demeanor when negotiating a loan. The relationship between the hospitality executive and lender is based on mutual trust. Therefore, it is invaluable for the hospitality executive to be able to interact with the lender in the most candid and honest manner possible. If the hospitality executive has been turned down for a loan by some other institution, he or she should not try to hide this fact from the lender. Because a potential lender will ultimately know a great deal about the executive, the lender's chances of discovering a previous turndown is quite high. If this information was in fact kept from the lender, he or she might reject the loan on the basis of dishonesty or lack of trust. Trust is also important when the hospitality firm faces a crisis and there is serious concern over the possibility of repaying the loan. By alerting the lender to problems as soon as possible, the hospitality executive and the lender may have the opportunity to work out a possible solution in lieu of foreclosing on the loan and closing the property.

The *capacity* of the borrower to pay back the loan is also highly regarded by lenders. Operating a hospitality property efficiently and profitably is, of course, a necessity for the loan to be repaid. The ability to repay a loan is demonstrated by showing projected financial balance sheets, income statements, and cash flow statements for generally the first three to five years of operation. Furthermore, because hospitality firms generally operate with lower working capital requirements than other types of businesses, the hospitality executive must explain this fact to the lender who may have little experience in handling hospitality industry loan requests. Another concern for the hospitality executive is showing how cash flow will be affected by the seasonality of income, which often varies from season to season due to location, vacation periods, or weather. The lender will be most concerned about how the hospitality executive plans to handle shortfalls due to these factors.

As mentioned earlier, in addition to financial statements, the hospitality executive should also have prepared the exact amount of the loan requested and be able to explain how the loan proceeds will be utilized. The lender will want a detailed plan outlining how the hospitality firm will pay back the loan. It would also be in the hospitality executive's best interest to show several different scenarios to help assure the lender that the loan will be paid back even in less than ideal circumstances.

Lenders are also very interested in how much *capital* the prospective hospitality firm and executive possesses with which to pay back the loan if the firm's operations do not live up to expectations. Although in most cases the hospitality firm itself obtains the loan, the lender will insist that the principal owners of a smaller hospitality company guarantee the loans made to the firm. Additionally, the larger the equity contribution made by the participants, the greater the likelihood of the loan being approved. Lenders like to see a large equity contribution, not only for reducing the risk of a bad loan but also for making the penalty of walking away from a troubled hospitality firm more expensive to the participants.

Finally, the lender will insist on *collateral* for the loan. This often includes liens on the firm's equipment and furniture. However, since lenders realize that most hospitality firm equipment has a high rate of depreciation and a low resale value, the lender may also insist on that the principal owners include their personal property as collateral in addition.

After all the requirements of the lender have been met, the hospitality executive must still negotiate the terms of the loan. The hospitality executive must be cautious because unreasonable restrictions can result in unfavorable consequences. For example, most loan agreements allow the lender to recall the entire amount of the loan if the borrower defaults in any manner from the loan agreement. Although the lender seldom enforces this, it does afford an opportunity to get the delinquent borrower into the office to discuss the problem. The lender may use the recall provision by placing additional restrictions upon the borrower or by renegotiating the entire loan.

Cash controls are other restrictions likely to be imposed by the lender. For instance, the lender may insist that cash balances be maintained at a certain level. As mentioned previously, the borrower must inform the lender about the hospitality industry's practice of carrying cash balances smaller than those in most other businesses. Another popular restriction is to insist that the borrower not sell any assets of the hospitality firm without permission from the lender. The lender may also stipulate that the hospitality firm may not use equipment as collateral for additional loans. Furthermore, the lender may demand that certain debt-to-equity ratios be maintained so as not to leverage the hospitality firm operations beyond levels deemed safe by the lender.

Lenders commonly believe that hospitality firms are a high risk. Thus, it is imperative that the hospitality executive spends a great deal of time preparing the loan proposal. From a feasibility study to a less formal preparation of loan documents, the borrower must remember that the goal is to assuage any concerns the lender may have. At the same time, he must allow him or herself the greatest amount of freedom possible in operating the hospitality firm. By spending the time to prepare the loan proposal properly, the executive is in the best possible position for obtaining the required loan.

APPRAISING HOSPITALITY PROPERTIES

Before a mortgage can be granted by a lending institution, the lender will want an independent third party to appraise the hospitality property. The appraisal business is an art, not a science. The appraiser gives an opinion about value, and there is no scientific way of proving that value. Even so, the developer should examine closely the background of the firm conducting the appraisal. Because the hospitality industry is so different from other businesses, the appraiser should be experienced in valuing hospitality properties.

There has been much controversy about the appraisal profession. One need only look at the savings and loan industry disaster to realize that many loans were made on poor appraisal analysis. A good appraiser will not only be familiar with the hospitality industry but will also gather sufficient data to conduct the necessary market and site analysis. All the major assumptions shoud be analyzed closely for their reasonableness. The appraiser should be able to support the valuation with the data collected.

Once the data has been collected and sorted, the appraiser gives an accurate value of the hospitality property. It should be noted that there are fundamental differences in appraising hotels and restaurants. There are, of course, many similarities, but because the dollar value of hotels is usually larger than that of restaurants, this section focuses on hotels. The three basic methods of valuing a hospitality property are:

1. Cost approach
2. Sales comparison approach
3. Income capitalization approach

Cost Approach

The cost approach is based on the assumption that a buyer will pay no more for a hospitality property than the cost of building another facility. Therefore, a potential buyer should be able to determine a building's worth by estimating the cost to replace that building, less all current depreciation. For purposes of the cost approach, depreciation is defined as any decrease in the value of the building and improvements resulting from physical depreciation, functional obsolescence, and economic obsolescence.

The problem with the cost approach is that the value of the depreciation deductions is subjective. A recently constructed hospitality property may be able to use the cost method, but other properties would find this method too subjective to be of much use. Not only does the cost approach method ignore economic factors such as cash flow, but many adjustments have to be made to determine the remaining useful life of the property, making the cost approach method very difficult to use.

Sales Comparison Approach

The sales comparison approach determines the market value of a particular hospitality property by analyzing sales of comparable properties. Of course, no two properties are the same, and the appraiser must adjust the valuation by differences in the property. These differences can be perceived subjectively and thus require an appraiser who is very familiar with the local market.

The most common use for the sales comparison approach is for smaller independent hospitality properties such as restaurants, where there are fewer and less complex factors to analyze. The more complex properties (such as resort hotels) require more subjective adjustments. This makes valuation by the sales comparison approach difficult. Also, because the hospitality industry is so service oriented, a large portion of a property's value is determined by the quality of its management.

Another difficulty with the sales comparison approach is that there are usually only a limited number of sales of comparable properties in the area. Market conditions could have changed dramatically since those sales. Also, the terms of the sale may have influenced the sale of a particular property. For example, the Ace Hotel was sold last year for no money down. The buyer agreed to pay the full asking price in consideration for the seller agreeing to finance 100 percent of the purchase price. Thus, the hotel's selling price would be higher than if the buyer had placed a 20 percent downpayment and the seller had agreed to take a money-purchase mortgage on the remaining 80 percent. Unless the appraiser had first-hand knowledge of the terms of the sale, he or she would assume that the property was purchased for its fair market value.

For these reasons, the sales comparison approach is not very useful in evaluating most hospitality properties. However, the sales comparison approach can be useful in determining the broad range that hospitality properties are sold for in the area. However, this dubious aid is best used when the data needed to make the comparisons is readily available and the appraiser is very familiar with the local market.

Income Capitalization Approach

The income capitalization approach is the most accurate method for obtaining value of a hospitality project. As the name suggests, this method of determining value takes the income stream from a hospitality operation and applies the appropriate capitalization rate. The theory here is that an investor will only purchase a hospitality property for an amount that returns a certain amount of cash on the original investment.

Net operating income is not the same as net income per the income statements. Net operating income is the cash flow from a hospitality project after deducting operating expenses but before payments on debt service. An analysis is then made of the debt portion of the hospitality property and the anticipated yield on the investment or equity to arrive at the value of the hospitality property.

Stabilized Net Income

Ideally, the appraiser analyzes each projected year's operating income. However, to derive net income in this manner is too cumbersome and inaccurate for most hospitality properties. So the appraiser anticipates the income that the hospitality firm should make after it is fully operational and has established its market. This income is known as the firm's "stabilized net income."

A great deal of expertise is required to analyze many hospitality projects, especially hotels. This is due to the many factors that come into play when forecasting the stabilized net income. For instance, what impact will the local economy have on the occupancy of the hotel? What effect will competitors have if they build additional hotel rooms in the area? How should other factors such as appreciation of underlying real estate be considered? These and other questions must be answered by the appraiser before issuing a report.

Capitalization Rate

The selection of the capitalization rate is the key to valuing a hospitality property. Simply put, capitalization rate is the percentage by which future cash flow is converted into present value. The capitalization rate for the debt is the mortgage constant which is needed to service the debt. The capitalization rate for the investment or equity component is the rate of return acceptable to buyers when compared to other similar investments. For instance, if 30-year U.S. Treasury Bills currently yield 10 percent, one would assume that an investor would want a higher return for the higher risk of operating a hospitality property—assuming a constant real estate value.

Viewed from a different perspective, the capitalization rate can be determined by dividing the percentage rate into the stabilized earnings of the hospitality project. For example, if the stabilized income for a restaurant is $60,000 for one year, and due to the risk involved a 15% capitalization rate is a reasonable return for the risk involved, then the value of the restaurant would approximately be $400,000, ($60,000 ÷ 15%).

As this example shows, the capitalization rate is vital to obtaining a hospitality property's value. The method of selecting the capitalization rate is not cast in stone, as one person may be willing to pay more for a property and take a lower return than someone else. For instance, many foreign buyers of U.S. hotel properties can obtain higher returns in this country than in their own, even though the return accepted in this country is lower than what another U.S. buyer may be willing to pay.

When selecting a discount rate, the appraiser also has to consider such factors as the property's age, location, quality of management, inflation outlook, and other relevant factors.

A simplified example of how a 200-room hotel would be valued utilizing a one-year stabilized net income is shown on page 123.

Mortgage 70% of Purchase Price	
Equity Contribution 30% of Purchase Price	
Mortgage Rate (20 Year Mortgage)	11.00%
Equity Return Desired	14.00%
Mortgage Constant	12.39%
One Year Stabilized Income for the Hotel Property	$3,000,000

The value of the hotel is calculated by weighing the mortgage constant and the equity return desired to arrive at the average rate. The one-year stabilized income ($3,000,000) for the property would then be divided by the average rate (12.87%) to arrive at an approximate value of $23,300,000, as calculated below:

Mortgage Constant	12.39% × 70% =	8.67%
Equity Return	14.00% × 30% =	4.20%
Average Rate		12.87%

Value of hotel = $3,000,000 ÷ 12.87% = $23,310,023 or
$23,300,000

Again, it must be emphasized that the above calculation is merely an estimate of value and should not be used in setting the selling price of the property. Numerous other factors influence the property's selling price. (See Chapter 11 on buying and selling a hospitality property.)

To calculate the earnings at which the hospitality project is valued, divide the capitalization rate into 1. For example, a 10 percent capitalization rate means that the hospitality firm is valued at 10 times its stabilized earnings ($1 \div 10\% = 10$).

SUMMARY

Financing hospitality projects is an ever-changing area that requires the developer to be constantly alert to financial methods available for constructing or buying a property. The amount and cost of financing a hospitality project is one factor that determines whether the project will be profitable or not.

The method of financing a proposed hospitality project is more complicated than that for purchasing an existing property. The hospitality developer usually needs to search for an ideal site and then negotiate the loan to purchase the property along with the cost of financing the loan. Also, the developer must obtain construction and permanent financing for the hospitality project. Note that the developer may be able to obtain through one lender financing for the entire project, from acquisition of land to permanent mortgage.

Existing hospitality projects are generally financed by a long-term mortgage. This is easier to obtain because the property has an operating history. Also, there is a greater likelihood that the seller of an existing property will assist in the financing of the purchase price by taking a money purchase mortgage, a land contract, or even a second mortgage position on the property.

Many different types of mortgage or deed of trust loans are available to the hospitality developer. The person borrowing the money is called the "mortgagor" and the lender is called the "mortgagee." The mortgage is security for repayment of the loan. The lender may also require other forms of security, such as guarantees by the principal owners to repay any deficiencies if the property proceeds are not adequate. The main difference between the mortgage and the deed of trust is mainly in the foreclosure methods.

The most common hospitality loan is the conventional mortgage. Traditionally, this is a fixed-rate loan that is amortized between 10–20 years with equal payments each month. With the onset of inflation in the 1980s, variable-interest rate loans became popular. Usually, the borrower will have his or her loan adjusted periodically to match the change in the lender's prime rate. The multiple is usually two to four percentage points above the prime lending rate.

Other mortgage methods include the balloon mortgage, in which the entire principal is due in a relatively short period; the participation loan, in which the lender participates with the borrower in the profits of the hospitality project; and the convertible mortgage, in which the lender has a right to convert the loan into ownership interest in the hospitality project. Less common is the zero coupon mortgage, which requires the right circumstances to be useful to the hospitality firm.

Junior or second mortgages take lower priority in the event of default to the first or primary mortgage. The wraparound mortgage is a form of the second mortgage that helps the buyer of a hospitality project to obtain an lower mortgage cost than if he or she had purchased the property using a new mortgage.

Many times, the seller helps finance the purchase of a hospitality project by issuing a purchase-money mortgage, accepting a land contract, or taking a second mortgage for the part of the purchase price that another lender will not help finance. Seller-financed transactions can be found for all different types of hospitality sales, but they are very common with smaller hospitality property sales.

Most short-term financing needs are best met with the line of credit or revolving line of credit arrangements. Property should not be purchased through short-term debt. Short-term debt is best for handling operations shortfalls.

No matter what type of financing is available, the borrower wants to obtain it at the lowest possible cost. To obtain a loan, the borrower must understand what the lender desires. Generally, the four C's of credit (character, capacity, capital, and collateral) are guidelines in planning for a loan. The lender is primarily interested in knowing how the loan will be repaid. The more confident the lender is in getting paid back, the greater the chances of obtaining a loan. The borrower should be well prepared when seeking a loan, able to answer difficult questions about the proposed hospitality business.

Finally, the lender will want an independent appraisal of the proposed or existing hospitality property. This will help determine whether there is sufficient value in the property to repay the loan if the borrower fails to make timely mortgage payments. The three accepted appraisal methods are the cost, sales comparison, and income capitalization approaches. The cost and sales comparison approaches require too many subjective adjustments to be of much use. The income capitalization approach is much better for valuing a hospitality project. The income capitalization approach uses the anticipated or actual stabilized income from a hospitality property. The required capitalization rate is obtained and divided into the stabilized income to obtain an approximate value for the property. The value obtained is only the appraiser's best estimate. The developer and lender must realize that appraising is more art than science, and they should carefully examine the appraiser's assumptions.

GLOSSARY

Appraisal   The estimate of the value of a property by a qualified person(s).

"Assume" clause   A clause that states the person accepting the property is accepting the mortgage as well. This means that the person accepting the property will be held liable by the lender for any deficiency in the proceeds from a foreclosure sale. This differs from a "subject to" clause in which the original borrower is still held liable on the mortgage.

Balloon note   A note that will not be fully paid off over the life of the note but instead will show a large balance at the end of the loan term (balloon).

Capitalization approach   A method of determining value of a property by use of its projected income.

Cost approach   A method of determining value by determining the replacement cost of a property, minus depreciation plus land cost.

Construction loan   A short-term loan used to finance the construction of a hospitality property to followed by permanent financing when the project is completed.

Convertible mortgage   A mortgage that entitles the holder to convert the loan into an equity interest in the hospitality project.

Deed of Trust   A device similar to a mortgage, except that title is held by a trustee as security for the loan. The property is sold by the trustee to satisfy the debt if the purchaser defaults on his loan payments.

Deficiency judgment   A court order to pay the remaining mortgage debt to the holder of the mortgage if the foreclosure sale fails to discharge the entire mortgage loan.

Escrow   The use of a third party to insure that all requirements are meant before title is given to the buyer. A third party (escrow agent) holds the deed until all the requirements in the escrow agreement have been complied with.

First mortgage   The highest priority mortgage that entitles the holder to the proceeds of any sale of the property to satisfy the outstanding debt before junior mortgage instruments.

Junior mortgage   Any mortgages that is lower in priority than the first mortgage.

Foreclosure   The method of taking the property and selling it to satisfy a mortgage loan that is in default.

Land contract   A seller finance device whereby the seller finances the purchase of the property and retains legal ownership of the property until the land contract is paid off. The buyer of the property has equitable title, which merges with the legal title when the land contract is paid off.

Line of credit   A short-term loan unsecured loan made for a limited period of time.

Loan commitment   A commitment by the lender to provide the permanent mortgage upon completion of construction.

Mortgage   A device giving the lender a lien on the property financed.

Mortgage loan   A loan that is secured by a mortgage.

Mortgagee   The party that lends the money secured by a mortgage.

Mortgagor   The party that borrows the money and gives the mortgage as security for the loan.

Participation loan   A loan device that permits the lender to participate in the income of the property, thus potentially increasing its yield.

Promissory note   A promise to repay funds borrowed.

Purchase-money mortgage   A seller finance device whereby the buyer agrees to give a mortgage to the seller on the property purchased for part or all of the purchase price.

Revolving line of credit   An unsecured loan commitment that may be drawn against over a number of years.

Sales comparison approach   A method used to determine the value of a property by comparing the property to other similar properties sold.

Statutory redemption   The time period given by state law that gives the owner the right to redeem property sold in foreclosure.

Secured loan   Any loan whereby property is pledged as security for repayment.

"Subject to" clause   A clause that states the person accepting the property is taking the property with mortgage attached or "subject to." The original mortgagor is liable for any deficiency upon any foreclosure and sale of the property by the lender.

Variable interest rate mortgage   A variable type loan whereby the interest rate changes from year to year. The interest rate is usually set as some premium over an established index or cost of money.

Wraparound mortgage   A second mortgage that "wraps around" an existing first mortgage so that the borrower is indirectly paying the first mortgage.

Zero coupon mortgage   A loan that defers the payment of interest until maturity.

References

Dasso, Jerome, and Kuhn, Gerald. *Real Estate Finance.* Englewood Cliffs, N.J.: Prentice-Hall, Inc., 1983.

Eyster, James J., and Sommer, William L. "Lending to the Hotel Industry." *The Journal of Commercial Bank Lending.* December 1982, pp. 72–76.

Eyster, James J. "Creative Debt-Financing Vehicles." *Cornell HRA Quarterly.* May 1983, pp. 28–35.

Lewis, Bertram. "Hotel Financing after Tax Reform." *Real Estate Finance Journal.* Summer 1987, pp. 52–55.

Rushmore, Stephen. "The Appraisal of Lodging Facilities—Update." *Cornell HRA Journal.* November 1984, pp. 35–46.

Rushmore, Stephen. "The Valuation of Hotels and Motels for Assessment Purposes." *Appraisal Journal.* April 1984, pp. 270–288.

Seldin, Maury. *The Real Estate Handbook.* Homewood, Illinois: Dow Jones-Irwin, 1980.

Recommended Reading

Boykin, James H. "Criteria Used in Selecting Real Estate Appraisers and Consultants." *Appraisal Journal.* January 1985, pp. 82–89.

Morton, Tom. *Real Estate Finance: A Practical Approach.* Glenview, Ill.: Scott, Foresman & Co., 1983.

Reynolds, Anthony. "Current Valuation Techniques: A Review." *Appraisal Journal.* April 1984, pp. 183–197.

Rushmore, Stephen. "The Valuation of Hotels and Motels for Assessment Purposes." *Appraisal Journal.* April 1984, pp. 270–288.

Tarras, John. "Obtaining a Loan." *Restaurant Management.* June 1987, pp. 30–31.

Chapter 7

Raising Capital

INTRODUCTION

It is very difficult for hospitality developers to raise the necessary cash to construct or purchase a hospitality business. Today, hospitality executives must be creative when looking for the financing for a project. Traditional sources are not always available. For example, the savings and loan industry was beginning to be an important source of financing for the hospitality industry before the scandal associated with the industry occurred in the late 1980s.

The money put into a project by a developer, investor, or limited partner is usually called "equity." The funds borrowed by the hospitality business is called "debt." Although it is possible to have a hospitality project built with all equity or all debt, the usual method is to combine the two. The developer wants to invest a minimum in the project, and the lending institution generally wants the developer to share substantially in the risk by making a large equity contribution.

Frequently, debt and equity become interchangeable. For instance, a developer may contribute money to a project, but for business reasons he or she may want the contribution to be in the form of debt. On the other hand, a lender may be willing to loan money to a hospitality project but wants to participate in the earnings of the project and thus be more like an equity contributor.

However, for legal purposes it is important to distinguish between debt and equity. For example, if a hospitality developer has contributed funds to a project mainly in the form of debt, the Internal Revenue Service can reclassify part or all of the debt as equity. Also, debt generally has to be repaid on a schedule while equity return depends on the project generating income.

There are many different sources of financing for a hospitality project. These include the traditional sources such as commercial banking, investment banking, and life insurance companies. The individual investor often participates in the hospitality industry by investing as a limited partner or taking back a purchase-money mortgage upon the sale of the hospitality operation. Institutional funding such as pension funds and Real Estate Investment Trusts (REIT) are playing a bigger role in providing capital for the hospitality industry. Finally, government programs such as the Small Business Administration's guaranteed loan programs and direct loans and Urban Development Action Grants (UDAG) provide needed funds for the development of hospitality projects.

This chapter discusses the various sources of capital to discuss how each functions and how each can be a valuable funding source for the hospitality industry.

TRADITIONAL SOURCES

Life Insurance Companies

Life insurance companies are some of the largest holders of mortgages in the United States. They can invest funds in long-term loans because they are required to carry reserves on premiums collected. Many life insurance companies also help manage pension funds that can be used to finance hospitality projects. Because life insurance companies can predict when reserves will be needed for payment on the various policies they have underwritten, they can invest funds for longer periods to coincide with when the benefits must be paid.

The government regulates how life insurance companies can invest their funds very little. Therefore, life insurance companies can invest in projects that will yield the highest rate of return within acceptable risk criteria. This is an important consideration because when alternative investments produce investment returns higher than investments in the hospitality industry, life insurance companies will most likely invest in the higher-yielding securities. Thus, there is sometimes less money available for investment in the hospitality industry. This can result in many worthwhile hospitality projects not receiving funding from life insurance companies.

Although not exclusively, life insurance companies tend to invest in large-scale investments such as major hotels or resorts (as opposed to independent restaurants or smaller hotel properties). Another factor to consider is that life insurance companies are more likely than other lending institutions to seek equity participation in various projects and not just be content with loaning funds.

More and more life insurance policies are written to compete with other financial offerings. These "variable rate policies" require that the life insurance industry invest in properties that are a good hedge against inflation and can offer an above-average return. This has been a plus for hotel development because hotels usually can raise rates quickly as costs rise during inflationary times.

Commercial Banks

Commercial banks constitute the largest financial institutions in the United States. They generally hold most of their deposits in demand accounts that their customers can drawn upon almost immediately. Because of the necessity to maintain liquidity for honoring checks, commercial banks have traditionally engaged in short-term lending. For the hospitality industry, this meant that commercial banks were interested in issuing construction loans with a short maturity. Commercial banks insisted that hospitality executives secured permanent financing from other lenders.

In recent years, commercial banks have become more interested in issuing permanent mortgage financing. Thus, the commercial bank may not only issue the construction loan, but also grant the developer the permanent mortgage from the bank or its wholly-owned mortgage subsidiary.

The commercial bank is still the most likely source of funding for short-term debt needs such as the line of credit or revolving line of credit. (See Chapter 7 for details.)

Savings and Loan Associations

Before the collapse of the saving and loan associations (S&Ls) industry in the late 1980s, they were instrumental in financing many hospitality projects. S&Ls were originally set up primarily as savings institutions for small investors. S&Ls would then loan these funds as long-term mortgages primarily for single-family homes. A major change occurred when the S&Ls were deregulated in 1981. This deregulation allowed S&Ls to offer checking accounts and, later, commercial loans.

Lending money for various real estate projects, including hospitality properties, brought many abuses. That practice, and other questionable lending policies, have led to the collapse of many S&Ls. Currently, the S&L industry has retrenched, and it appears that it will return to its traditional forte of providing financing for single-family homes.

Mutual Savings Banks

Mutual savings banks (MSB) were originally set up for lower-class working people to have a place to deposit their savings. Most MSBs are located in the Northeast. Thrift institutions similar to S&Ls, MSBs are not as prevalent today as S&Ls. MSBs have mainly invested in residential mortgages. MSBs can issue commercial loans and have been making more adjusted variable rate loans in recent years. As with other institutions with portfolios of low fixed-rate mortgages, when inflation and the deregulation of interest rates occurred in the early 1980s, the MSBs have been looking for investments that offer a higher total return on funds loaned.

INDIVIDUAL INVESTORS

Individuals

Very few individuals earn a living funding hospitality projects. An individual is most likely to be involved in financing a hospitality project when he or she is selling a hospitality property and is helping the seller finance it through a purchase-money mortgage or a land contract. (See Chapter 6 for a detailed discussion of this financing device.)

The circumstances under which a individual helps finance part or all of the purchase price are too numerous to discuss here. Generally, a seller who is motivated to sell is more likely to help finance the purchase price than a seller who wishes to sell but does not have to sell. (See Chapter 11 about buying and selling hospitality properties.)

Another source of individual investing in a hospitality project is through family members. Parents, grandparents, other relatives, business associates, and friends often loan or invest directly in hospitality projects. Care should be taken so that funds contributed are structured properly to avoid future problems to protect everyone concerned. For instance, a relative may wish to invest in another relative's hospitality project but does not want to risk more than his or her initial investment. In this situation, the hospitality project may be organized as a limited partnership to minimize risk of loss to the relative. (See Chapter 2 on choosing a business entity.)

Limited Partners and Syndications

Many individuals wishing to invest in the hospitality industry simply do not have enough funds or are not willing to risk a large investment on any one project. On the other hand, they many find that being a limited partner is a hospitality limited partnership is ideal for investing. Because the limited partnership plays such an important role in funding many hospitality projects, this section discusses in detail the more important aspects of the syndication process and how it affects the individual investor. (See Chapter 2 for details of the limited partnership.)

Developers of hospitality properties (especially hotels) have for years syndicated or sold equity interest using the limited partnership. The advantage to the developer was that he or she did not need to put in all the money and could share the risk of the project with the investors. The investors received an equity interest in a hospitality project to use as a tax shelter. Over time, the hospitality project would hopefully appreciate in value so that the investor would receive a large capital gain upon its sale. Many hotels were built in the early- and mid-1980s because they offered excellent tax shelters with good economic potential. Many experts feel that the generous tax rules contributed to the overbuilding of the hotel industry.

The Tax Reform Act of 1986 (TRA 1986) eliminated most of the tax advantages of the limited partnership by introducing passive income and losses and eliminating favorable capital gain treatment. (See Chapter 3 for a detailed discussion on the tax aspects for hospitality properties.)

Today, hotel syndication is still a viable method for raising capital, but now investors are looking solely at the economics of the project because of the elimination of most of the tax benefits. Thus, investors look closely at the return on invested capital and future appreciation of the underlying real estate as the most important factors in analyzing the project as an investment.

Syndication as a Security

Although a detailed discussion on security laws is beyond the scope of this book, a general discussion is important to understand their importance in following proper procedures when syndicating even a small hospitality property. The Securities and Exchange Commission (SEC) has consistently held that the offer of interest in real estate projects constitutes a security under Securities Act of 1933 and the Securities Exchange Act of 1934. This has serious implications for the developer wishing to syndicate a hotel property or properties.

Basically, the syndicator of a hospitality project has to either file all the required documentation with the SEC or qualify under one of the many exceptions. A syndication that requires a filing and approval from the SEC is known as a "public offering." A public offering has the advantage of raising a large sum of money from a large number of potential investors. A public offering is almost always issued through a stock brokerage firm, and initial investments can be as small as $1,000.

Investors in public limited partnerships usual invest in a specified-property syndicate or in a blind-pool syndicate. A specified-property syndicate is constituted when a particular property of group of properties is identified for purchase. A blind-pool syndicate is constituted when the syndicator first raises the target investment amount and then purchases property of the type explained in the blind-pool offering circular.

The private offering of a limited partnership interest relies on the rules promulgated under

Regulation D of the Securities Act of 1933. A private syndication is one that, if all the requirements are met, does not require the syndicator to file with the SEC. The syndicator still must provide each potential investor an offering circular that thoroughly discusses the project along with projected financial statements.

State laws may differ from federal laws, and the syndicator must review the state law in which the property is located and where the investors reside to learn the proper filing requirements. There are other exemptions to registration with the SEC, but most private syndications rely on Regulation D.

Although the rules under Regulation D are rather complicated, the most important one is the limitation of allowing only 35 nonaccredited investors to invest in the project. The partnership may admit any number of accredited investors. (Accredited investor is defined below.)

The private placement cannot engage in general advertising for investors. The more common method of raising funds through a private placement is through a brokerage firm that has clients interested in investing in a hospitality project. The market for private placement has been weakened somewhat after passage of the TRA 1986. A syndicator may have trouble raising equity capital even if the project is attractive.

The other exemptions to registering with the SEC that may be used by the syndicator include the intrastate offering exemption, the small offering exemption, and the accredited investors exemption.

The intrastate offering exemption is available only in those rare instances in which the sale is local and the offering amount is small. This exemption is very difficult to use because if any interstate instrument is employed (e.g., the U.S. mail), the exemption does not apply.

The small offering exemption under Regulation A is available to a syndicator who issues in a 12-month period an aggregate offering amount of less than $1.5 million. This exemption does not preclude a registration requirement if the exemption is used, but it means only that the syndicator is permitted to file a short-form registration statement. Generally, an offering circular must be filed for any offering exceeding $100,000.

"Accredited investor" is defined as financial institutions such as banks, employee benefit plans, insurance companies, registered investment companies, etc. An individual cannot be an accredited investor. Because the law requires that these types of institutions have available the expertise to evaluate projects, it was felt that they did not need protection against unscrupulous syndicators. Thus, a syndicator is permitted to have any number of accredited investors and still qualify for any of the exemptions to registration listed above.

Analyzing the Offering Circular

Whether an investor is analyzing a public or private offering for a hospitality project, he or she should take time to analyze the offering memorandum. Many investors do not have the expertise to determine whether a potential investment is appropriate for the investor. Therefore, many individuals should engage a financial professional who is familiar with hospitality projects to analyze the offering. A good starting point for the investor is to ask a CPA or other trusted financial advisor to review the offering.

The first step in reviewing the offering circular is to examine the syndicator who is putting the deal together. What is the syndicator's experience in syndicating hospitality businesses? The investor must closely review the syndicator's background and current operations. Have their previous projects been successful? In the very competitive field of hospitality development, experience is important in the success of the hospitality project.

The second step of review involves examining the manager of the property. Most private placements are hotels or resorts. The management company selected to operate the property is critically important to the success of the property. Unfortunately, many management companies are not very good at operating hotel properties. Also, the management company selected should have experience operating the type of property syndicated. The investor should also examine the management fee arrangement between the partnership and the management company. What is the split between the basic fee and the incentive fee? What would happen if the property had cash flow problems? How will the management company subordinate any amount owed to them until the project turns around and shows positive cash flow? Does the management company have an equity interest in the project? (See Chapter 9 on management companies for further discussion.)

The third major area of review concerns the compensation the syndicator receives from the project. There are basically three ways the syndicator takes fees out of a project: (1) front end fees, (2) operational fees, and (3) back end fees.

In order to organize a hospitality project, a syndicator often spends his or her own money to prepare the property for syndication. The syndicator, therefore, will almost always want to reclaim personal expenses with money raised from the syndication offering. There are also commissions to be paid to brokers who sell interest in the limited partnership. The investor should review the fees to be charged against the partnership to ensure they do not exceed a reasonable dollar amount, usually no more than 25 percent of the total amount raised. The syndicator is almost always a general partner, and if he or she provides services to the limited partnership it is reasonable that fees be collected for this effort. The investor should determine that the fees are reasonable for the services provided. For instance, if the general partner provides accounting services for the project, the fee should be reasonable for the time necessary to prepare the annual reports.

The investor should be cautious of fees for extraordinary services such as a turnaround fee for rehabilitating an older property. The investor should determine that the syndicator actually has special qualifications for turning around such properties.

Finally, the investor should examine the amount of any fees the syndicator or general partner receives at the termination of the limited partnership. Usually, a limited partnership is sold after a specified number of years so that the partners can realize any gains made over the years. The syndicator usually receives a fee for arranging for the disposition of the hospitality property. Again the investor should review the back end fees in a similar manner as the front end fees. The question centers on what the syndicator did to earn the fee and whether the fee is reasonable in comparison to the effort expended.

The fourth major area to review is the acquisition price to be paid for the property and the corresponding debt structure. Just prior to syndication, the investor should investigate whether the syndicator has purchased the property for an amount stubstantially less than what he or she is currently selling it to the partnership for. If the price is overly inflated, the return to the limited partners can be substantially reduced. The purchase and subsequent sale of a property by the syndicator is known as "flipping" and should be reviewed carefully.

Another concern of the investor is the manner in which the hospitality property is financed. The investor should be wary if the debt structure is such that the loan cannot be repaid from operations of the limited partnership. Many hospitality limited partnerships are structured so that the debt can be repaid only when the property is sold. Although this may be a legitimate financing technique, the investor should be aware of the risk involved if the property is not sold for the price anticipated.

The fifth major area to review is the financial projections and underlying assumptions that are an integral part of the syndication. The financial projections consist of several schedules showing profit and loss, cash flow, and projected benefits for the limited partners. Although each syndication has its own unique characteristics that must be examined by an investor and a financial advisor, there are several important sections in the financial schedules that should be examined closely.

The first thing the investor should review in the financial projections is whether the underlying market analysis makes sense. (The criteria used in doing a market feasibility study in Chapter 4 should be used as a guideline for the information to be examined.) The investor should look at the major assumptions used in establishing the gross revenues. For example, the underlying assumptions of a hotel syndication concern the average occupancy rate and average room rate. Do the occupancy and room rates seem attainable and likely in the market in which the hotel would be competing?

The investor next wants to review the reasonableness of expenses in relation to the gross revenues generated. The investor should examine closely for reasonableness any special or incentive arrangements such as the incentive management fee and any fees paid to the general partner. (See the discussion on page 22 on fees paid to the general partner.)

Finally, the limited partner should examine the profit and loss of the partnership over the projected years. Projected losses from the partnership are considered passive and thus not likely to be deducted by a limited partner until some future date. (See Chapter 3 on key tax considerations for more detail.) The investor should determine how many years it will take before the property starts showing a profit so that losses can be deducted.

More importantly, the limited partner is likely to pay more attention to cash flow statements. Hotel projects are very capital intensive and, as such, generate large depreciation expenses, which are non-cash expenses. Thus, a hotel often shows losses on the financial statements but is actually generating positive cash flow. The limited partner will want to examine the cash flow and determine whether the rate of return is acceptable for the risk to be taken. (See Chapter 5 on how to measure the rate of return.)

TRA all but eliminated traditional tax shelters. As a result, today's investor wants more than ever a good economic return on his or her money. Therefore, it is not uncommon for syndicators to offer a guaranteed minimum rate of return for investors. The syndicator may also guarantee the lender a portion or all of the mortgage debt in order to make the deal more attractive to investors.

Foreign Investors

In recent years, there has been a great influx of foreign buyers in the hospitality industry, particularly hotel properties. The Westin, Holiday Inn, and Bel Air hotels are examples of properties bought by foreign buyers. In addition, foreign *developers* are entering the U.S. market (e.g., Hilton International and Nikko hotels).

There are several reasons why international companies find the U.S. an attractive place in which to invest in hospitality properties. The foreign investor can usually borrow funds in his or her own country at very low interest rates. As mentioned, the rate of return on investment in the United States is often greater than that received in the investor's own country. Finally, the United States is seen as a stable political environment in which to invest funds.

Another advantage the United States has for foreign investors is the large inventory of properties that can be purchased and the absence of major restrictions on the purchase of property by foreigners.

INSTITUTIONAL INVESTORS

Pension Funds

A rather recent phenomenon has been the increasing use of pension funds in hospitality financing. With assets in the billions of dollars, pension funds represent a lucrative source of financing for the hospitality industry. However, the pension fund manager operates under stricter government regulations than private companies in that the there are specific limitations concerning the investment of funds. Pensions are regulated under the Employee Retirement Income Security Act (ERISA). One of the most important restrictrions on the investment vehicles that a pension fund manager may utilize is the "prudent man rule." Basically, this rule is a test in which the pension manager is measured against how a reasonable person would invest his or her own money. Because of this subjective rule, the pension fund manager is not as free to invest in various hospitality projects as, for example, a life insurance company would be.

However, one of the main themes of ERISA is diversification, and a well-run hospitality property that returns a superior return than stocks and bonds with similar risk factors certainly can meet the prudent man rule and help the pension plan diversify its holdings. The rules have been relaxed to allow many pension funds to invest in real estate. For instance, tax laws now permit qualified pension funds to invest in real estate projects without incurring unrelated business income tax (UBIT), where leveraged financing is used, as long as certain restrictions are complied with.

Normally, pension fund incomes are tax exempt. This means that they pay no taxes on earnings. However, so as not to give pension funds an unfair advantage with tax-paying entities, Congress enacted UBIT on earnings derived from business dealings and not investments. There are several exceptions to the UBIT, and a hospitality developer must investigate specifically what a pension fund is permitted to invest in without incurring the UBIT.

Real Estate Investment Trusts

The real estate investment trust (REIT) is a special form of real estate entity that can be used to invest in the hospitality industry. This special entity was created so that many small investors who purchase stock could invest in real estate with a diversified portfolio of properties. The REIT then can either invest in real estate ownership or lend funds in the form of mortgage loans. The REIT sometimes combines the ownership aspect with mortgage lending to form a hybrid trust.

The REIT has a big advantage. If the complicated tax laws are followed, the REIT acts much like a partnership. It is not taxed on any income. Instead, the income is passed through to the individual shareholders, who pay income tax on the income received. REIT requirements are that a significant portion of its assets be maintained in real estate assets, cash, and government securities. In addition, a REIT must distribute 95 percent of its taxable income to shareholders each year.

Many REITs have been formed specifically to invest in the hospitality industry. Since the primary purpose of most REITs is investment in income-generating properties, the REIT may be the preferred investment vehicle now that individual tax rates have been reduced and favorable capital gain rates have been eliminated.

GOVERNMENT PROGRAMS

Frequently, hospitality developers want to develop a site as a hospitality project but the economics of the project do not justify the financial risk. Often, these projects are in economically disadvantaged areas or the community has been stagnate or declining over the years, increasing the risk of building. Usually, inner city locations come to mind when one thinks of these type of developments. But the scenario can also include hospitality developments in impoverished rural areas as well.

Federal, state, and local governments have long realized that in order to improve economically disadvantaged areas, government incentives would be needed to attract developers. Unfortunately, in recent years federal budget deficits have resulted in cuts to government subsidy programs aimed at developing distressed areas. Many programs, although in existence, do not have the impact they once had. However, government financing can still be an effective financing tool for the hospitality developer who is willing to spend time locating these incentive programs.

Urban Development Action Grants

Urban Development Action Grants (UDAGS) were started in President Carter's administration to help distressed urban and rural counties rebuild their economies. The UDAG program has been scaled back in recent years but still represents a major source of funding for hospitality projects, especially hotels.

Basically, a UDAG is a grant given by the federal government to localities for projects that have received federal approval. The UDAG program is administered by the Department of Housing and Urban Development, which selects the localities based on selected criteria and their order of application. The locality then can loan the grant money to a developer at a very favorable interest rate so that the hospitality project becomes feasible to develop.

As with all government programs, the rules for qualifying for a grant are complicated. Criteria that must be met are:

1. The hospitality project must be in an area that is considered distressed ("distress" is defined by HUD, and a list of distressed cities and counties is published in the *Federal Register*).
2. Financing must be in the form of equity and/or loans to the project that equal five dollars for every one dollar of UDAG financing.
3. The project must not be feasible except for the financing obtained by use of the UDAG. In other words, if the project is not feasible on its own merits but requires special below-interest financing to make it feasible, a UDAG is appropriate.
4. The city or county must meet federal equal opportunity standards.

Hotel projects have been a popular vehicle for UDAG financing because they employ many unskilled laborors. Also, hotels often are a necessary component in making a community an attractive site for conventions and other business developments.

UDAG's have not been issued in the past few years, and with the current budget cuts, it may not be revived anytime soon. However, this has been a popular item with Congress, and it may become a practical source of financing once again.

Small Business Administration

The Small Business Administration (SBA) was formed during the 1950s to help small business companies get started when traditional lending organizations felt that the ventures were too risky. In the hospitality industry, the SBA has been used mainly by small hotel and restaurant operations, usually those that are family-owned.

The SBA has two major programs, the loan guarantee program and the direct loan program. The loan guarantee program is larger in scope than the direct loan program. Under the former, a borrower goes through a bank that participates in the SBA loan guarantee program and becomes, for all intents and purposes, the bank's customer. For qualified borrowers, the SBA then guarantee the loan principal up to 90 percent or $750,000, whichever is lower.

To qualify for an SBA guaranteed loan, a hospitality firm must meet the definition of "small." For restaurant and hotels, "small" is based on total sales volume. To qualify, the restaurant's annual sales cannot exceed $2 million dollars; hotels cannot exceed $3 million dollars.

The direct loan program requires the lender to deal directly with the SBA. This program has been scaled back over the years due to federal budget cuts and has not played a significant role in financing hospitality projects. The one exception is that some money has been earmarked for minority developers. To qualify for a direct loan, the borrower must demonstrate that financial assistance cannot be obtained from a lending institution or that the applicant is unable to secure an SBA guaranteed loan.

The SBA provides other services that may interest the small hospitality firm. For instance, the SBA operates business loan seminars, prebusiness workshops, and financial counseling for small business executives. The Service Corps of Retired Executives (SCORE) consists of retired financial executives who offer free counseling services about the feasibility of starting a hospitality business. SCORE also provides counseling for established businesses that are having financial difficulties.

State and Community Funding

Many states have begun to stimulate their own economic development by making direct contributions to businesses that they consider important. This aid can take many forms, from venture capital to below-interest loans. Hospitality properties represent a chance for hiring many unskilled workers, and thus many states encourage their development.

Local communities often support hospitality organizations by being the recipients of these federal funds. Also, local communities often get involved in providing financial assistance to hospitality firms by various methods. Some communities have established formal community development funds to invest directly in businesses that will have a positive economic impact. Also, many communities have policies whereby desired businesses can receive property tax abatements for a number of years. Hospitality developers should look seriously into obtaining financial assistance from these local community economic development offices.

SUMMARY

There is little doubt that the hardest aspect of developing a hospitality project is obtaining the capital to launch the business. Whether it comes from all equity contribution, all debt, or, more likely, some combination of the two, the hospitality developer has to be creative in discovering sources of funding for the project.

Smaller hospitality projects are more likely to obtain their funding from the more traditional sources of financing vehicles, such as a local banker or SBA. Also, family members are more likely to help finance a small hospitality operation than the large hotel developments that require millions of dollars in investment capital.

Traditionally, life insurance companies have supplied the majority of capital for large hospitality developments. With a stable source of insurance premiums to work with, a life insurance company can better match its inflows with long-term outflows and thus take the long-term view when investing in hospitality projects.

Commercial banks are another major figure in financing hospitality projects. Traditionally, commercial banks were more interested in providing construction loans. As commercial banks became more active in other profit opportunities, they have expanded their services to include long-term financing.

Savings and loan associations were making headway in financing many hospitality projects in the early 1980s. However, the collapse of the savings and loan industry in the late 1980s has all but put an end to their being a force in financing hospitality projects.

The private and public syndications have played a major role in financing hospitality projects over the years. Public offerings permit the small investor opportunities to invest in a hospitality project for just a few thousand dollars. Private offerings usually require the investor to possess substantial net worth to participate, and minimum investment requirements usually are in six figures.

The sale of limited partnership interest in hospitality projects is considered a security by the Security and Exchange Commission. Therefore, syndications require the developer or syndicator to disclose substantial amounts of information so that the investor can make an informed decision.

However, the investor should review certain key points in the offering memorandum to be certain that the investment has a reasonable opportunity for success. The potential investor should review the background of the syndicator for experience in hospitality projects. Along with this background check, the investor should make sure that the property being sold to the partnership is not unduly marked up and that the financing is realistic. Also, the investor should investigate who will manage the property. The investor should inspect closely for reasonableness the fees charged by the syndicator. Finally, the investor should review the financial statements for reasonableness of the assumptions underlying projected income and loss and projected cash flows.

In recent years, foreign investors, particularly the Japanese, have begun purchasing hospitality properties and companies. Not only are many hotel chains being purchased by foreigners, but many foreign corporations are also establishing properties in this country (e.g., Nikko Hotels).

Institutional investors such as pension plans have billions of dollars in cash that could be used for developing hospitality projects. The role of pension funding has been growing steadily over the past few years. However, the manner and amount of cash a pension fund may invest is limited, and pension fund managers must always be aware of the "prudent man rule." The hospitality developer must understand these limitations and work to make the project attractive as an investment for pension funds.

Real Estate Investment Trusts (REIT) have been around for a number of years and represent yet another source of potential funding for the hospitality industry. The REIT is given favorable tax treatment under the Internal Revenue Code and is an attractive device for investors who lack the capital to fund hospitality projects directly.

The hospitality developer must stay abreast of government programs designed to spur development in designated economically distressed areas. Although restricted by budget cuts recently, the Urban Development Action Grants (UDAG), which are given to economically distressed cities and counties, have been used by hotel developers to help finance otherwise uneconomical projects.

The Small Business Administration (SBA) has helped smaller hospitality firms for more than 30 years. The loan guarantee program is the largest program offered by the SBA. The smaller program of direct loans assistance has been used recently to help develop minority businesses. Other valuable services offered by the SBA include feasibility reviews, business workshops, and business consulting from the Service Corps of Retired Executives (SCORE).

State and local communities have also set up programs to aid the development of businesses that they consider beneficial. This aid can range from direct financing to tax breaks, such as property tax abatements, or a combination of the two. Local communities can be very flexible in tailoring financial programs to hospitality firms' needs. However, these programs should be investigated thoroughly before a hospitality project is undertaken.

GLOSSARY

Commission   A percentage paid to a qualified person for selling an interest in a limited partnership. Also, a percentage paid to a person for services connected with selling a property.

Guarantee   A promise of responsibility for an obligation if the primary obligor fails to honor the debt.

Limited partnership   A form of business run by at least one general partner who is personally responsible for the debt of the partnership and that has, as passive investors, one or more individuals known as limited partners. The limited partner is liable for partnership debts only up to the amount of his or her contribution to the partnership.

Pension   A plan established by an employer to provide retirement benefits to its workers.

Private offering   An offer of sale of a limited partnership interest to a limited number of qualified persons.

Prudent man rule   A term designating how a prudent man would invest his own money. Used by the courts to scrutinize transactions by pension fund administrators.

Public offering   An offer of sale of a limited partnership interest to the public in general.

Real Estate Investment Trust (REIT)   A special business entity created by the Internal Revenue Code that confers favorable tax treatment for shareholds for qualified real estate investments.

Regulation D   A Securities and Exchange Commission (SEC) regulation that defines which types of security offerings are exempt from SEC registration.

Securities and Exchange Commission   A federal agency that administers federal security laws.

Small Business Administration   A federal agency developed to aid the small business organizations with financial assistance and counseling.

Syndication   A business that is organized by a group of interested investors. Usually interests in the project are sold to outside investors and operated as a limited partnership.

References

Bruggeman, William B., and Stone, Leo D. *Real Estate Finance.* Homewood, Ill.: Richard D. Irwin, 1981.

Adelstein, S. Thomas. *How to Read, Analyze, and Select Private Real Estate Offerings.* Chicago: Longman Financial Services Publishing Inc., 1985.

Cymrot, Allen. "How to Read a Syndication Prospectus." *Real Estate Review.* Winter, 1984, pp. 66–70.

Dasso, Jerome, and Kuhn, Gerald. *Real Estate Finance.* Englewood Cliffs, NJ: Prentice-Hall, Inc., 1983.

Jarchow, Stephen P. *Real Estate Syndication.* New York: John Wiley & Sons, 1985.

Ostroff, Allen J. "Hospitality Industry Specializes, Upgrades to Attract Institutional Investment." *National Real Estate Investor.* September, 1985.

Rozek, Hohnathan M. "If It's so Good Why are You Offering It to Me?" *Real Estate Review,* Fall, 1986, pp. 56–59.

Stanger, Robert A. and Allaire, Keith D. *How to Evaluate Real Estate Partnerships.* Shrewsbury, NJ: Robert A. Stanger & Co., 1986.

Weisner, Philip J. "Real Estate Syndications: Is There Life After Tax Reform?" *Journal of Accountancy.* May, 1986, pp. 116–127.

Wolfert, Jeffrey D. "A Case for Specialization." *Mortgage Banking.* April, 1983, p. 62.

Recommended Readings

Adler, Robert, and Lenz, Michael "How to Evaluate the Offering Memorandum for a Real Estate Syndication." *Real Estate Review.* Spring, 1985, pp. 38–45.

Sirota, David. *Essentials of Real Estate Finance,* 4th ed. Chicago: Real Estate Education Co., 1986.

Stanger, Robert A., and Allaire, Keith D. *How to Evaluate Real Estate Partnerships.* Shrewsbury, NJ: Robert A. Stanger & Co., 1986.

Weisner, Philip J. "Real Estate Syndications: Is There Life After Tax Reform?" *Journal of Accountancy.* May, 1986, pp. 116-127.

Chapter 8

Leasing

INTRODUCTION

A lease is defined simply as an agreement by which an owner of real property or personal property gives its right of usage to another for a specified time period and for a specified rental payment.

This chapter focuses on leasing real property as a means of financing. Leasing real property is very prevalent in the hospitality industry, especially for restaurants. There are many reasons why a hospitality firm would choose to rent rather than own. For instance, many restaurateurs simply do not have the capital to build or buy their own buildings. Many times, they would rather invest capital in expanding their restaurant businesses, and leasing is viewed as a way of financing that expansion. Also, because location is so important for the success of most restaurants, many times the restaurateur's only option is to rent a desirable location from the landowner.

The lease is unique under the law because it conveys possession only. Not only does a lease transfer the right to possession of real estate, but a contract also specifies the rights and duties established between the tenant (lessee) and landlord (lessor). At the expiration of the lease term, the landlord has the right to possession of the property.

This chapter also discussed the importance of negotiating the different terms of the lease agreement so that both parties have a mutual understanding of their rights and obligations under varying circumstances. The business world is becoming more complex every day, and it is important for the hospitality owner to understand key terms in the lease agreement to make intelligent decisions.

Besides the obvious important clauses such as the length of the lease and rental payments, this chapter discusses the different types of rental payments, including those favoring the landlord and those favoring the tenant under different circumstances.

The hospitality owner must understand exactly the nature of the property being rented. This includes answering the following questions:

- What will be the ultimate disposition of improvements made to the property?
- Who is responsible for maintaining and repairing the building?
- What restrictions on the use of the property are contained in the lease?

Because lease agreements generally favor the landlord, it is important that the tenant negotiate any changes he or she feels are important to successfully operate a hospitality operation.

Negotiating important clauses is discussed in detail in the course of this chapter, but the tenant and landlord should not be afraid to add clauses that will be mutually beneficial. For instance, the tenant and landlord will want to consider adding an arbitration clause to the lease whereby the parties agree to settle any problems by binding arbitration. This clause will keep attorney and court fees lower than if the parties had to litigate the problem in the court system. It is usually quicker to arbitrate a problem than to resolve it through litigation.

TYPES OF LEASES

Under the law, there are four different types of leases:

1. Estate for years
2. Estate from period to period
3. Estate at will
4. Estate at sufferance

Estate for Years

The estate for years is the most common type of lease interest used by restaurants. This lease is for a specified number of years and expires automatically at the end of the lease term. The lease may contain renewal options that could extend the lease term for another designated period of time.

Estate From Period to Period

The estate from period to period lease is usually created from month to month but does not state a specific time period for its expiration. Many smaller restaurants have this type of lease.

Under this lease arrangement, the landlord is required to give reasonable notice of termination to the tenant. The length and type of notice required to terminate are governed by statute in each state. For example, most states require that at least 30 days written notice be given by either party. Obviously, this type of lease would be inappropriate for any restaurateur who must spend a considerable amount of money preparing the property for use.

Estate at Will

The estate at will is used very seldom in leasing arrangements for restaurants. It is simply an oral agreement to rent property for as long as it is convenient for both parties. Because there is no written agreement, this form of leasing is discouraged and should be viewed as suspect by a restaurateur.

Estate at Sufferance

The estate at sufferance is a special situation under the law in which the lease term has already expired but the tenant has not yet vacated the property. This is simply a tenant holding over at the expiration of the lease. The estate created may require the landlord to give notice before the tenant must vacate, as the holdover is conducted with the landlord's consent.

The preceding categories of leases are important under the law because they provide different rights and obligations for both the landlord and tenant. However, the main thrust of any lease is the specific rights and obligations actually spelled out in the lease agreement. The following sections highlight key elements in the lease agreement to which both parties should pay close attention when negotiating a lease.

LEASE AGREEMENT: RENT CLAUSE

Fixed Rental

The most important clause in any rental agreement concerns the rents to be paid by the tenant. The most straightforward method is the fixed rent agreement. The rent is stated as a specific amount of money due per month. This type of rental payment is most sought after by tenants because the rent amount is certain and the tenants can plan accordingly, thus reducing their financial risk if inflation increases significantly.

However, because of the high inflation of the early 1980s, landlords have been reluctant to offer fixed rate rental agreements. They often find themselves incurring additional expenses without being able to pass on those costs to tenants. Therefore, it is not uncommon for landlords to ask for an indexed clause based on the Consumer Price Index (CPI) or some other index to protect them from inflation. (See "Escalation and Indexed Rental" on page 146 for further discussion.)

Tenants should pay close attention to the index used to ensure that it correlates reasonably to the actual rising costs experienced by landlords. For instance, an index based on the CPI may not be as accurate as one that measures factors more appropriate to real estate costs. Items to be measured by an index might include property taxes, insurance, and costs of building materials. This type of index might be fairer to both tenants and landlords than the CPI.

Fixed rental agreements are sometimes used for leases of a short duration—one or two years. Landlords would not be reasonably expected to accept fixed terms for leases of a longer duration.

Graduated or Step-up Rental

This type of rent agreement provides for agreed-upon rent increases during the term of the lease. For example, rent during the first year may be fixed, but specified increases in subsequent years could be built into the lease.

The graduated or step-up rental agreement is used very often when a hospitality firm has just begun doing business. At this time, the landlord is usually willing to assist the new venture with a lower rental rate, with the hope of recapturing the lost rental money in later years when the restaurant is in a better position to pay.

Escalation and Indexed Rental

Almost all modern lease agreements contain some sort of escalation clause, based either on some outside index or on an incremental increase in property taxes or yearly operating expenses. Whether the lease is based on a percentage of sales or a fixed rent amount, the commercial lease will probably contain some sort of escalation provision.

The index closest to actual increases in real estate taxes or operating expenses is the fairest one for determining rent increases. The tenant and landlord must negotiate which index is the most appropriate method of passing on the increases in operating expenses from year to year.

Tenants usually want landlords to provide audited financial statements showing the increases in the operating expenses for properties. Unless tenants fully understand the operating expenses to be included in the index, they will be at a disadvantage when negotiating the lease agreement.

Many times, tenants and landlords agree on escalated rental increases based on some sort of independent index. The major advantage for landlords is that they do not have to provide audited operating expense statements justifying the rental increases.

The most popular independent indexes used are based on the CPI, published by the U.S. Department of Labor Bureau of Statistics. This index measures the purchasing power of consumers' dollars from year to year. The index base of 100 was established for the period 1982–1984, and subsequent years' increases are measured against this base. (See Exhibit 8-1 below for a schedule of the CPI.)

An example of how rent can be adjusted using the CPI follows:

> The Bell restaurant is operated by Mr. Bell under a lease that provides for annual rental adjustments based on the percentage change in the CPI. For the year 1987, Mr. Bell paid $3,000 per month in rent. His rent is to be adjusted for 1988 by the percentage change in the CPI for years 1986 and 1987, which is calculated to be 3.65 percent [from exhibit 8-1, $(113.6 - 109.6) \div 109.6 \times 100 = 3.65$ percent]. Mr. Bell's monthly rent will increase by $110. ($3,000 \times 3.65\% = 110$) to $3,110 per month.

EXHIBIT 8-1
Consumer Price Index

Year	Index
1982	96.5
1983	99.6
1984	103.9
1985	107.6
1986	109.6
1987	113.6

Source: U.S. Bureau of Labor Statistics.

Other types of indexes are also used (e.g., the Wholesale Price Index, Prime Interest Rate, and the Commodity Price Index). Tenants should be careful to select an index that accurately reflects the landlord's increased costs.

Percentage Rentals

With the increase in the inflation rate in recent years, many landlords are refusing to accept fixed rental agreements. Instead, they are asking that rent payments from restaurateurs be based on a percentage of sales. The logic here is that as inflation increases, tenants will have to increase prices to compensate for rising food and labor costs.

Landlords commonly ask for the greater of a minimum fixed annual rental payment or a stated percentage rate. Some restaurant leases are based strictly on a percentage of sales, but these generally relate to establishments for which the landlord has a very good idea of the restaurant's anticipated sales.

Tenants and landlords must agree upon what constitutes gross sales. Also, both parties must agree whether sales taxes, free meals given to customers, and customer service charges are to be included in gross sales calculations.

Because landlords share in the success of failure of the establishments, they may wish to incorporate into the lease agreements a recapture clause that enables them to regain the property if the restaurant is not successful over a period of time. This allows the landlords to re-rent the property to another property if the restaurant is not performing as the tenant projected.

Landlords are also likely to insist upon putting in the agreements the hours and days in which the restaurants will be open. Also, because many restaurants are located in tourist locations where business is seasonal, landlords may insist upon a minimum rent payment during the slow months so as to meet their out-of-pocket costs.

TERM OF THE LEASE

Initial Term

The term of length of the lease is another major area of negotiation. Generally, a restaurant lease ranges between three and eight years. Although rare, some restaurant leases have an initial term of up to 20 years. If the lease is tied to a percentage of sales, landlords are likely to agree to a longer lease term because they can be better protected against inflation. On the other hand, if tenants wish to pay rent on a fixed basis, landlords are most likely to agree to a one-year or two-year lease arrangement.

Option to Renew

Many hospitality leases contain options to renew clauses after the initial lease term expires. This is especially true for restaurants because their locations are usually so important to their continuing success. Thus, many restaurateurs negotiate an option clause into their leases.

Some of the more important factors to be negotiated in an option agreement include the following:

- *Renewal rental.* Landlords generally want an increase in rent if tenants are successful at the location and wish to renew. Although the rent can remain flat, landlords will more likely want some sort of increase for the right of renewal. Often the parties cannot agree on what the renewal period rent should be. In this case, the most common method for setting future rent is for the parties to rely on some independent third party or other outside standard to set the rent. The parties could agree, for example, that a reappraisal be done on the property by a third party or that rent be established by arbitration. More likely, however, the lease states that rent at time of renewal will be the rent of similar properties at the time of renewal. Whatever method is chosen, the parties should spell out in detail exactly how the rent amount is to be calculated so as to leave as little room as possible for disagreement.
- *Renewal term.* The option period may specify only one right to renew or several renewal periods.
- *Notice of renewal.* Tenants are given the right to renew the lease. However, the option clause should specify when and how the notice to renew should be given. Landlords usually want a long notice of renewal (up to one year's notice) in order to find another tenant for the property. Obviously, tenants want to make the notice as close as possible to the expiration of the original lease term.

DESCRIPTION OF THE PROPERTY

The description of the leased premises should be clearly stated in the lease. If the entire structure is to be rented, an address should be sufficient for proper identification.

However, if a tenant leases a portion of a building or space in a mall or strip shopping center, a complete description of the property is critical. It may be wise to attach a diagram to the lease identifying the lease property clearly.

IMPROVEMENTS BY THE TENANT

In the hospitality business, it is likely that tenants will have to make significant improvements to the property. Because landlords have a vested interest in their properties, they will require advance approval on all improvements.

Tenants and landlords often negotiate who pays for the improvements. Often, landlords pay for part or all of the improvement as part of lease negotiations to obtain a desirable tenant. This is often the case when a shopping center needs a reputable restaurant to help attract customers for the other tenants.

An important question concerns who owns the improvements. Unless agreed to in the lease document, landlords own the fixtures at the expiration of the lease. If improvements are to be removed, the lease agreement should provide for tenants to restore the property to its original condition. For example, a restaurateur purchases an antique bar and installs it in his restaurant. He had an agreement with the landlord to remove the bar upon the termination of the lease. If improvements are to remain, landlords will want to claim ownership upon their installation so as to avoid any later claims by third parties.

Under the Tax Reform Act of 1986 (TRA 1986), tenants are able to depreciate the costs of improvements over their useful lives. For instance, if an improvement has a useful life of 10 years and the lease runs for eight years, the tenant will depreciate the improvement using the 10-year useful life. Any unused depreciation on the improvements at the end of the lease is deductible when the lease expires. In the example, if the lease did end at the end of eight years, then the remaining balance on the assets would be written off at the expiration of the lease. (See Chapter 3 for details of depreciating leasehold improvements.)

TRADE FIXTURES

Usually, leases contain a clause dealing with trade fixtures. Leases should specify that all trade fixtures purchased by the tenant are his or her property. The fixtures should be identified in the lease so as to avoid confusion as to what is a trade fixture and what is an improvement when the lease terminates. Many times, landlords contribute trade fixtures, which should also be identified in the lease to avoid problems with third parties who may claim an interest and to prove ownership at the termination of the lease.

SIGNAGE

This item recently became more important in leasing hospitality properties because of government restrictions on the size and placement of signs. For example, sign restriction is greater in an urban area than in the country. Tenants must determine how important the sign exposure is for the future success of their properties.

This brings up an important point: The tenant should be aware of any laws that will affect his hospitality operation. The tenant should be careful not to rely exclusively on the landlord to provide the correct information, because the tenant will ultimately suffer if the landlord is not correct.

In addition, landlords may place restrictions in the lease concerning the size and placement of signs. For instance, if a hospitality firm is located in a shopping center, the establishment's sign may be placed alongside many other signs that make the hospitality firm's business difficult to spot from the highway.

Tenants may want to make certain that their leases contain nothing that would permit landlords from placing signs on the properties without the tenant's permission. Tenants may also be concerned about any restrictions on colors than can be used on signs.

MAINTENANCE AND REPAIR

This section spells out tenants' and landlords' duties concerning those parts of leased properties for which each is responsible. It is common for tenants and landlords to enter into a net lease arrangement for maintenance in a free-standing building. (See the discussion of net leases on page

153 for additional details.) The operator of the hospitality property located in a shopping center must examine which sections the landlord controls and which the tenant controls.

Generally, landlords are responsible for maintaining the outside structural of the buildings, although this can be modified in the lease agreements. Landlords are usually responsible for the public areas of the shopping center and parking lots, outside lighting systems, and drainage and sewer systems.

In most cases, tenants are responsible for repairs to and maintenance of the restaurants themselves. In addition, under the terms of the lease, tenants are responsible for the sidewalks in front of the operations. Tenants are generally responsible for all areas that are under their exclusive control. For example, service connections to utilities, air conditioning and heating actually controlled by the tenants, and roofs are exclusive to the tenants' properties (a strip shopping center). Finally, almost all leases hold tenants responsible for repairs necessary due to their negligence.

USE RESTRICTIONS

The hospitality firm that wants to rent a premise will undoubtedly be faced with many restrictions concerning the use of the property. In addition, the hospitality firm will want to restrict the landlord from renting part of the premises to a competitor. Depending on the location of the property, the importance of these restrictions varies. For instance, in a large enclosed mall, the landlord is unlikely to agree to a clause that allows only one restaurant. On the other hand, a similar restriction is possible and desirable in a smaller strip mall.

Tenants will first want to examine the properties for restrictions on the buildings that may prevent them from operating the hospitality businesses. They should ensure that the properties are properly zoned for the types of businesses proposed. For example, if a property is in the process of being rezoned, the tenant should make the lease contingent on the rezoning decision.

The value of contingent clauses should be noted. When negotiating for any substantial types of contracts such as leases, tenants should keep as many options open as possible. After all, if the property doesn't fit the needs of the tenant, he or she should be able to back away from the proposed lease. Unfortunately, if tenants do not place contingent clauses in their contracts for possible negative events, they may be required to fulfill the original contract terms or pay substantial damages for breaching the contract.

Also, tenants should beware of covenants and restrictions on the property that may prevent them from engaging in the hospitality businesses intended. For example, the lease for a restaurant adjacent to land owned by the landlord may contain a clause restricting any other restaurants from operating on that property.

If property is located in a shopping center, a tenant should ensure that there are no lease restrictions preventing him or her from operating the hospitality firm. It is a good idea to have the landlord sign a representation that no such restrictions exist.

Landlords can restrict use by the tenant with a positive statement of the type of business that will be renting the location or a negative restriction statement that spells out which businesses the tenant may not operate. Either way, the landlord will want to make certain the property being rented is used for the purpose originally agreed to.

ASSIGNMENT AND SUBLEASE

A tenant (assignor) can assign his or her lease to any third party (assignee) if the lease does not prohibit it. Many landlords include a clause in the lease that permits an assignment of the lease only if the landlord consents. The assignee is then obligated to pay rent to the landlord and perform all of the other obligations specified in the lease agreement. Many leases contain an out-and-out prohibition of any assignment or sublease by the tenant.

As assignment differs from a sublease in one very important aspect. Under a sublease, the original tenant remains obligated under the lease, while in a true assignment the assignee steps into the shoes of the original tenant who then has no further obligations under the lease.

As previously mentioned, almost all leases that permit assignment or sublease of the property do so only with the consent of the landlord. In most jurisdictions, a landlord cannot unreasonably withhold his or her consent. This clause should describe the type of business that is permitted, the legality of its proposed use, and the obligations of the original tenant.

Often, a landlord wants to include other restrictions in the lease agreement. For instance, a landlord may want to share in any profits that the tenant makes from subleasing a portion of the property. If the landlord does not provide for profit sharing in the lease agreement, he or she will be prevented from claiming any profits later. Many restaurants have successfully subleased all or part of their leased space, often at very high profits, in areas where rents have escalated quickly.

Another clause that is often inserted by landlords concerns their right to terminate the lease within a certain number of days at their option if the tenant subleases the premises. Many times, a restaurant tenant spends a great deal of money to improve the property and consequently would be very unlikely to agree to a lease clause whereby he or she could lose much of that investment.

MORTGAGE SUBORDINATION

A lease is generally subordinated to a mortgage on the property, and a tenant's rights are subject to the terms of the mortgage instrument. This usually means that the lease may be cancelled by the mortgage holder at his or her option upon foreclosure. If the lease is taken out prior to any mortgage placed on the property, the lease will survive the foreclosure proceedings.

Many times, a tenant wants and can obtain from the mortgage lender a nondisturbance agreement that allows the tenant to continue under the original lease. A tenant can also reserve the right to cure any default by a landlord on the mortgage and to recover any expenses incurred in curing the default.

INSURANCE

This section of the lease agreement spells out the duties and obligations of the parties concerning insurance. A lease almost always requires that a tenant insures the landlord and the property from risks resulting from the operation of the hospitality business. Landlords are especially concerned that insurance is purchased to cover risks associated with property damage (casualty insurance) and with negligent acts of the tenant (liability insurance).

Often, landlords insist that they be named additional insureds on the tenant's insurance policy. This means that if a tenant's employee causes injury to a third party while on the property, the tenant's insurance company is required to defend the landlord's interests also. For example, if a landlord leases a building for use as a restaurant, the landlord would want to be named in the lease as an additional insured to protect the building if an injured customer sues the landlord and the tenant for negligence.

An area often overlooked by a hospitality firm concerns naming suppliers who enter the property to make deliveries as additional insured. Suppose a distributor backs into a customer's car, causing serious injuries to the car's occupants. If the distributor has named the tenant an additional insured on his policy, his insurance company would be required to defend the hospitality firm also. Many times, the expenses associated with defending a lawsuit are more costly than the actual damages resulting from the accident.

The landlord should examine the certificate of insurance carefully. A certificate of insurance is a document that shows evidence of an insurance policy. Tenants should also demand to see certificates of insurance from any parties doing business with their firms. For example, when a contractor comes onto the hospitality firm's premises, the tenant should see a certificate of insurance as evidence of insurability. In addition, the owner should also place a "hold harmless" clause in the contract for maximum protection before the contractor begins work. This hold harmless clause, or indemnity clause, is an agreement by a tenant not to hold the landlord liable for losses that occur on the lease property, whether or not the landlord was at fault. But the hospitality firm should be aware that some courts in some jurisdictions have found hold harmless clauses invalid.

In many leases, the landlord seeks a hold harmless clause from the tenant to cover all losses on the landlord's property whether or not the tenant is at fault. Tenants should seek to limit their exposure by inserting a requirement that the hold harmless clause applies only if the tenant is negligent or if the landlord was actively involved in the activity causing the loss. Generally, courts uphold hold harmless clauses as long as the landlord was not willfully negligent.

The landlord and tenant should define abatement of rent in the lease agreement if the property is damaged by casualty. Most courts no longer follow the harsh common law holding that the landlord has no obligation to repair property damaged by casualty and that no abatement of rent occurs because of the casualty. However, tenants and landlords should spell out in detail in the lease who will be responsible for the repairs and what, if any, rent abatement will be allowed during the construction period.

CONDEMNATION

Like other provisions of the lease, common law provides a solution to problems that are not dealt with in the lease document. However, the parties may find that their own solutions to problems are more equitable and time saving. This is the case with condemnation proceedings. The general rule is that upon condemnation, a tenant is entitled to recover the value of the leasehold. The leasehold value is simply the discounted value of the current lease rentals and the discounted value of the current market rental value of the property (the amount of rent the property could currently bring).

The lease clause can provide that the lease terminates upon the condemnation of the entire property. This is a satisfactory solution if the hospitality tenant has not made any substantial improvements. However, most hospitality businesses make substantial investments in leasehold improvements that will be lost upon condemnation. The tenant and landlord will then have to agree to some schedule whereby the tenant recovers the depreciated value of the improvements.

Another issue in the lease clause on condemnation concerns what to do if a government agency seizes part of the property. This is particularly important for many restaurants, where seating capacity is very important. The lease clause should provide how much of the property seized justifies canceling the entire lease. Also, if the lease is to be cancelled, the tenant should ensure that he or she has sufficient time to move to another location by making the lease cancellable before the condemnation takes place.

Other issues concerning partial condemnation must be addressed in the lease. What, if any, rent will be reduced? Also, how will proceeds be divided between the landlord and tenant? These same issues must be addressed in cases of complete condemnation. Finally, which party will be responsible for the restoration of the property from the proceeds of the condemnation award?

DEFAULT AND TERMINATION OF THE LEASE

Landlords usually specify that the occurrence of certain events will cause the lease to be in default or terminated. The usual default events relate to the tenant's failure to pay rent when due or failure to comply with obligations promised in the lease agreement. Most states specify a number of days during which the tenant may cure the default without the lease being automatically terminated.

Generally, a tenant's only recourse against a landlord who defaults on obligations under the lease is to sue the landlord to obtain damages for breach of the lease. The tenant may also contend that the landlord's actions amount to an eviction, and therefore the lease is in effect terminated. Sometimes, as in a net lease, a landlord has no duties under the lease other than to collect the rent, in which case the landlord would not have to provide the tenant with a default provision.

A termination clause generally states that the leased premises will be turned over to the landlord at the end of the lease term. The termination clause should spell out in detail whether the tenant is to restore the premises to their original condition by removing all improvements or whether the improvements are to remain. If the lease is silent on this point, the general rule is that the improvements are the property of the landlord.

SPECIAL LEASE ARRANGEMENTS

The Net Lease

As previously mentioned, net leases are very popular in the hospitality industry. Generally, a net lease covers a single structure, such as a free-standing restaurant. A true net lease is one in which the tenant pays the landlord an agreed upon rental payment and assumes the obligation to pay the property taxes, insurance, repairs, maintenance costs, and other expenses associated with the property. The net lease is basically a guaranteed return to the landlord without any obligations on his or her part to maintain the property during the lease term.

Sometimes, a true net lease is referred to as a triple net lease. If the lease is not a true net lease, it is sometimes called a net lease, a net-net lease, or a net-net-net lease. Under the net lease, a tenant pays only the operating expenses for the property. Under the net-net lease, a tenant pays operating expenses and insurance premiums. Finally, if the terms net-net-net lease or triple net lease are used, the tenant pays operating expenses, insurance premiums, and real estate taxes.

A landlord's advantages in renting property to a hospitality operation is that he or she does not have to calculate a rental amount to cover expenses that are difficult to estimate. A satisfactory rate of return on the property can be calculated, and the tenant is then responsible for maintaining the property in good working order.

A tenant's failure to care for the property properly is always a major concern to a landlord. Thus, landlords should satisfy themselves about the credit worthiness of potential tenants and take precautions in the event of default of lease obligations by tenants. For example, a landlord will want to be named on the insurance policy along with the tenant. A landlord may want to ensure that there is money available to pay real estate taxes by requiring the tenant to escrow the taxable amount each month. Finally, a landlord may want the tenant to purchase rental insurance to cover at lease one year's rent, insurance, and property taxes.

The Ground Lease

The ground lease is an agreement between tenant and landlord to lease land. They almost always agree that the tenant should construct or purchase a building when assuming the underlying ground lease. Obviously, because of the large inherent investment in a building, the ground lease ranges from a minimum of 20 years to a maximum of 99 years. Ground leases are used quite often in the hotel industry, especially in large cities.

Due to the length of a ground lease, a landlord usually wants it to be a net lease with rent based either on a percentage of gross revenue or fixed rent tied to an inflation index. When the parties cannot agree on the value of the land, they may consult an appraiser to determine the fair market rental value of the property.

The building on the leased land reverts to the landlord at the termination of the lease. Therefore, if a building is to be constructed on the property, the parties should agree in the lease upon a financial settlement for when the lease terminates. Again, the parties may stipulate that an appraiser be contracted if they cannot agree on the property's value at the end of the lease term. There may be little need for this provision if the term of the ground lease matches the economic life of the hospitality property.

Most provisions in a ground lease are similar to those in commercial leases discussed in this chapter. However, when constructing a building, the tenant often has to obtain a mortgage upon the property. Because the ground lease is the tenant's most valuable asset, lending institutions want a mortgage on the leasehold as collateral for the loan. Therefore, the tenant should ensure that the lease gives him or her the right to mortgage the lease interest. The tenant should also make sure that the lease requires the landlord to notify the lending institution of any defaults by the tenant so that the lending institution can step in to cure the default before the lease is terminated.

Because a tenant has such a large investment in the building on the land, he or she will want assurances that if the landlord sells the land, the tenant's lease is protected. Therefore, the lease agreement should state explicitly that the buyer of the property takes the property subject to the ground lease.

The main advantage of a ground lease to the landlord is that he or she receives periodic income for use of the land and any appreciation of the property, since he or she owns the property. The tenant has the advantage of being able to deduct the lease payments as a business expense. Also, if the hospitality firm feels that it can generate a greater return than the expected rate of appreciation on the land, it may wish to lease and invest the capital back into the business.

Sale-Leaseback

The sale-leaseback is an arrangement by which the owner and user of a hospitality property sells the property to an investor and immediately leases back the property on a long-term basis. The advantage to the hospitality firm is that it is immediately infused with cash that can be used for business expansion purposes without losing the use of the property. The hospitality organization retains the burdens of ownership, and the buyer (lessor) is able to take depreciation on the property. The lease is structured as a net lease. The leases entered into are long-term and, depending on the remaining useful economic life of the property, can run from 20 to 60 years. As with any financing technique using real property, there are important economic and tax considerations to be considered before entering into such a transaction.

Characteristics of the Sale-Leaseback

The sale-leaseback permits the seller (the hospitality firm) to obtain cash for business expansion while retaining the use of the premises. A major consideration for entering into the sale-leaseback is that the seller is able to obtain 100 percent of the fair market value of the property. The hospitality firm is not likely to receive more than 75 percent of the fair market value from a mortgage taken out on any property.

Although the seller loses the depreciation deduction on the property after it is sold, he or she can deduct the rent paid to the buyer. Thus, the seller can take a deduction for land costs that were not previously deductible. TRA 1986 has increased the depreciation deduction of business property to $31\frac{1}{2}$ years, reducing the advantages of keeping the depreciation deduction.

The hospitality firm should also consider is whether the sale will trigger a taxable event. Generally, most hospitality properties have appreciated in value over time, and a subsequent sale is likely to generate a substantial taxable gain to the seller.

Tax Problems With the Sale-Leaseback

Because the sale-leaseback is a form of financing, the hospitality firm needs competent tax advice to structure the sale-leaseback agreement so that it does not appear to be a loan, but rather a true lease. The Internal Revenue Service (IRS) carefully reviews sale-leaseback transactions to determine whether the transaction is a sham or a true lease.

If a hospitality firm agrees to repurchase its property at the end of the lease at a bargain price (one that is substantially below market value), the IRS is more likely to attack the transaction as a loan instead of as a lease. Another factor that may determine whether the transaction will be treated as a loan is if the rent paid is below market value. The rent options are examined to see that they are true options instead of mere formalities. Finally, the lease must cover the property for the entire projected economic life of the property.

In *Frank Lyon v. United States*[1], the U.S. Supreme Court set forth criteria for a true lease in contrast with a loan arrangement. Although the case is rather complex and the facts are not likely to be similar to a hospitality firm, the method by which the Court reached its decision is important. The Court used many of the points discussed above to reach its decision. The Court concluded, "So long as the lessor retains significant and genuine attributes of the traditional lessor status, the form of the transaction adopted by the parties governs for tax purposes." Therefore, anyone contemplating a sale-leaseback should study the Lyon case before entering an arrangement in order to structure the lease terms to comply with the criteria set forth by the Court.

OPTION TO PURCHASE

Frequently, a hospitality firm wants to rent a particular location and take out an option to purchase the property at some future date. The option to purchase lies with the tenant, and he or she may exercise that right according to the terms of the lease. The right of first refusal, on the other hand, entitles the tenant to bid on the property only if an outside party makes an offer on the property. Under the right of first refusal, the tenant has the right to purchase the property at any time only when the landlord offers the property for sale. The advantage to the hospitality owner of having an option to purchase or right of first refusal is that if the location is desirable, he or she has a chance to retain the goodwill built up at that location.

Negotiating an Option to Purchase

The critical considerations in negotiating an option to purchase agreement are price and time of exercise. Because the option to purchase is very similar to any purchase agreement, the parties should include all the details that are provided in all real estate purchase agreements. (See Chapter 11 on the purchase of hospitality property for more details.)

Price

The parties can either agree upon a fixed and determinable price at the time of the agreement or set forth procedures to determine the price if and when the option is exercised. Many times, the parties set a price as determined by an appraiser. In such a case, the parties should agree on who will select the appraiser, the method the appraiser is to use, and what to do if the appraisal does not appear adequate.

---

[1]Frank Lyon Co. v. United States, 435 US 561 (1978).

Time of Exercise

The parties can either agree for the option to be exercisable any time during the lease period, at the termination of the lease, or at certain periods of time during the lease term.

Negotiating a Right of First Refusal

When negotiating a right of first refusal, the landlord should seriously consider the reasons for entering into the agreement. Although the advantages to the tenant are quite evident, the landlord may have difficulty selling the property if he or she so desires because a third party may not want to enter into serious negotiations only to have the tenant purchase the property from under him or her.

If right of first refusal is negotiated into the lease, it should specify clearly that the right of first refusal applies only to purchase offers from bona fide outside parties. This avoids the mere transfer of property under a corporate reorganization, buy-sell agreement, and by death.

Common problems in a right of first refusal should be handled in the agreement so as to avoid trouble at the time of the exercise. For instance, the parties should agree how long the tenant has to respond to an offer made by a third party. The tenant will want a reasonable time in which to secure any financing required to purchase the property. Another potential area of disagreement concerns whether the tenant must match the gross offer or the net offer (subtracting the brokerage commission). Generally, the landlord insists on the tenant meeting the gross purchase price, but this factor should be specified in the agreement.

SUMMARY

A lease can be viewed simply as a means of financing a hospitality business. A tenant rents the property for the use intended and thus is not tying up large sums of money in the land and building. A landlord receives money for the use of the premises plus any appreciation in the underlying value of the property over time.

A lease can be a valuable asset for the tenant because he or she can sublet part of all of the premises. Upon the sale of a hospitality firm, an affordable lease is one more valuable asset for the tenant to sell along with the other assets of the business.

When negotiating the lease terms, the hospitality owner must carefully consider all clauses contained in the lease document. Or the other hand, once a lease is signed, the tenant has to live with the clauses agreed to, and it is in his or her best interests to know exactly what is agreed to and ensure that the agreement is appropriate for the hospitality firm.

Rent payments are likely to be based on a minimum fixed rent payment with some sort of indexing of the minimum rent in future years. A landlord will often want to make rental payments based on the higher of the minimum rental payment and a percentage of gross sales. The theory is that the landlord will share with the hospitality firm the good fortune of increasing sales. In effect, a landlord shares the economic risk with the tenant.

The length of the lease is another major consideration for the hospitality owner. Although the tenant generally wants a long-term lease of about 20 years, he or she is unlikely to want to be committed for that length of time. Therefore, the tenant and landlord may want to consider using an initial five-year lease with options for three additional five-year periods at the discretion of the tenant.

Many times, the tenant may be able to negotiate with the landlord for contributions to improvements in the restaurant or the abatement of rent while remodeling is being done to ready the property for business. This is especially true in shopping centers where, many times, a restaurant is a major draw for customers to other tenants. Either way, the tenant and landlord should agree in writing on who will own what and how improvements will be removed from the property once the lease expires.

These and other planning opportunities abound when negotiating a lease. The tenant and landlord are about to enter into a long-term relationship that should be beneficial to both sides. Only through informative negotiating by both sides can this be possible.

GLOSSARY

Arbitration clause A clause in a lease that establishes the method of settling a dispute without using the legal system. Usually, an impartial third person is chosen by the parties to the lease to settle disputes arising from the lease. The parties usually agree beforehand to abide by the decision of the arbitrator (binding arbitration).

Assignment A transfer of rights by the tenant (assignee) to a third party (assignor) to use leased property.

Cancellation clause A clause in a lease that spells out in detail the criteria to be used in terminating a lease by either or both parties.

Consumer Price Index An index published by the Bureau of Labor Statistics of the U.S. Department of Labor that tracks the prices of a representative group of goods and services. This index is used to measure the differences in the cost of living from year to year.

Cost of Living Index An index published by the government which measures the increase or decrease of living costs for the average person.

Escalation clause A clause establishing how and on what basis future rent will be increased (see Cost of Living Index).

Fixed-rent lease A lease in which the rental payments are fixed for the duration of the lease.

Graduated-rent lease A lease in which the rental payments are initially fixed and are then increased by a specified percentage at designated times.

Gross lease A lease in which the landlord (lessor) is obligated to pay the real estate taxes, utilities, insurance, and all other operating expenses for the property being leased.

Ground lease A lease for the use of vacant land, exclusive of any improvements.

Hold harmless clause A clause whereby a tenant agrees to assume the liability for operating the property, thereby relieving the landlord of any responsibility.

Improvements Any additions to the original property that make the property more valuable. Improvements generally are additions to the building structure, not merely repair or maintenance.

Lease An agreement whereby one party (landlord) agrees to give possession to another party (tenant) for a specified time period and for consideration in the form of rent.

Leasehold A nonfreehold estate that is established by a lease.

Leasehold improvements Any improvements made by the tenant to the leased property.

Lessee The person (tenant) who is given the right of possession to the leased property.

Lessor The person (landlord) who owns the property and rents it to the tenant.

Maintenance The work done to a property to keep it operating efficiently.

Net lease A lease in which the tenant pays the maintenance expenses of the property in addition to rent.

Net-net lease A lease in which the tenant pays the maintenance and insurance expenses of the property in addition to rent.

Net-net-net lease A lease in which the tenant pays the maintenance, insurance, and property taxes of the property in addition to rent. Sometimes known as a triple net lease.

Percentage rent The amount of rent due that is stated as a percentage of gross sales from the hospitality firm.

Personal property Property that is not designated as real property under the law.

Reappraisal lease A lease in which the escalation of rent is determined by a reappraisal of the property at the agreed-upon time stated in the lease.

Renewal option The right of the tenant to extend the lease for another specified period of time.

Rental agreement A lease.

Sale-leaseback A prior-agreed-to-sale and subsequent lease from the buyer back to the seller.

Sublease A transaction in which the tenant leases his or her leasehold interest to another party.

Subordination To make the lease lower or junior to the mortgage interest on the property.

References

Arnold, Alvin. *Real Estate Investor' Deskbook.* New York: Warren, Gorham & Lamont. 1987.

Cohen, Elliot. "Rental Foundations are Built on a Solid Lease." *Business Insurance.* September 3, 1984, p. 37.

Godfaden, Raymond. "Stopping the Clock on Lease Foreclosures." *Cornell Hotel & Restaurant Administration Quarterly.* May 1986, pp. 28–32.

Hanford, Lloyd. "Re-Examining Assignment-Sublease Clauses." *Journal of Property Management.* May/June 1986, p. 67.

Hanlin, Roy. "Establishing Equitable Tenant Allowances." *Journal of Property Management.* May/June 1985, pp. 30–31.

Harris, Richard. "Enforceability, Equality and Fairness in Commercial Leases: A Tenant Trap." *Real Estate Review.* Summer 1986, pp. 24–27.

Lundberg, Donald. *The Restaurant: From Concept to Operation.* New York: John Wiley & Sons, 1985.

Main, Bill. "Negotiating Your Lease: Part I." *Restaurant Management.* July 1987, pp. 27–28.

Main, Bill. "Negotiating Your Lease: Part II." *Restaurant Management.* September 1987, pp. 24–26.

Main, Bill. "Negotiating Your Lease: Part III." *Restaurant Management.* November 1987, pp. 26–27.

Ominsky, Harris. "Reading Between the Lines of Your Lease. *Restaurant Hospitality.* December 1985, pp. 33–36.

Selling, John. "Selecting a Lease Index." *Journal of Property Management.* May/June 1985, pp. 62–63.

Recommended Readings

Cory, Robert N., Shedd, Peter J., and Floyd, Charles F. *Real Estate and the Law,* New York: Random House, 1982.

Goldfaden, Raymond. "Stopping the Clock on Lease Foreclosures." *Cornell Hotel and Restaurant Administration Quarterly.* May 1986, pp. 28–32.

Ominsky, Harris. "Reading Between the Lines of Your Lease." *Restaurant Hospitality.* December 1985, pp. 33–36.

Stefanelli, John. *The Sale and Purchase of Restaurants.* New York: John Wiley & Sons, 1985.

Chapter 9

Franchising and Management Contracts

Franchising has been part of the U.S. economic system since the 19th century, when Singer Corporation introduced it as a way of selling sewing machines. Basically, a franchise is the right to sell someone's product or service. The owner of the business is the "franchisor," and the person who is granted the right to sell the product or service is the "franchisee." Generally, the franchisee pays a one-time initial fee and then a monthly royalty fee based on the gross sales of the franchise business.

The collector of the royalty fee based on gross sales has an advantage in that both the franchisor and franchisee have a vested interest in the business. The higher the gross sales, the more likely that the franchisee will be more successful; the increased sales mean that the franchisor will receive larger monthly royalty checks. The franchisee can also increase wealth by having a large enough territory to open up more than one outlet. The franchisor benefits again because this expansion increases the royalty fees that he or she will receive.

Many people mistake entrepreneurial activity with franchising. In franchising, a person buys a proven method of doing business. This is especially true in the hospitality industry. People who desire to be their own boss usually will not want to be a franchisee. On the other hand, with the high failure rate among independent hospitality firms, a trade of some independence for a better opportunity at success makes the franchise operation very attractive to many individuals.

There are no guarantees in any business venture. Even though the failure rate for franchises is lower than that for independent operations, many franchises do fail or make insufficient profit to the franchisee for the time and effort put into the business.

Most hospitality franchises can be broken down into the restaurant segment and the hotel segment. Both types depend on name recognition, reputation, and a standard method of doing business. Such well-known companies as McDonald's, Wendy's, Holiday Inn, Chi Chi's, Comfort Inn, and others owe their growth to the franchise system.

Any person who wants to obtain a franchise must assess his or her reasons for doing so. Some franchises require that the franchisee actually work in the business and not be merely a passive investor. Other franchises restrict the territory or opportunity to expand beyond a certain limited territory.

Types of Franchise

Restaurants

The restaurant segment and the hotel segment dominate franchising in the hospitality industry. There are far more restaurant than hotel franchises because it generally costs more to construct a hotel than to open a restaurant.

The restaurant franchising segment is dominated by the fast-food industry. The largest single segment within fast food segment is the hamburger market. This segment has been dominated by McDonald's, Burger King, Wendy's, and Hardee's. Other important markets include chicken, Mexican food, seafood, steak, sandwich, pancake, ice cream, and yogurt.

Although restaurant franchising has enjoyed tremendous popularity, especially in the past 30 years, there are indications that the restaurant market is becoming saturated. As a result, many franchise companies have folded in recent years, notably the D'lites restaurant chain. Today, restaurants compete not only with themselves but also with other service-oriented businesses such as party stores, supermarkets, and department stores.

To remain competitive, many restaurant franchises now operate within hotels and motels to be closer to demand generators. Another trend is combining two or more franchises in a single building to help reduce real estate and management costs. Many older restaurant franchises are rehabilitating older properties to give them a fresher look to compete with newer franchises.

Hotels and Motels

The hotel and motel industry is broken into many segments, with franchising dominating the budget motel segment. (See Chapter 1 for a discussion of the various segments in the lodging industry.) In general, the cost of obtaining a hotel or motel franchise is greater than that of a restaurant because of the necessity of building the hotel. Therefore, there are not as many potential investors for hotel and motel franchises as for restaurants.

The most affordable lodging franchises are in the budget hotel segment. Many full-service hotel chains do not franchise. If they do, they franchise only to certain management companies. The cost of a full-service hotel can run into millions of dollars, which limits the number of potential franchisees.

A typical budget motel costs between $10,000 and $20,000 per room, excluding land cost. This means that, depending on the size of the operation, even for a budget motel the total construction cost could run between $200,000 and $2.5 million. In addition, the initial franchise fee may cost several thousand dollars. There are many more start-up expenses, such as the cost of furnishing each room, that require the franchisee to have sufficient resources prior to opening a hotel.

Offering Circular and Contract

Offering Circular

The legal relationship between the franchisee and the franchisor is defined in the franchise contract. However, due to widespread fraud in recent years, the Federal Trade Commission (FTC) and several states require that the franchisor provide the prospective franchisee with an offering circular at least 10 days before signing any franchise contract.

The offering circular provides sufficient information to the franchisee to allow him or her to make an intelligent decision about obtaining a franchise. However, the FTC does not review the offering circular for accuracy. The offering circular is not the franchise contract, and important provisions may be left off the document. It is very important for the prospective franchisee to review both the offering circular and the franchise agreement with an attorney who is an expert in franchise law. The following items are required in the offering circular, according to the FTC:

1. Identification of the franchisor and its affiliates. The circular must identify by address the franchisor, addresses of affiliates, and any predecessor companies.
2. The business experience of each of the franchisor's officers, directors, and key management.
3. Any previous bankruptcies involving the franchisor and its officers, directors, and key management. It is much easier to trust someone who has a clean history in business dealings. However, the fact that key personnel have been involved in failed businesses in the past does not mean this business also will fail. But the franchisee should satisfy him or herself that the reasons for failure were not due to the franchisor's incompetence.
4. Any lawsuits involving the franchisor and its officers, directors, and key management. It is important to analyze the types of lawsuits and their frequency because they may indicate the franchisor's management style. Also, could the lawsuits place the franchisor in financial difficulty?
5. The initial franchise fee and other initial payments to be paid by the franchisee to obtain the franchise. This section states the fee to be paid up front by the franchisee and any other fees required to obtain the franchise. The method of payment is discussed at this point. The manner in which the initial franchise fee may be refunded if the franchise agreement is terminated prior to opening is also defined.
6. The continuing expenses the franchisee will be responsible to pay the franchisor once the business is open. This includes royalties and any other costs such as advertising, equipment, and supplies. This section does not include those expenses that are a normal part of the business operation such as payroll, taxes, and supplies to outside vendors.
7. Any financial assistance available from the franchisor or its affiliates to the franchisee for purchase of the franchise. This does not happen very often. However, several of the more established franchisors do have programs for assisting qualified minority businesses set up a franchise.
8. The type and quality of goods and services used in the franchise. This includes any requirements about their having to be purchased from the franchisor and any restrictions concerning purchases from the franchisor or its affiliates. In this section, the franchisor must disclose the standards for each product. Generally, it is illegal to require that the franchisee purchase from the franchisor goods and services that can be reasonably purchased from a third party. However, there are exceptions. For instance, a restaurant franchise can require that the franchisee purchase perhaps one brand of soft drink from a third party for consistency among stores. However, a requirement to purchase paper products only from the franchisor may not be legal. Nevertheless, the franchisor may establish standards that the paper products must meet in order to maintain consistency among the franchises.

9. Products or services the franchise is permitted to sell and any restrictions on what may be sold by the franchisee. This section informs the franchisee about what is permissible to sell in the business and the restrictions the franchisor places on the sale of other products or services.

10. Any territory limitations. Each franchise has a certain limited territory in which the franchisee expects exclusivity. If the territory is too large, the franchisor loses potential sales because the franchisee may not be able to serve the market. If the territory is too small, the franchisee will compete with other franchisees or company stores in an area where there are too few customers to make the territory profitable.

11. Any restrictions on the franchisee in the operation of the business. This is a very detailed list of what is expected of the franchisee in the actual operation of the business. For example, the agreement may require that the floors of the restaurant be washed every two hours. These restrictions on operation can be quite cumbersome and the franchisee should understand that by agreeing to them he or she is obliged to conform to the agreement.

12. Criteria used for terminating, renewing, and transferring a franchise. This section details conditions that may cause the franchise to terminate, be renewed, and transferred to a third party. It is important to understand what constitutes a termination of the franchise agreement; failure to do so could result in the franchisee losing the franchise. Also, many companies permit regular renewal. However, there is usually an additional cost for renewal, and the fees may be substantial. This is especially true if the franchise is very successful.

13. Training programs provided to franchisees. In the hospitality business, customer service is very important, and this section must be examined closely for exactly what kind of training will be provided to the franchisee and his or her employees. The service industry is becoming extremely competitive, and the need for a well-trained staff is a must.

14. Any approval necessary for assistance provided in selecting a site for the franchise. The hospitality industry is driven by getting customers in the door, and location is extremely important. It is important to know if any assistance is provided to help the franchisee locate a good site. At a minimum, most hospitality franchisors require their approval of a site before awarding a franchise.

15. The franchisor's financial statements. The franchisor is required to show the latest financial reports to the franchisee. These include balance sheets and income statements. They should be examined closely to determine the franchisor's financial health. The franchisee should be extremely suspicious of financial reports that have not been audited by an independent certified accountant.

16. Statistical information concerning the franchises. This section contains the raw data on present franchises, the number of terminated franchises, the renewal rate of franchises, the repurchases of franchises, and the projection of future franchises. This data does not name any particular franchisees, but it is intended to give the franchisee an idea of what has been happening in key areas of the franchise. There are almost always franchises that do not work out, so the fact that a small percentage of them have been terminated should not alarm a potential franchisee unduly. However, if more than 20 percent of franchises have been terminated, the franchisee should inquiry more closely about the reasons.

17. The involvement of any celebrities in the franchise. Many franchises use celebrities to pitch for a particular business. However, these celebrities are often not owners but merely paid spokesper-

sons for the franchise. It is a mistake to base an investment on a franchise business because of a celebrity speaking for the franchise.

18. The participation required of the franchisee in the operation of the franchise. Many hospitality franchises, especially restaurants, require the franchisee to work full time at the franchise. Many franchisors do not permit the franchisee to operate any business in the same field as the franchise business. For instance, a restaurant franchise may prohibit the franchisee from operating another restaurant franchise.

19. The basis for claimed earnings, if presented. Franchisors very seldom predict what a franchisee will earn in the franchise business. This is to prevent lawsuits by disgruntled franchisees if their earnings do not materialize.

20. A list of the names and addresses of other franchisees so the franchisee can contact them to get their opinions about the franchise business and the franchisor.

Many franchisors have decided that showing projected operating profits that the franchisee may earn is too risky because the franchisee might treat the earnings projections as a guarantee of future earnings and involve the franchisor in litigation for misrepresentation if they fail to meet earnings projections. Therefore, most offering circulars do not state any earnings projections.

Publications and organizations can assist the prospective franchisee select a franchise operation. The largest such organization is the International Franchise Association (IFA), 1025 Connecticut Avenue, N.W., Suite 707, Washington, DC 20036, which provides its members with valuable publications about how to get started in the franchise business and how to evaluate franchise opportunities.

Another valuable resource is *Franchise Opportunities Handbook,* published by the U.S. Department of Commerce (USDC). This book lists more than 1,000 franchisors and provides data such as names and addresses of the companies, descriptions of the operations, the amount of equity capital needed. Other books and pamphlets related to franchise operations are available from the IFA and USDC.

The Franchise Contract

The offering circular is very helpful, but the franchise agreement specifies the legal rights and obligations of the parties. Also, many items are not included in the franchise agreement that are covered in the franchise contract. The franchise contract is drafted by the franchisor, and thus terms and conditions will favor the franchisor in most instances. This is why it is so important for the franchisee to seek someone with franchise experience to help review and negotiate the franchise contract.

The first step for many franchisees is not actually signing a franchise agreement but rather a purchase agreement. In the purchase agreement, the franchisee puts down a deposit as a good-faith gesture that he or she will execute a franchise agreement in the near future. This deposit is usually required because the franchisee may need assistance locating a suitable site or obtaining a desired lease before the franchise can be obtained. The deposit shows that the franchisee intends to go ahead with the franchise if the site is obtained. As such, the deposit is usually refundable if a desirable location cannot be obtained. However, if the franchisee wants to end the relationship for other reasons, the deposit is usually forfeited as liquidated damages.

Franchise Cost and Fees

Restaurant Franchise Costs

Many fees are associated with most franchise operations. It is important when evaluating a franchise opportunity to understand all of them. For example, the cost of building the restaurant structure could be hundreds of thousands of dollars. That is why many restaurant franchisees rent rather than build. But even if the franchisee rents, he or she will probably have to spend several thousand dollars on leasehold improvements to bring the property up to the standards of the franchisor. In addition, the franchisee must purchase equipment for the restaurant, and this can easily run into thousands of dollars. The franchisee will also have to purchase an initial inventory supply, incur pre-opening expenses such as hiring and training, and provide sufficient working capital for the operation of the restaurant. Other non-operating costs of obtaining the franchise are:

- *Franchise fee.* This is the initial franchise fee that is charged to open each operation. This can range from free for a new franchise attempting to get off the ground to several thousand dollars. This fee may be refundable in part if the franchisee is unable to obtain financing. The franchise fee compensates the franchisor for the use of its name and trademarks and to defray the expenses the franchisor incurs in selling franchises, consultation, training, and assistance to franchisees before the opening of each restaurant.
- *Royalty fee.* After the restaurant is open, it pays a royalty fee based on a percentage of gross sales from the operation. This fee can vary significantly from franchise to franchise, but it is usually in the single digits for most franchises. Established companies such as McDonald's can command double-digit royalty fees.
- *Advertising fee.* Most national franchisors charge a fee based on gross receipts, usually one to four percent. This fee is usually placed in a special fund that can only be used for advertising and public relations. Often the franchisor contributes to this fund for company-owned stores.
- *Local advertising.* In addition to requiring the franchisee to pay a fee for national advertising, many franchisors also require the franchisee to spend a minimum amount for local advertising, usually a percentage of gross receipts.
- *Renewal fees.* Most franchisors charge a renewal fee when the franchise contract expires for the franchisee to retain the franchise.
- *Upgrade costs.* Most franchisors insist that the franchise be upgraded to remain competitive. Usually, the franchisee is responsible for the entire cost of renovation.
- *Transfer fee.* The franchisor charges a fee for the transfer of ownership of an approved franchise. Generally, the fee is lower if the transfer is to an existing franchisee.
- *Training costs.* Many franchisors provide the initial training for free. Even if there is no charge for training, the franchisee is usually responsible for travel, lodging, and personal expenses.
- *Other costs.* Other expenses may arise or are contingent upon certain events. For instance, many restaurant franchises require that new franchisees spend a certain amount on the "grand opening" of every store. Also, most franchisors require that if an audit of the books reveals that revenues were understated by more than a certain percentage, the franchisee is required to pay for the audit as well as the royalty shortage.

Hotel Franchise Costs

Many expenses common to restaurants also apply to hotels. The single biggest difference, however, is that hotels and motels are usually constructed and thus renting property is not an option. This makes the hotel franchise a larger business investment. Hotel and motel franchises usually require a minimum number of rooms for each property. The cost to build a hotel (including the land financing, legal fees, site construction, furnishings, fixtures, and equipment) could amount to a few thousand dollars per room for budget hotels to hundreds of thousands of dollars per room for luxury properties. The franchisor offers almost no help in financing the construction of these properties.

Other likely costs beside normal operating costs in obtaining a franchise are:

- *Franchise fee.* This initial fee is usually based on a dollar amount per room plus a minimum amount regardless of the number of rooms. This fee covers the cost of training and assistance provided to the franchisees and the cost of quality control inspections and support of the main office staff. For example, a hotel may charge an initial franchise fee of $300 per room and a minimum fee of $40,000.
- *Royalty fee.* This fee is based on a percentage of gross room revenue, and it varies among hotel chains. Some hotel chains levy a fixed charge per room rather than a percentage of room revenues. The royalty fee is usually two to six percent of gross room revenues.
- *Advertising fee.* This fee is usually based on a percentage of room revenue, and it supports national and regional advertising. The advertising fee is usually one to three percent of gross room revenues.
- *Reservation fee.* This fee is charged either as a percentage of room revenue (usually one to three percent) or as a fixed amount per room or reservation. This fee supports the hotel or motel chain's national reservation system. Many lodging chains require franchisees to purchase or lease reservation equipment.

Analyzing Different Franchise Agreements

There is no single method to help the franchisee evaluate one franchise over another. There is always an element of risk in choosing any franchise; the newer the franchise is, the more riskier the investment becomes. In evaluating alternatives, the franchisee must select a method of evaluating the return on the total investment required on discounted return method. (See Chapter 5, "Measuring Rate of Return," for a discussion of the various methods to measure rate of return.)

The initial investment by the franchisee includes the franchise fee and other start-up costs. Many times, investors make franchise decisions based only on the cost of obtaining the franchise. This is a mistake because some established franchises, such as McDonald's, are expensive to obtain but also offer the closest thing to a guaranteed return as there is in the hospitality industry. Another factor that makes evaluation difficult is correctly estimating the support the franchisor provides for the fee charged. The ultimate success of any franchisee depends on the support and financial strength of the franchisor. The franchisee can learn a lot about the franchisor by talking to other franchisees.

The other major cost is the continuing expenses associated with the franchise. This includes the royalty fee, advertising fee, and reservation fee. Again, each prospective franchisee should evaluate his or her return on investment after all expenses have been considered. This is difficult to do unless the franchisee reviews the return after total costs are considered. For instance, some franchisors charge a lower-than-average initial franchise fee but then impose a higher-than-average royalty fee.

Franchise Evaluation Checklist

Various state governments have literature to assist prospective franchisees evaluate any given franchise. The "Checklist for Evaluating Franchises" was prepared by the State of Michigan. Anyone contemplating investing in any franchise should contact his or her state government for help in deciding about investing in a particular franchise.

MANAGEMENT CONTRACTS

Management contracts became increasingly popular in the past 10 years. In the past, most hotels were owned and operated by the same company or leased to a hotel operator. However, as hotel financing became riskier and more complicated, lenders began to insist that hotels be professionally managed. Also, the increase in real estate prices in the late 1970s and early 1980s convinced many hotel companies that it would be more profitable for them to sell hotel properties and enter into long-term management contracts to operate the hotels.

However, criticism has suggested that the new management companies have not operated hotel properties any better than they were in the past. As a result, a new field, "asset management," has evolved in which the owner oversees the operation of the property to ensure that it is run properly. Some hotel are run by the asset managers with the management company merely carrying out the owner's wishes.

A hotel management contract is simply an agreement by the owner or developer and the operating or management company. The owner retains the risk of real estate ownership; the management company, agents for the owner, is responsible for operating the property. In return for operating the hotel property, the management company receives a fee. The fee may be a base fee only, an incentive fee only, or (more likely) a combination of base and incentive fees.

As in any contract between two parties, almost all the provisions are negotiable, and the relative strength of the two parties in the negotiating process determines which contract provisions will favor which party. Also, the parties must remain flexible in which strategies and tactics are applied in negotiating a contract because what may be effective in today's economy may not work a month later as conditions change.

All sections of the management contract are important and should be dealt with carefully. Some of the more important provisions are discussed below.

Period of the Management Contract

The period or duration of the management contract balances the strength of the management company against that of the owners. The initial term of the management contract could be from one to 50 years, depending on the strengths of the negotiating parties. For instance, an independent management company that manages a few properties is not in the same bargaining position as the Marriott Hotel Management Company and would generally accept a shorter operating term agreement than the Marriott.

The contract may or may not provide for renewal of the management contract provisions. General renewal terms are longer with chain or first-tier management companies than with independent operators or second-tier companies. As with the initial term, the frequency and length of renewal depends on the strength of negotiating parties. Renewal periods may run from one to 10 years.

The duration of management contracts is important because if the management company does a poor job it may be difficult to terminate the contract. (See termination section on page 170.) Another consideration is when the owners wish to sell the property. The remaining length of the contract may influence the sale price of the real estate. If a prospective buyer wishes to utilize his or her own management company and there is no termination provision in the contract, the buyer may lose interest in purchasing the property because of the time remaining in the contract.

Management Fees

The management company expects to be paid for services it renders to the owners. However, the exact form this payment takes is often subject to intense bargaining. Basically, the management contract includes a base-fee provision and an incentive-fee arrangement. However, a management contract may provide for a base-fee arrangement only or an incentive-fee arrangement only.

A typical base-fee arrangement is usually based on a percentage of gross operating revenue and typically consists of between three to five percent of this revenue. The incentive fee, on the other hand, is usually based on gross operating profit, usually net income after fixed charges or on cash flow from the property. The incentive fee could run anywhere from 10 to 25 percent of the net operating profit.

There are many reasons why management contract fees vary greatly from property to property. Following the reputation of the management company, the next consideration is whether the fee structure consists mostly of a basic fee or an incentive fee arrangement. Management companies normally prefer the basic fee on gross revenue to assure themselves a profit no matter how the hotel actually performs. Hotel owners prefer that the operator takes greater risk in the operation of the property and thus prefer to pay the management company on an incentive-fee basis. Therefore, the owner and management company must negotiate the fee arrangement to the satisfaction of both parties.

The incentive fee arrangement has to be negotiated so that the hotel property will be able to pay the incentive fee and still be an operating entity. Because a property can generate operating income without necessarily generating positive cash flow or sufficient rate of return to the owner, the hotel representatives may wish to include a clause in the contract to limit payout of the incentive fee. This limit can relate to minimum cash flow generated by the property, rate of return on the owner's invested capital, or some other mutually agreed-upon limitation.

The management fee, minus the limitation, is due and payable with interest when and if the property reaches the stated objectives or the property is sold. The limit could even be set up so that if the property failed to reach its objective, an incentive fee would be eliminated that year. If that were the case, the management company could bargain for a higher incentive fee rate.

Management Company's Responsibilities

Most management contracts grant the management company the exclusive right to operate the hotel property. This includes the normal operation of the hotel and establishing prices for hotel services. However, the owner may wish to negotiate for provisions that require the management company's consent for major purchases or changes in management. If the owner cannot negotiate these provisions, he or she may at least require final approval for budgeting and capital expenditures to ensure proper appropriation of funds.

At a minimum, the management company should be required to inform the owner of any major policy changes that will affect the property. Thus, many owners establish a reporting system to ensure that the management company is doing everything it has stated it would do.

Financial and other reports must be complete and presented in a timely manner so that the owner can take action if it is necessary. The time period for reporting annual audited profit and loss statements is generally 45 days, although there may be an allowance for up to 120 days. Other important reports that must be received in a timely fashion include daily operating reports and monthly operational and financial reports.

Owner's Responsibilities

The owner assumes the risk and rewards of ownership. Thus, it is important for the owner to monitor the management company to ensure that profitability goals are being met. In addition, the owner is usually responsible for providing working capital to the property. The owner must also pay for repairs necessary for the operation of the property.

Although the management company purchases supplies, licenses, and permits for the property, the owner must pay for those supplies.

Performance and Termination Clause

Management contracts generally define what shall cause the termination of the management contract for either party. Generally, the owner will want some sort of performance clause included in the contract to measure the effectiveness of the management company. Unless there is a provision for this measurement, the owner usually can remove the management company only if he or she can prove gross negligence—a difficult circumstance to prove.

Much management contract litigation has occurred because owners feel that management companies have not operated their hotels adequately. As with most contracts, the more detailed the contract's definition of adequate performance, the more likely it is that an expensive lawsuit can be avoided. One method of measuring performance is negotiating an acceptable rate of return on the property's assets after the property has operated a few years. This eliminates the start-up variability common to new properties.

Many management contracts do not accurately define what will cause the contract to terminate. Therefore, it may be in the parties' best interests to subject any disagreements to binding arbitration. Arbitration is less expensive and quicker than the civil court system. The parties may then allow the arbitrators to establish the termination payout (if any) that the owner will have to pay the management company.

Management Company's Equity Investment

For years, the driving force behind the management contract was the profitability of these contracts for the management companies in light of comparatively little risk. Today, many owners require the management company to contribute to the equity of the hotel property in some form. For instance, in the start-up phase of a newly constructed hotel, the management company may contribute equity in the form of working capital, pre-opening expenses, furniture, fixtures and equipment, or as joint ventures or partnerships. These contributions can be structured as debt and be treated as any other loan amount, or the management company could be given preference to payment when cash flow becomes available.

Miscellaneous Provisions

Many provisions make up the management contract, and they must be examined carefully by both parties to ensure they accomplish what the parties want. Some common provisions are:

- The management company may implement a suitable accounting systems for the property.
- The management company may negotiate, at the owner's request, leases for commercial leases.
- The management company may have the power to make emergency expenditures when necessary to avoid immediate danger to life or property.
- The owner may have the right to select outside accountants and to inspect records at any reasonable time.
- The owner may be required to maintain a minimum ratio of current assets to current liabilities and sufficient cash in the property to fund expenses for a specified period of time.
- The owner will obtain all necessary licenses and permits for the property.
- The management company will be reimbursed for any reasonable expenses incurred for the property.
- The owner will provide all insurance coverage for the property.
- The management company will be deemed an independent contractor for the owner under the contract.
- The management company may seek an agreement whereby it will not be held accountable for all losses, costs, expenses, liabilities, or damages arising or alleged to have arisen from any acts or omissions (except fraud, willful tort, and gross negligence).
- The management contract is binding upon and ensures the benefit of the parties and their respective successors and assigns.
- The contract will be in default if any party files a petition for bankruptcy or consents to an involuntary petition in bankruptcy, or if either party fails to perform under the contract terms.

- Default will occur if the owner fails to pay the management company under the terms of the contract.
- No partnership or joint venture is deemed to have been created by the parties entering into the management contract.

HOTEL CONDOMINIUMS

The hotel condominium is a creative financing device often used by hotel developers, especially in resort areas. The hotel condominium is a traditional hotel in that it sells rooms to guests. The main difference from other hotels, however, is the ownership structure. In a hotel condominium several individuals own the rooms instead of a single owner.

The main advantage of the hotel condominium to the developer is that he or she can obtain financing for the project from other than traditional financing sources. The condominium owner usually needs only to obtain construction financing, and the permanent financing is provided by the individual investors.

The hotel condominium is usually managed under a management contract with a reputable firm. The developer or subsidiary of the developer may operate the hotel under a separate management contract. The management contractor receives a fee for operating the property and passes on any profits to the individual owners. (See page 168 of this chapter for further discussion of management contracts.) A reputable management company should be selected because investors may not be willing to invest in the project unless they are reasonably sure the project can return a profit.

Generally, individual investors share in room revenues either through the actual individual room rentals or the rental pool.

Under the actual individual rooms rental method, each unit is given its share of room revenue for each guest who stays in that room. This method works best when the individual rooms are separate and unique units.

The more common method is shared rental pool. Under this method, guest revenues are pooled, and each owner receives a pro rata share. Often, the method selected is based on the rates of the rooms. Thus, the larger rooms receive a larger portion of the pooled income than the smaller rooms.

Many times, the owner wants to use his or her room at the hotel facility. Arrangements must be made for when the owner can occupy the unit (usually in the off season) in the condominium contract. The owner may not be allowed to participate in the rental pool arrangement while occupying the room.

Prior to the Tax Reform Act of 1986, hotel condominiums were very popular with individual investors because they were able to own part of a hotel investment and they could also deduct mortgage interest, operating expenses, and depreciation expenses. In effect, the government helped the individual investor finance the purchase of the hotel condominium. Today, the expenses from a hotel condominium are considered passive because most investors are not active in the hotel business, and losses from the investment are deferred unless the investor has other passive income (See the discussion of Passive Activity Rules in Chapter 2 for details of this limitation on the deduction of losses.)

With the current glut of hotel rooms and the reduced tax benefits to investors in hotel condominiums, this device as a financing tool will probably be limited to hotel projects that show a very strong economic potential. The more glamorous resort hotel projects located in up-and-coming locations still have the best potential for attracting investors who are willing to invest in a hotel condominium.

TIME SHARING

Time sharing is a type of real estate ownership whereby ownership is split among individuals on the basis of time. The "property interest" of the owner is his or her right to use a particular property for a specified period of time. This interest is usually called a "fee interest time-share." The title to the property is divided into 52 intervals. The purchaser and heirs have the right to use a particular unit for a specified week each year for the life of the property.

The owner purchases the time-share unit for the specified time period, and usually the time-share units are furnished. An annual fee usually covers utilities, taxes, telephones, insurance, cleaning, maintenance, and replacement reserve for the furnishings. This fee is variable and is likely to increase as the cost of maintaining the time-share units increases.

Time-share projects provide a swamp program that allows owners to exchange time segments with one another. Resort Condominiums International is an organization through which owners can exchange time segments with owners at other time-sharing units in the United States or some foreign countries.

For the developer, time-sharing units can be very profitable because they sell for several times more than if the units were sold outright to individual buyers. The reason is that for many properties, the parts are greater than the whole. The owner has basically purchased a large segment of his or her total vacation cost and can benefit from any appreciation in his interest.

The negative publicity that time-sharing has had in recent years is due to unscrupulous developers who failed to maintain properties in good condition or who fraudulently took investors' money. This has made the public very wary of time-sharing. Most states have enacted legislation to protect time-share purchasers. However, buyers should carefully investigate the reputation and record of any project developer before investing.

SUMMARY

Franchising is an important part of the U.S. economy and is expanding rapidly into international markets. The advantage of the franchise arrangement is that it allows the franchisor to expand rapidly into markets with little capital outlay and offers the franchisee/investor to enjoy a good rate of return based on the proven methods of the franchisor. It is for this reason that franchising is really not an entrepreneurial activity but more of an investment opportunity. Although franchises have been known to fail, the failure rate is lower than that for independent businesses.

There are two types of franchises in the hospitality industry: restaurants and lodging. The restaurant franchise market is dominated by the fast-food segment, with the hamburger segment predominant. Other important segments include chicken, Mexican food, seafood, steak, sandwich, pancake, ice cream, and yogurt. Franchising in the lodging industry is represented in all segments, but the budget segment has the greatest number of franchise units. With stiff competition in both the lodging and restaurant segment, many franchisors are attempting to increase profits by placing franchised fast-food establishments within lodging properties.

The franchise arrangement has had a history of fraud and misrepresentation by franchisors. To protect the public better, the Federal Trade Commission requires that a discloser document called the Uniform Offering Circular (UFOC) be distributed to each potential franchisee before a franchise agreement is signed. Basically, the UFOC requires the franchisor to disclose specific information about key personnel within the franchise company along with legal and financial information to help the potential franchisee make a decision.

Once the UFOC has been reviewed and the potential franchisee decides to invest in the franchise, he or she signs the franchise agreement. The franchise agreement is the document that spells out the rights and duties of the franchisee and franchisor. It should be reviewed by an expert in franchise law. The franchisor normally charges a fee for the franchisee to have the right to operate the franchisor's business. Whether a franchisee is operating a restaurant or hotel, there is usually an initial franchise fee to cover the cost of setting up franchises by the franchisor. In addition, there is a royalty payable on gross revenue for the right to continue to use the franchisor's products and methods of business. Also, most franchisors charge an advertising fee. A reservation fee is also common for hotels. These fees are in addition to the other normal operating costs that the franchisee incurs in running the business.

When analyzing franchise opportunities, it is important to include all relevant costs in obtaining the franchise. The most important consideration in evaluating different franchises is to estimate as accurately as possible which one has the greatest return on the investment. Too often, potential franchisees base their investments on the cheapest franchise cost and not on the potential return possible from a well-run franchise.

In the past two decades, management contracts have played an ever-important role in the management of hotel properties. As hotel operators discovered that they could make more money with less risk by just operating the hotel properties, the use of management companies has grown tremendously. The management is given the right to run the property as agents for the owners. The owner retains the risks and rewards of owning the hotel.

The management company and the owner negotiate the terms of the management contract based on the strengths of the parties. The first major item to be negotiated is the period or duration of the management contract. Generally, the better the reputation of the management company, the longer the management contract term.

The management company is usually compensated by a combination of basic and incentive fees. The basic fee is often paid as a percentage of gross sales, usually between three and five percent. The incentive fee is usually based on some definition of gross operating profit and is usually deferred if there is insufficient cash flow from the operation in a given year.

There are many areas that must be negotiated between the management company and the owners of a hotel property. Some of the more important negotiation points that should be considered besides the term and fees are the performance criteria, termination clause, and equity investment by the management company.

The management of hotel condominiums represents an opportunity for management companies. A hotel condominium is much like any other hotel, but the ownership is divided among many owners who own individual rooms. Hotel condominiums have been most popular in resort areas and are another form of financing available to developers.

Generally, once the hotel is built, the property is managed by a management company, and the owners share the rent by the actual room rental method or the more common pooled rental method.

With limitation on generous tax benefits, it is difficult to predict how well hotel condominiums will do in the future. The investor has to analyze such opportunities more on the basis of sound investment criteria than as a tax shelter.

Time-sharing is another creative method for financing and selling resort properties. Here, a person purchases the right to use a facility for a specified period of time. The title to such a property can be divided into 52 intervals. The time-share owner can swap his or her time with other members or through national organizations with other time-share owners.

The developer of the time-share units has a high profit margin since the individual time periods can be sold for several times more than if the units were sold outright to one buyer. However, due to unscrupulous developers in recent years, many states have began to regulate time-share developments in order to protect the public.

GLOSSARY

Franchise   A legal relationship between one party (franchisor) who agrees to provide the know-how and/or product and a second party (franchisee) for a fee. The franchisor agrees to assist the franchisee through advertising, promotion, and other advisory services as part of the franchise contract. The franchisee agrees to operate the business according to the terms of the franchise agreement.

Franchisor   An individual or company that grants a right to someone else to use the business concept (franchise).

Franchisee   An individual or company that is given the right to conduct a business concept granted by the franchisor under a franchise agreement.

Management contract   A contract for operating a hotel property entered into between the owner of the property and a management company. The contract describes the duties and obligations of both parties, including the fee to be paid to the management company.

Management fee   The fee paid to the management company to operate a property. This fee usually consists of two parts: the basic management fee (which is usually based on a stated percentage of gross sales) and the incentive management fee (which is usually based on a percentage of net income defined by the parties).

Royalty fee   The fee paid by franchisee to the franchisor for use of the franchise. This fee is usually based on a percentage of gross sales and may include an additional percentage for national advertising.

Time-sharing   Exclusive ownership for a period of time each year of a vacation condominium. The ownership is shared with other individuals who own other exclusive periods of time throughout the year.

Trademark   A symbol protected by law that identifies the commercial operations of a company, including the name of the company, various products, and services.

Uniform Offering Circular (UFOC) The discloser document required by the Federal Trade Commission to be given to a prospective franchisee before any investment is made in a franchise business.

References

Eyster, James J. *The Negotiation and Administration of Hotel Management Contracts* (Ithaca N.Y.: School of Hotel Administration, Cornell University, 1988).

Smart, J. Eric. *Recreational Development Handbook* (Washington, D.C.: Urban Land Institute, 1981).

Siegel, L. Siegel. *Franchising* (New York: John Wiley & Sons, Inc., 1983).

Tarbutton, T. Lloyd. *Franchising, The How-To Book* (Englewood, N.J.: Prentice-Hall, Inc. 1986).

Webster, Bryce. *The Insider's Guide to Franchising* (New York: American Management Association, 1986).

Suggested Reading

Eyster, James J. *The Negotiation and Administration of Hotel Management Contracts* (Ithaca N.Y.: School of Hotel Administration, Cornell University, 1988).

Ingleby, Steven L. and Boyer, Ted. *The Resort Time Sharing Handbook* (Chicago: Real Estate Education Co., 1984).

Kostecka, Andrew. *Franchising Opportunity Handbook* (Washington, D.C.: United States Printing Office, 1988).

Rusmore, Stephen. "Structuring an Incentive Management Fee." *Lodging Hospitality,* June 1987, 52–54.

Tarbutton, T. Lloyd. *Franchising, The How-To Book* (Englewood, N.J.: Prentice-Hall, Inc., 1986).

Chapter 10

Buying and Selling Hospitality Properties

INTRODUCTION

A difficult aspect of negotiating purchase or sale of hospitality properties is the degree of wariness the parties should assume. At some point, the business assets must be verified and all major assumptions involved in the transaction checked for accuracy. The details to consider in the purchase or sale of a hospitality property could easily fill an entire book.

The sale is very complicated and involves a great deal of negotiation to reach agreement about the terms. The seller will try to get the best price possible for the business, while the buyer will want to pay a price that will ensure a targeted rate of return.

Often, the seller of the property will have considerations other than just obtaining the best sales price. For instance, the seller may be concerned about what will happen to employees after the sale, how the money will be paid (e.g., in a lump sum or paid over a period of time), whether the property's customers will receive the same high-quality service as in the past, etc.

The buyer is concerned with issues such as the future market for this type of establishment, his or her own business acumen, whether customers will show the same loyalty, etc. These and other important considerations must be satisfied by the seller before the buyer will be comfortable with a purchase agreement.

Although this chapter deals with the seller's and buyer's separate issues, it must be kept in mind that the issues facing one party are also important to the other. Also, many concepts covered in previous chapters apply to the buy-sell agreement. For instance, the valuation of a hospitality property discussed in Chapter 7 also applies to valuing a business entity.

The buyer must arrange an analysis of the site location, especially concerning business generators and competition in the area. Therefore, a quick review of factors involved in the feasibility study in Chapter 4 will help determine the desirability of a particular business, especially forecasting likely future income.

The buyer will have to decide what business entity he or she will use to operate the newly purchased business. Refer to Chapter 2 for a thorough discussion of the advantages and disadvantages of the sole proprietorship, general and limited partnership, corporation, and S corporation.

DECISION TO SELL

The decision to sell a hospitality property has many important considerations. No two people view a business outlook the same way. In late 1989, Marriott Corporation decided that it no longer saw the food service industry as profitable as the lodging industry and decided to sell its restaurant and food catering businesses. We may never know Marriott's motivation for selling its food divisions, but another major corporation almost certainly would have seen this sale as an opportunity to expand in the restaurant business. And other corporations would no doubt see the market for the future profitability of restaurants differently from Marriott.

Motivation

What is the motivation for the seller's putting his business up for sale? This is usually the buyer's first question. Is the owner selling because of poor health? A disagreement between partners? The death of the founder? Retirement plans? Business failure? Or have market conditions changed?

Understanding the seller's motivation is very important. For example, a buyer purchases a small hotel in a small town, hoping to run a successful but leisurely business only to discover that a new Holiday Inn is being built in the town that will force the motel owner to lower his or her rates to remain competitive. He learned the seller's motivation too late.

It is important to determine if the seller's motivation is due to factors that can be controlled or shifting market conditions. In the example above, if the buyer had been aware of the planned Holiday Inn, he or she could have analyzed its potential impact on the desired motel and offered a more realistic price for the property. But if the business had simply been poorly run and the buyer had identified the reasons for poor sales as being easily corrected, the buyer would have been in a much better position to offer a fair price for the property. He or she would have had a chance to turn the operation around and made it profitable. Making these determinations is a real skill in the purchase of a property. Many times, a buyer will purchase a hospitality property thinking that he has superior operating abilities only to discover that factors beyond his control are causing sales to slump.

The buyer's motivation is as important as the seller's. Why does he or she want to buy the property? Does he or she have the skills to operate the property successfully? These are important questions the seller will want answered, especially when the seller has to finance part of the purchase price himself with a money purchase mortgage or land contract. The seller wants a successful sale so he or she does not have to run the property again. This is a real concern for owners who want to retire.

To better understand the motivation of the parties, each side will want as much information about the other as possible. Generally, the buyer of a hospitality property will want to begin by focusing on:

1. Market analysis
2. Financial information
3. Debt and legal obligations

Much of this information may be difficult to obtain. If it is available, it must still be verified. This is why both parties need to proceed cautiously in the sale and purchase of a property. This is also why consummation of the sale can take many months.

Market Information

Much of Chapter 4 (Feasibility Studies) applies to the purchaser's and seller's determining the value of a hospitality business. Such analyses as competitive analysis, site analysis, and demand analysis should be conducted by the potential buyer. (Review Chapter 4 before continuing.)

The remaining portion of this section focuses on what the buyer should obtain from the seller to help determine actual or potential market conditions. At the very minimum, the buyer should obtain back sales data for at least three years (longer, if possible) from the seller. How well the company records were maintained will tell the buyer a great deal about how the business was run.

The smaller the business, the more likely it is that sales records will be useless to the buyer. If this is the case, the buyer may have to substitute other methods of verifying sales. These could include observing the actual operation of the business or interviewing present and past employees and management personnel. Another method is to examine sales tax records to figure the sales per store. Most states require that records be maintained for a certain minimum number of years for audit purposes. Either way, it is important to have an accurate picture of how well the business performed in the past and in the present.

Another internal source for determining the business market is in-depth interviews with customers about why they patronize the establishment. The buyer should also observe the general condition of the premises for cleanliness, professionalism of the staff, and management style. The layout of the restaurant, for instance, may play a direct role in negotiating the purchase price of the property, especially if the new owner would like to change the floor plan but can't because of the physical layout of the property.

Finally, the buyer should not overlook past efforts to increase sales. Was an effective marketing plan in place, and was it carried out effectively? By analyzing the sales effort and comparing it to actual sales, the buyer may be able to determine potential market capture.

Financial Information

Some of most important information the buyer needs is in the hospitality firm's financial statements. These can include not only the balance sheet and income statement but also income tax returns, sales tax returns, payroll tax returns, cash flow statements, bank balance statements, purchase orders, and inventory amounts. Other statements, such as operating ratios, will also help the buyer decide whether to make an offer for the business.

The starting point of the review process usually occurs when the buyer analyzes the balance sheet and income statement. The balance sheet is often considered a snapshot of the business at any given time. On the other hand, the income statement shows a summary of the year's transactions. Both are valuable for determining the state of the business, but there are problems with using these statements.

The buyer's biggest concern is verifying the data on the balance sheet and income statement. For example, the balance sheet lists the assets of the business at cost, less depreciation. But this may not be the fair market value of the assets. In fact, property is probably more valuable than what is stated, and the fair market value of furniture and equipment is less than the statement claims.

Analysis of the financial statements requires that the buyer understand how they were prepared. The buyer should examine the accounting controls used and how they were applied. For instance, many smaller hospitality companies prepare their statements based on unacceptable accounting methods that make comparison of data from another firm difficult. This is why it is often advisable for the buyer to involve his or her own accountant as early as possible in the negotiation process.

The biggest obstacle the buyer faces is verifying the amounts on the financial statements. As mentioned earlier, many smaller firms prepare their own financial statements, and the data supplied may not be accurate. The optimal situation is when the seller can provide the buyer with audited financial statements prepared by a reputable certified public accountant (CPA), who expresses his professional opinions about how fairly the financial statements reflect the true condition of the hospitality business. Note that the audited statements are not meant to guarantee the accuracy of the financial statements, and the buyer should conduct his or her own analysis. However, audited statements are much more likely to be accurate than owner-prepared statements.

The buyer will also want to analyze the firm's income tax statements. Remember that the name of the game is to pay as little tax as is legally permissible. The income statement should be prepared in accordance with the Internal Revenue Code. As such, income and deductions may be treated differently on the income tax return than on the financial statement. The buyer must examine these differences and then be able to reconcile the income shown on the income tax return with that on the financial income statement.

One of the biggest problems for a buyer of smaller hospitality firms (especially restaurants) is that the seller often says that the income tax statements are understated because the owner skimmed income from the operation in order to reduce the taxable part of the earnings. How can the buyer verify if the seller is telling the truth or merely trying to justify an increased sales price for the establishment? One possible way to verify sales is to observe business during normal operating hours and then try to project future sales. In many cases, the buyer has to observe the operation over a long time to collect a representative data sample for the business income for the year. Other methods of verifying sales include examining purchase orders, reported tips from the wait staff, and examining any other data that may provide a clue about the firm's true sales.

A seller should take one precautionary measure before supplying information to a potential buyer. Sometimes, the person posing as a purchaser may be planning to open a competing business and is only interested in gathering information. Therefore, the seller should first qualify the buyer before supplying any information. This can be accomplished using several different methods, from checking references to having the buyer put down a good-faith deposit before entering into serious negotiations.

Debt and Legal Obligations

It is very important for the purchaser to verify the debt outstanding on the business to determine if liens on the property will be assumed by the purchaser or discharged through acquisition of the business. It is also important to verify the debt outstanding by visiting the holder of the debt instruments and learning if payments have been made on a timely basis.

If the seller has been making late payments to the lender, this could be a valuable clue about the seller's motivation for putting the business up for sale. In many cases, a buyer may be able to work out favorable borrowing terms with the lender if the lender feels that the new owner will be able to salvage a declining business venture. Therefore, the purchaser should interview any lenders in depth about the possibility of their financing a hospitality project.

Another potential problem area for the purchaser is the discovery of legal problems that may affect the operation of the business. The most common legal problem turns on whether the seller has a valid title to transfer to the buyer. Title issues were discussed in detail in Chapter 1. The main goal of sales transactions is the transfer of a valid title. There would be little problem if the transfer involved only a single piece of land that the buyer wished to purchase. But the problem is compounded for an on-going business by the fact that there is not only a transfer of land title but also of licenses, inventory, furniture and fixtures, lease rights or obligations, receivables, etc. Because each asset has its unique ownership characteristics, the ownership of each must be verified at the time of transfer.

The buyer must also know about past liabilities that may affect his or her ownership interest or reduce his or her value in the business. For example, if the seller has not paid property taxes and the city has a lien on the property, the buyer will be obliged to pay the taxes if the seller has not paid them by the time of transfer. Another reason for investigating potential liabilities is that they may reveal other facts about the business that have to be corrected to reduce future liabilities. For instance, if a township has initiated a tougher liquor enforcement policy, the buyer may find that he or she must initiate a liquor awareness training for the employees to reduce future liquor liability exposure.

The buyer also must be concerned with legal contract obligations with suppliers, customers, employees, lessors, etc. In most cases, the buyer assumes the seller's contractual obligations as part of the purchase of the business. Therefore, it is important for the buyer to understand and accept the obligations that he or she will want to assume. In addition, many obligations cannot be transferred to the buyer without the consent of third parties. For instance, if the buyer assumes the seller's mortgage, the lender must agree in advance that the assumption will be permitted and that the seller will remain liable if the buyer defaults in the future.

If the premises are covered by a lease, the buyer should obtain a copy and review the provisions relating to the amount of rent, terms of payment, expiration, renewal options, subleasing, improvement clause, exclusivity of business operation, permissible business operations, etc.

Buyers often overlook insurance contracts currently in force protecting the property. By examining these contracts in detail, the buyer can learn if insurance coverage on the property is adequate. Also, the insurance contracts may pinpoint the kinds of liabilities the buyer is likely to face upon assuming the business. Finally, this review will give the buyer a better understanding of the cost of insurance coverage for various risks, which may help him or her plan how best to reduce future insurance cost through an effective risk management program.

Local government and law must also be taken into account when considering possible problems that may arise after the purchase. These can include local zoning and building ordinances to determine if there are any nonconforming uses of land or violations of building codes. These may cause the government entity to intervene and enforce expensive modifications to the property. Also, the buyer should review master plans for possible rezoning or changes in traffic patterns that may affect the business in the future. For instance, a proposed major highway project for a bypass of the current business location could be the seller's motivation for placing the property on the market.

The buyer must consider every possible source of information to guarantee making the best possible decision. A decision based on faulty or inadequate information could result in lengthy litigation or even financial disaster.

Valuing

The value of the hospitality business is based on the conclusions drawn from the analyses done by the seller and buyer. However, the parties may disagree about the amount of that value. Valuing the business almost always comes down to measuring its profit-making potential.

The seller's biggest mistake usually in pricing the property is including a value based on the original investment or the effort put into the business over the years. Although the cost of the assets may bear on the selling price, it is seldom directly related to the sale price. The fair market value of the assets themselves may not be as important as how much income they can generate.

On the other hand, the buyer generally prices the business to bring a satisfactory return on the original investment. Thus, he or she is likely to discount the future cash flow estimates by a percentage rate that reflects a fair return on the investment, given the risk involved. The buyer's estimate of future inflation rates and the ability of the business to generate increases in revenue to offset these increases is another consideration.

The buyer compares his or her investment in the hospitality business with that of alternative investments, such as government bonds or the stock market. (These and other discounting procedures were discussed in detail in Chapter 5.)

Purchase Price

Many people confuse the sale price of a property with its value. Value is what the hospitality property is worth, while the sale price is the amount for which the property is transferred from the seller to the buyer. There are many reasons why the value and the price are almost always different. The buyer and the seller may arrive at different valuations of the hospitality property by assuming different future assumptions.

Also, the sale price is usually based on many factors other than just what the property is worth. For example, the owner may be motivated to sell the property because of debts unrelated to the hospitality business. Or the owner may be gravely ill and wants to sell the property before he or she is totally incapacitated.

Another factor that often changes the selling price is the terms of the sale. For instance, a buyer may be able to obtain a large discount off the selling price if he or she offers cash for the business. On the other hand, the selling price may be increased substantially if the seller is forced to accept 100 percent financing (where the buyer makes little or no down payment). The increase compensates the seller for the additional risk of loaning the whole purchase price to the buyer.

The parties will probably wish to assign values to the various assets purchased. For instance, certain portions of the purchase price for a restaurant will be allocated among the liquor license, furniture and fixtures, equipment, land, building, etc. The buyer usually wishes to allocate as little as possible to nondepreciable assets such as land and the liquor license. The allocation of assets should be based on a supportable basis that reflects the fair market value of the assets. See Exhibit 10-1 on page 188 for an example of how a typical purchase price is allocated among the various assets of a restaurant.

Often, it is a good idea to allocate the purchase price among the assets early in price negotiations. This will help the parties reach a quicker understanding about which assets are to be transferred at the time of sale. Many times, the owner wishes to reserve for himself certain assets and should list those assets so as not to mislead the buyer about the items included in the sale.

Another contributing factor to the final selling price is the obligations that the buyer must assume. For instance, will the existing mortgage be paid off or will the seller assume that liability? If the sale of the business involves the sale of common stock instead of the assets of the corporation, will the price of the stock reflect the debt that the new corporate buyers are assuming upon the purchase of the stock?

When the purchase price is settled upon, it is imperative for the parties to put their agreement in writing. The resulting document is much more than a mere recitation of the purchase price and terms of the sale. It should include all possible contingencies and how they will be handled at the time of sale or later. For instance, it is usually a very good idea for the buyer to insist that the seller sign a "covenant not to compete" agreement. This will prevent the seller from competing with his or her former business.

A typical purchase agreement will detail which assets are being sold, the purchase price, method of payment, and financing arrangements with the seller or a third party. In addition, the contract should spell out:

- Adjustments to be made if assets are not as represented
- Warranties given by the seller
- Buyer's assumptions of any contracts and liabilities
- Seller's responsibilities before closing, including risk of loss
- Covenant not to compete
- Closing arrangements
- Indemnification by the seller and security deposit for liabilities not expressly assumed by the buyer
- Legal forum for the resolution of disputes

Negotiation

Throughout this book, many of the key aspects of hospitality financing require participants to negotiate. For instance, leases are negotiated between two parties, and franchise agreements are the result of negotiation between two parties for permission to use a business method of one of the parties.

What is negotiation and what are the parties really bargaining for when a hospitality business is bought and sold?

Negotiation can be best defined as the attempt by one person to influence another person to engage in a transaction that will change the status quo. This broad definition of negotiation can be narrowed to the context of buying and selling hospitality properties to be defined as an agreement intended to eventually exchange ownership interest for consideration.

Negotiation can take place only between individuals. Institutions or corporations cannot negotiate; only the representatives of the organizations can. Thus, negotiation involves influencing human behavior for one's own or a group's mutual advantage. Generally, a prerequisite for negotiation is one party's ability to hurt or help another in some manner. Negotiation is really the satisfaction of needs of the parties involved.

Goals

Before any negotiation process begins, it is important the parties understand what they want. They do this by writing down exactly what they hope to accomplish. For instance, the buyer must know the type of hospitality business he or she really wants to purchase, the amount of money he or she is willing to spend for the property, the acceptable conditions of the purchase agreement, etc.

The seller engages in the same type of thinking when preparing to sell the property. It is important for the seller to understand and express his or her reasons for selling. Also, the seller should list on paper the things important to him or her when selling the business. The price of the property is probably the most important, but other considerations may be equally important in the decision to sell. For instance, the owner may wish to ensure that long-term employees can keep their jobs after the property has been sold.

Strategies

Once the parties have established their goals, it is important for them to develop strategies to accomplish those goals. One could develop an exhaustive list of strategies for negotiating any given situation, but the following general guidelines should help develop specific strategies.

a. Information Valid information is the most important asset a negotiator can have. Verified financial statements and records are examples. Relevant information will help the parties understand where the other side is coming from. Of course, the other party may not want to disclose all pertinent facts that would aid the other side. For example, the strategy of one of the parties may be to disclose as little information as possible about the reasons for wanting to enter a transaction. If a seller knows that a major restaurant chain is planning to build next door to his property and this may result in a significant loss of business, he or she may choose to withhold this fact to the potential buyer. It is the buyer's responsibility to obtain that information. This is why the information that is obtained must be objective.

When negotiating, it is important to understand the difference between facts that can determined independently and assumptions. Facts can be proven to exist or not exist. Assumptions, on the other hand, are beliefs that an individual feels are true even though they cannot be proven. For example, when we drive down the highway we assume that a car coming at us will not cross the median and hit us. It is not a fact until the car in the opposite lane actually passes, but in order for us to function in society we must make that assumption. Fortunately, it is almost always true that the other car does in fact stay on the other side.

However, many assumptions made when negotiating are not so reasonable. For instance, it is not always correct for the buyer to assume that the most important consideration for the seller is the purchase price. The seller may wish to obtain a fair price but is actually more concerned that employees retain their positions after the business is sold. If the buyer follows that assumption without attempting to gather more information, he or she may miss an opportunity to bargain for a reduced price in consideration for retaining the employees. Or worse, the buyer may lose the sale completely because he or she is not satisfying the seller's needs.

Both parties must understand their assumptions and whether there is better information. They must also know how best to obtain the better information. Many deals are ruined because a party failed to verify an important assumption made during the negotiation process.

b. Communication Negotiation can occur only if there is adequate communication between the parties. This means that each party must understand what is being said to him or her and how the other side perceives what he or she is saying. There is a great amount of information available about the importance of communication in the negotiation process, and the major conclusion is that conveying the intended meaning is a key element of communicating.

In many cases, communication consists not only of what is said but what is not said. For instance, an attitude may convey an entirely different meaning from what is actually said. Tone of voice and mannerisms can often convey important information to the other party.

We also communicate with body language. What is the other party really saying with his or her gestures? This can be very difficult to determine, especially if you have had limited contact with that person in the past. However, a good negotiator will listen to what is being stated and watch how the other party reacts to statements and actions.

Needs

One of the more important aspects in negotiating is understanding the needs of the other negotiators. Everybody has different needs that must be satisfied. The best negotiators find a way to satisfy the other party's needs and wants while taking care of his or her own. To do this, the negotiator must have intimate knowledge of his or her own needs.

This does not mean that a negotiator will surrender position or even compromise for the sake of satisfying the other party's needs. But it does mean being sensitive to them. For example, when purchasing a small hotel at an estate sale, the buyer may recognize that the heirs want cash from the sale. The buyer may offer a cash sale but at a substantial discount from the asking price. The need of the heirs to obtain cash is real, and the buyer's need to obtain the property at a good price can be realized. If both parties feel they have their needs met, a sale will likely take place.

Tactics

Finally, once the negotiator has determined the other party's needs as well as possible, he or she will then implement tactics that are consistent with the strategy developed to achieve the stated goals. Negotiating tactics are too numerous to mention in detail. Only a few of the more common are discussed here.

The point is that different tactics work best at different times. A tactic is a tool that aids in achieving a desired goal, and it should be discarded if it does not work. Many negotiators use a very limited number of tactics.

There are thousands of tactics that can be used in the negotiation process; here are some of the more common ones:

1. *Time limit.* Here, a party places a limit as to when an offer will be accepted. This could in fact be a real limit, but more likely it is a tactic used to hurry the negotiations along before the other party has all the relevant facts. The other party must determine whether the deadline is real or not. If the deadline appears arbitrary, it probably is and should be ignored. Other variations of the time limit are "take it or leave it" or "this is my last offer." One should never invest a large sum of money in a project without being sure of having all the information necessary to make a wise decision.

2. Lack of authority. Many times, the other party states that he or she cannot bind the deal but first must get permission to close the sale. Anyone who has purchased a car will recognize this technique. It is designed to get the second party to concede to important points while leaving the first party free to modify or reject the terms. The first rule of negotiating is to seriously negotiate only with someone who has the authority to act.

3. *Silence.* This tactic is very effective for many people who can handle silence well. The party says very little and waits for the other party, who cannot handle silence, to make concessions. Silence is very hard for many people to overcome; they want to fill the vacuum and many times will concede more than they intended only because they felt uncomfortable. If a party cannot remain silent for long (and many cannot), he or she should devise a method of talking about non-related topics to fill the void. This will prevent unintended consessions.

4. *Screaming.* This person yells and tries to intimidate the other party into making a less-than-satisfactory deal. Although this can be one of the most upsetting tactics of negotiating, it can be defeated by simple refusal to be intimidated. Often, the only response needed is to tell the offending party that continued yelling will force you to deal with another party. Although losing its popularity, screaming is still encountered. The injured party can end any negotiation situation over which he or she has lost control.

5. *Feinting.* This tactic is making a major issue over minor points in the negotiating process so that the other side feels obliged to concede something—often the major point. This is often effective because parties may feel that having got what they wanted on one point, they should concede a point in return. This can result in giving up more than one wants just for the sake of compromising. The best defense to this tactic is to measure how important the issue is to the other party and to oneself. One must never lose perspective as to how important the issue is no matter how the other party is acting at the time. Also, each issue in the negotiating process is usually independent of other issues and should not be used as a one-for-one compromise unless they are equal in value.

These are just some of the major tactics that may be used in the negotiating process. The best negotiation process, however, is one in which both parties feel they got a fair deal. Under those conditions, the sale will more than likely proceed quickly and efficiently than if one party feels he or she had been taken. Often, a party who feels that he has been cheated will do almost anything to disrupt the sale. This can happen even if the other side is successful in a lengthy and expensive litigation that could have been avoided if the party had been more sensitive to the other's needs.

PURCHASE

Locating Property to Purchase

Before a hospitality property can be purchased, there must be potential purchasers who are aware that the property is for sale. There is no one method of placing a property for sale, but often a seller runs ads in local and trade publications announcing a property for sale.

The most common form of listing a property is through a commercial real estate brokerage firm. These firms specialize in selling commercial properties. The potential buyer should be cautioned that the broker is under contract to the seller and is obliged to get the highest price possible. Many would-be buyers mistakenly believe that the broker is working for them.

Other indirect methods of locating a hospitality property to purchase include discussions with leading local businesspersons about their knowledge of properties for sale. Also, the potential buyer may discuss purchasing a hospitality property with salespersons who service the kind of business the buyer wishes to purchase. Finally, the potential buyer may contact property owners directly to determine whether they are willing to sell their business in the near future.

One of the most difficult parts of locating property for sale for the buyer is obtaining verifiable information that will allow him or her to analyze the property confidently. Some of the best opportunities to buy occur in businesses that the buyer already knows. Therefore, the potential buyer may want to start inquiring from people with whom he is comfortable about leads in a suitable property to purchase.

Use of Options

One way to tie up a desirable piece of property without being obliged to purchase it is through an option. The option is really a low-investment technique for real estate investors and developers to review the desirability of a particular property.

Basically, an option is the exclusive right for valuable consideration to purchase property within a specified period. The person obtaining the option is known as the "optionee," and the "optionor" is the party who owns the property and grants the option. The time period in which the optionee has right to exclusively purchase the property is the "option period." If at the end of the option period the optionee has not exercised the right to purchase the property, the option will be deemed to have lapsed and the optionee has no further rights in the property.

Options come in many different forms to suit the purpose of the parties. The most common option is the "fixed option." Here, the optionee has the right to buy the property during a designated time period.

Another popular kind of option is the "full-credit option." Under this option, the optionee's cost of obtaining the option is credited toward the purchase of the property if the option is exercised.

Sale-Purchase Contract

When the parties reach an agreement about the sale and purchase of a property, it is committed to a written contract. (See Chapter 1 for the elements required for a valid contract.) The contract details the obligations and duties of the parties. It is very important for them to understand explicitly what the contract includes. This will avoid costly legal or financial surprises later.

The sale-purchase (sales) contract should not only include the duties and obligations of the parties but also procedures for handling any breeches of provisions in the contract or problems that arise later that were not contemplated by the parties when they made up the contract. For example, many contracts provide for arbitration of disputes that arise instead of expensive and often time-consuming litigation.

DESCRIPTION OF THE PROPERTY

The first thing that the sales contract usually contains is a thorough description of the location of the property. Usually, the full legal description of the property is given along with the street address.

The buyer should confirm that the description of the site matches the property being contracted for purchase. Also, the buyer and seller will want to make certain that the description is accurate and free from ambiguity; otherwise, the contract may not be enforceable.

Purchase Price and Financing

The sales contract shows the purchase price agreed to by the parties. In addition, the sales price is usually allocated among the various assets being purchased (land, buildings, furniture, fixtures, goodwill, etc.). Also, along with the purchase price, there is usually a provision for adjusting to the final sales price if any number of contingencies occur or if the property is slightly different from what was originally contracted for. For example, if the land purchased for a resort contains fewer acres than originally described in the contract, this provision could provide for an adjustment to the final sales contract based on a final survey of the property.

This section of the sales contract usually provides for earnest money or a good-faith deposit for the acquisition of the property by the buyer. This deposit shows that the buyer is serious about purchasing the property. Many times, this deposit is deemed to be the liquidated damages if the prospective buyer fails to go through with terms of the contract. The buyer usually insists that if the deposit is to be used for liquidated damages, certain conditions beyond the control of the buyer

EXHIBIT 10-1

Purchase Allocation for a Hypothetical Restaurant

Total Sales Price—$275,000

Allocation by Asset Category:

Land*	$ 20,000
Building	150,000
Liquor license*	80,000
Furniture & equipment	20,000
Inventory	5,000
Total	$275,000

*Nondepreciable asset

should not be deemed a default. Under the contract, the buyer would be entitled to get back the deposit under specified conditions. For example, a buyer may make the sale contingent upon receiving certain zoning changes necessary to construct the building. Failure to obtain the zoning changes would constitute an event that was outside the buyer's control, and thus he or she would be entitled to a return of the deposit.

This section of the sales contract may also contain the buyer's financing method. For instance, the sales contract may specify that the seller is to finance part of the purchase price (purchase-money mortgage), assume (or take "subject to") an existing mortgage, and/or obtain a new mortgage. Whatever combination of financing is used should be detailed in this section.

Other Considerations

The sales contract usually specifies that the property is to be conveyed by the seller and that the seller will provide the necessary proofs of ownership and transfer of licenses, and that the equipment to be transferred will be in good working condition unless noted in the agreement. Since there may be a lengthy period of time from the sale of the business to the actual closing date (where actual ownership is transferred between the parties), the buyer will also want to include a provision for the inspection and approval of any contracts that the seller may enter into on behalf of the business and the right to inspect the premises regularly. Also, the sales contract should indicate that the buyer has the right to be consulted about any management matters of the property and any personnel decisions.

The sales contract should also provide for the sale to be contingent upon the completion of a valid survey of the property. The survey will determine the exact parcel of property to be transferred. The survey also will indicate any easements on the property, right of ways, roads, and access to the property. The survey should be inspected carefully by both parties to ensure that the property being conveyed is the property agreed to and that any variances may result in an adjustment of the sales price.

The sales contract should provide for as many events as possible that may occur after the contract is signed and the closing date. The sales contract should state who will provide insurance on the property and proof that such insurance exists. Also, the parties should spell out what will occur if the property is taken by power of eminent domain or some other casualty. The general rule is that if the property is destroyed between the date of the sales contract and closing, the sale is to be canceled and the parties returned to their original positions. The more events that the parties can anticipate, the better are the chances that the transaction will proceed according to the wishes of both parties.

Finally, the contract should specify that good title will be passed from the seller to the buyer. The seller will usually convey to the buyer a title insurance policy as satisfaction of conveying good title. (See Chapter 1, page 10 for a discussion of title and title insurance.)

The final item in the sales contract is the closing date, when marketable title or some other agreed-upon title is passed from the seller to the buyer. (See Chapter 1, page 11 for a discussion of deeds.) The closing date can be ceremonial or complicated, depending upon the issues not covered in the sales contract. Many real estate transactions never get completed at the closing because of disagreements over terms in the contract or the inability to deliver on promises made.

Miscellaneous Considerations

Real Estate Broker

Sale of an existing hospitality business is a complex process that requires the participation of many professionals. One of the first professionals that a buyer or seller is likely to employ in a real estate transaction (other than accountants or attorneys) is a broker. A broker is someone who is licensed to bring buyers and sellers together and who receives compensation in sales commissions. The commission is based upon a percentage of the sales price, although the parties can agree to a fixed commission amount if they choose. The parties are not obligated to use a broker, but many sellers use them to list their properties in order to obtain the widest possible exposure to potential buyers.

The commission that the broker charges is usually paid for by the seller unless otherwise agreed to in the sales contact. Remember that the broker works for the seller, not the buyer. Also, the contract with the broker should spell out that the commission is payable only upon the title transfer. If for any reason the sale is not completed, the broker may be able to claim a commission due and payable unless stated differently in the brokerage agreement.

As with other contracts, the real estate listing contract with a broker is a negotiable instrument that should be reviewed by the seller to ensure protection from an incompetent broker. For example, although a listing contract usually gives the broker an exclusive right to list the property and receive a commission (even if the seller finds a buyer on his own), the seller can limit exposure by placing a time limit on how long the property will be listed. Another example would be for the seller to list prospects that he has contacted and exclude them from the listing agreement, so if one of these prospects buys the property, the seller is not liable to the broker for a sales commission.

Covenant not to Compete

Anyone buying an existing business will want to include as part of the sales contract a "not to compete clause." This is done so that the seller does not open a business in the area to compete with the one he or she just sold. In order to be enforceable in a court of law, the covenant has to be reasonable in the time and area limits that are placed upon the seller. Individual facts and circumstances dictate what the courts view as reasonable. The buyer should strive to make the limits reasonable to avoid litigation. For example, a court would consider unreasonable a stipulation that the seller may not open another restaurant in the entire state or that he or she may not enter into a competing business for 20 years. A court would hold the covenant unenforceable.

SUMMARY

The buying and selling of a hospitality business is a complex and time-consuming endeavor for both parties to the transaction. The seller wants to obtain the best selling price for the property along with other possible considerations, such as employee retention. The buyer wants to obtain the property at a price that will assure him of being able to obtain his targeted rate of return.

Although the general concepts that were introduced in previous chapters (such as feasibility study, valuation techniques, desired rate of return, choice of business entity, etc.) are part of the purchase decision, the biggest problem facing the buyer is the analysis of the existing business operation. A big part of analyzing any business operation is verifying claims made by either party.

The first consideration to both parties is the seller's motivation to sell. A less—but still important—consideration is the buyer's motivation to purchase. The buyer is especially interested in why the seller is putting the property on the market. Is the reason legitimate, or is the seller withholding something that is likely to occur in the future (a national chain building nearby, a manufacturing plant closing, etc.)?

The buyer wants to verify past sales to the maximum extent possible. Since smaller hospitality firms rarely have certified audits performed, the buyer may have difficulty verifying past sales. The buyer should then seek alternatives that lend confidence about the potential sales of the business, such as observe operations, talk to current and past employees, and perform ratio analysis on the financial statements presented to determine their reasonableness.

Financial statements such as the income and balance sheets, sales tax reports, income tax returns, payroll tax returns, purchase orders, and any records that would help the potential buyer verify the seller's data are useful and should not be overlooked.

The seller should be cautious about giving information to a buyer in the event that the buyer is only gathering information to open a competing business. Therefore, it is important for the seller to qualify the buyer, either through reference checks or through written testimony that the buyer is not going to open his or her own business.

The buyer will need to verify the amount of the business' outstanding debt and any liabilities owed by the business. Often, the buyer can obtain an accurate picture of how well the business is doing by talking to banking officials and analyzing the liabilities.

Other important legal considerations to the buyer are the status of outstanding suits, current insurance coverage and claims, lease obligations, and government claims against the property.

The final consideration that the parties will each arrive at separately is the value of the hospitality business. The value of most businesses is the future earnings. The seller often values the property based on its potential or sentimental value. The seller and buyer almost always value a property differently. This is due to different major assumptions used to obtain value.

Other factors enter into the final determination of the price of the hospitality property. These include the motivation of the parties, financing amount and costs, market conditions at the time of sale, etc.

If a sale is to take place, both parties enter into negotiation for the purchase of the property. Although there are various aspects to the negotiation process, the parties will likely meet their needs if they adhere to certain basic principles.

The first way of meeting one's needs in the negotiation process is to establish goals. The parties should write down what they hope to accomplish. Second, they should then develop specific strategies to meet those goals. Developing a strategy includes gathering relevant information and being able to effectively communicate with the other party.

One of the basic premises of negotiating is understanding one's needs and the other party's needs. Many sales have been lost because one party was not sensitive to the other party's needs. One must always assess whether meeting another's needs will result in a favorable negotiated settlement.

Finally, the negotiator has to develop specific tactics to help accomplish desired strategies. Although there are numerous specific tactics, a good negotiator chooses those that fit the situation best. The most common tactic used in the purchase of a business is to impose artificial time limits upon the other party about how long the property will remain available.

Before there can be any negotiation for the purchase of a hospitality property, the seller and buyer must come together. Usually, a seller lists the property with a commercial broker who then attempts through advertising or contacts to match the seller with a buyer. However, many hospitality firms are sold through word of mouth or through the buyer contacting a hospitality operator directly and asking if he or she would consider selling the property.

Once a desirable property has been located, the buyer may want to explore the property's desirability further while using an option such as a low-investment technique to secure property. An "option" is the exclusive right for valuable consideration to purchase property within a specified period.

Once the negotiation process is completed, the parties commit their agreements to writing. This is the sales-purchase contract, which defines all the details of the sale, including the description of the property, listing of assets included in the sale, any contingencies that must be met by either party, penalties for non-compliance of any of the contract terms, financing terms, covenant not to compete clause, closing date, and other terms parties deem important.

GLOSSARY

Acquisition costs   Cost usually assessed at closing to cover costs other than price of the property, such as escrow fees, title insurance, lender charges, etc.

Agent   A person authorized to represent the principal (usually the person selling the property).

Asking price   The initial listed price the seller sets for the property.

Breech of contract   The failure to honor all or part of a contract without sufficient legal reasons.

Cancellation clause   A clause in a real estate contract by which the parties may legally revoke the contract with or without penalties under specified circumstances.

Closing   The last procedure in the purchase and sale of real estate whereby the final documents are executed (transfer of title, deed, loan proceeds, etc.) and the sale is completed.

Contingency   Dependence upon an event to occur before a party is obliged to complete the contract.

Earnest money   Money give by the buyer to demonstrate good faith when offering to purchase a property.

Escrow   An account held by a third party that usually contains the legal documents and money necessary to complete the purchase of a property. The documents and money will be disbursed by the third party according to the instructions contained in the escrow agreement signed by the parties to the sale.

Exclusive listing   A written contract between the seller of a property and a real estate broker that provides for a fee to be paid to the broker if the property is sold during a specified period of time. The commission is payable to the broker even if the seller finds a buyer independently.

Legal description   The identification of a property that is referenced in a legally acceptable document.

Listing broker   A real estate broker who obtains a listing.

Mistake   In a real estate contract, the unintentional error or misstatement of the facts that permit the contract to be rescinded without liability to either party to the transaction.

Negotiation   The process of bargaining with another party to obtain something desired or to prevent something negative from occurring.

Option   The right, for consideration, for a party to be able to purchase a specific property for a specified price within a stated period of time.

Purchase agreement   A contract agreed to by the buyer and seller that sets the terms and conditions of the purchase of real estate.

References

How to Buy and Sell a Small Business. New York: Drake Publishers Inc., 1975.

Douglas, E. Gordon. *How to Profitably Sell or Buy a Company or Business.* New York: Van Nostrand Co., 1981.

Stefanelli, John. *The Sale and Purchase of Restaurants.* New York: John Wiley & Sons, 1985.

Suggested Reading

Nierenberg, Gerard I. *The Art of Negotiating.* New York: Simon & Schuster, 1981.

Stefanelli, John. *The Sale and Purchase of Restaurants.* New York: John Wiley & Sons, 1985.

Ware, Richard & James Rudnick. *The Restaurant Book.* New York: Facts on File, 1989.

Appendices

Appendix I

THE SUM OF ONE DOLLAR COMPOUNDED ANNUALLY FOR N YEARS

Year	1%	2%	3%	4%	5%	6%	7%	8%	9%	10%
1	1.010	1.020	1.030	1.040	1.050	1.060	1.070	1.080	1.090	1.100
2	1.020	1.040	1.061	1.082	1.102	1.124	1.145	1.166	1.188	1.210
3	1.030	1.061	1.093	1.125	1.158	1.191	1.225	1.260	1.295	1.331
4	1.041	1.082	1.126	1.170	1.216	1.262	1.311	1.360	1.412	1.464
5	1.051	1.104	1.159	1.217	1.276	1.338	1.403	1.469	1.539	1.611
6	1.062	1.126	1.194	1.265	1.340	1.419	1.501	1.587	1.677	1.772
7	1.072	1.149	1.230	1.316	1.407	1.504	1.606	1.714	1.828	1.949
8	1.083	1.172	1.267	1.369	1.477	1.594	1.718	1.851	1.993	2.144
9	1.094	1.195	1.305	1.423	1.551	1.689	1.838	1.999	2.172	2.358
10	1.105	1.219	1.344	1.480	1.629	1.791	1.967	2.159	2.367	2.594
11	1.116	1.243	1.384	1.539	1.710	1.898	2.105	2.332	2.580	2.853
12	1.127	1.268	1.426	1.601	1.796	2.012	2.252	2.518	2.813	3.138
13	1.138	1.294	1.469	1.665	1.886	2.133	2.410	2.720	3.066	3.452
14	1.149	1.319	1.513	1.732	1.980	2.261	2.579	2.937	3.342	3.797
15	1.161	1.346	1.558	1.801	2.079	2.397	2.759	3.172	3.642	4.177
16	1.173	1.373	1.605	1.873	2.183	2.540	2.952	3.426	3.970	4.595
17	1.184	1.400	1.653	1.948	2.292	2.693	3.159	3.700	4.328	5.054
18	1.196	1.428	1.702	2.026	2.407	2.854	3.380	3.996	4.717	5.560
19	1.208	1.457	1.753	2.107	2.527	3.026	3.616	4.316	5.142	6.116
20	1.220	1.486	1.806	2.191	2.653	3.207	3.870	4.661	5.604	6.727
21	1.232	1.516	1.860	2.279	2.786	3.399	4.140	5.034	6.109	7.400
22	1.245	1.546	1.916	2.370	2.925	3.603	4.430	5.436	6.658	8.140
23	1.257	1.577	1.974	2.465	3.071	3.820	4.740	5.871	7.258	8.954
24	1.270	1.608	2.033	2.563	3.225	4.049	5.072	6.341	7.911	9.850
25	1.282	1.641	2.094	2.666	3.386	4.292	5.427	6.848	8.623	10.834
30	1.348	1.811	2.427	3.243	4.322	5.743	7.612	10.062	13.267	17.449
35	1.417	2.000	2.814	3.946	5.516	7.686	10.676	14.785	20.413	28.102
40	1.489	2.208	3.262	4.801	7.040	10.285	14.974	21.724	31.408	45.258
45	1.565	2.438	3.781	5.841	8.985	13.764	21.002	31.920	48.325	72.888
50	1.645	2.691	4.384	7.106	11.467	18.419	29.456	46.900	74.354	117.386

Year	11%	12%	13%	14%	15%	16%	17%	18%	19%	20%
1	1.110	1.120	1.130	1.140	1.150	1.160	1.170	1.180	1.190	1.200
2	1.232	1.254	1.277	1.300	1.322	1.346	1.369	1.392	1.416	1.440
3	1.368	1.405	1.443	1.482	1.521	1.561	1.602	1.643	1.685	1.728
4	1.518	1.574	1.630	1.689	1.749	1.811	1.874	1.939	2.005	2.074
5	1.685	1.762	1.842	1.925	2.011	2.100	2.192	2.288	2.386	2.488
6	1.870	1.974	2.082	2.195	2.313	2.436	2.565	2.700	2.840	2.986
7	2.076	2.211	2.353	2.502	2.660	2.826	3.001	3.185	3.379	3.583
8	2.305	2.476	2.658	2.853	3.059	3.278	3.511	3.759	4.021	4.300
9	2.558	2.773	3.004	3.252	3.518	3.803	4.108	4.435	4.785	5.160
10	2.839	3.106	3.395	3.707	4.046	4.411	4.807	5.234	5.695	6.192
11	3.152	3.479	3.836	4.226	4.652	5.117	5.624	6.176	6.777	7.430
12	3.498	3.896	4.334	4.818	5.350	5.936	6.580	7.288	8.064	8.916
13	3.883	4.363	4.898	5.492	6.153	6.886	7.699	8.599	9.596	10.699
14	4.310	4.887	5.535	6.261	7.076	7.987	9.007	10.147	11.420	12.839
15	4.785	5.474	6.254	7.138	8.137	9.265	10.539	11.974	13.589	15.407
16	5.311	6.130	7.067	8.137	9.358	10.748	12.330	14.129	16.171	18.488
17	5.895	6.866	7.986	9.276	10.761	12.468	14.426	16.672	19.244	22.186
18	6.543	7.690	9.024	10.575	12.375	14.462	16.879	19.673	22.900	26.623
19	7.263	8.613	10.197	12.055	14.232	16.776	19.748	23.214	27.251	31.948
20	8.062	9.646	11.523	13.743	16.366	19.461	23.105	27.393	32.429	38.337
21	8.949	10.804	13.021	15.667	18.821	22.574	27.033	32.323	38.591	46.005
22	9.933	12.100	14.713	17.861	21.644	26.186	31.629	38.141	45.923	55.205
23	11.026	13.552	16.626	20.361	24.891	30.376	37.005	45.007	54.648	66.247
24	12.239	15.178	18.788	23.212	28.625	35.236	43.296	53.108	65.031	79.496
25	13.585	17.000	21.230	26.461	32.918	40.874	50.656	62.667	77.387	95.395
30	22.892	29.960	39.115	50.949	66.210	85.849	111.061	143.367	184.672	237.373
35	38.574	52.799	72.066	98.097	133.172	180.311	243.495	327.988	440.691	590.657
40	64.999	93.049	132.776	188.876	267.856	378.715	533.846	750.353	1051.642	1469.740
45	109.527	163.985	244.629	363.662	538.752	795.429	1170.425	1716.619	2509.538	3657.176
50	184.559	288.996	450.711	700.197	1083.619	1670.669	2566.080	3927.189	5988.730	9100.191

THE SUM OF AN ANNUITY OF ONE DOLLAR COMPOUNDED ANNUALLY FOR N YEARS

Year	1%	2%	3%	4%	5%	6%	7%	8%	9%	10%
1	1.000	1.000	1.000	1.000	1.000	1.000	1.000	1.000	1.000	1.000
2	2.010	2.020	2.030	2.040	2.050	2.060	2.070	2.080	2.090	2.100
3	3.030	3.060	3.091	3.122	3.152	3.184	3.215	3,246	3.278	3.310
4	4.060	4.122	4.184	4.246	4.310	4.375	4.440	4.506	4.573	4.641
5	5.101	5.204	5.309	5.416	5.526	5.637	5.751	5.867	5.985	6.105
6	6.152	6.308	6.468	6.633	6.802	6.975	7.153	7.336	7.523	7.716
7	7.214	7.434	7.662	7.898	8.142	8.394	8.654	8.923	9.200	9.487
8	8.286	8.583	8.892	9.214	9.549	9.897	10.260	10.637	11.028	11.436
9	9.368	9.755	10.159	10.583	11.027	11.491	11.978	12.488	13.021	13.579
10	10.462	10.950	11.464	12.006	12.578	13.181	13.816	14.487	15.193	15.937
11	11.567	12.169	12.808	13.486	14.207	14.972	15.784	16.645	17.560	18.531
12	12.682	13.412	14.192	15.026	15.917	16.870	17.888	18.977	20.141	21.384
13	13.809	14.680	15.618	16.627	17.713	18.882	20.141	21.495	22.953	24.523
14	14.947	15.974	17.086	18.292	19.598	21.015	22.550	24.215	26.019	27.975
15	16.097	17.293	18.599	20.023	21.578	23.276	25.129	27.152	29.361	31.772
16	17.258	18.639	20.157	21.824	23.657	25.672	27.888	30.324	33.003	35.949
17	18.430	20.012	21.761	23.697	25.840	28.213	30.840	33.750	36.973	40.544
18	19.614	21.412	23.414	25.645	28.132	30.905	33.999	37.450	41.301	45.599
19	20.811	22.840	25.117	27.671	30.539	33.760	37.379	41.446	46.018	51.158
20	22.019	24.297	26.870	29.778	33.066	36.785	40.995	45.762	51.159	57.274
21	23.239	25.783	28.676	31.969	35.719	39.992	44.865	50.422	56.764	64.002
22	24.471	27.299	30.536	34.248	38.505	43.392	49.005	55.456	62.872	71.402
23	25.716	28.845	32.452	36.618	41.430	46.995	53.435	60.893	69.531	79.542
24	26.973	30.421	34.426	39.082	44.501	50.815	58.176	66.764	76.789	88.496
25	28.243	32.030	36.459	41.645	47.726	54.864	63.248	73.105	84.699	98.346
30	34.784	40.567	47.575	56.084	66.438	79.057	94.459	113.282	136.305	164.491
35	41.659	49.994	60.461	73.651	90.318	111.432	138.234	172.314	215.705	271.018
40	48.885	60.401	75.400	95.024	120.797	154.758	199.630	259.052	337.872	442.580
45	56.479	71.891	92.718	121.027	159.695	212.737	285.741	386.497	525.840	718.881
50	64.461	84.577	112.794	152.664	209.341	290.325	406.516	573.756	815.051	1163.865

Year	11%	12%	13%	14%	15%	16%	17%	18%	19%	20%
1	1.000	1.000	1.000	1.000	1.000	1.000	1.000	1.000	1.000	1.000
2	2.110	2.120	2.130	2.140	2.150	2.160	2.170	2.180	2.190	2.200
3	3.342	3.374	3.407	3.440	3.472	3.506	3.539	3.572	3.606	3.640
4	4.710	4.779	4.850	4.921	4.993	5.066	5.141	5.215	5.291	5.368
5	6.228	6.353	6.480	6.610	6.742	6.877	7.014	7.154	7.297	7.442
6	7.913	8.115	8.323	8.535	8.754	8.977	9.207	9.442	9.683	9.930
7	9.783	10.089	10.405	10.730	11.067	11.414	11.772	12.141	12.523	12.916
8	11.859	12.300	12.757	13.233	13.727	14.240	14.773	15.327	15.902	16.499
9	14.164	14.776	15.416	16.085	16.786	17.518	18.285	19.086	19.923	20.799
10	16.772	17.549	18.420	19.337	20.304	21.321	22.393	23.521	24.709	25.959
11	19.561	20.655	21.814	23.044	24.349	25.733	27.200	28.755	30.403	32.150
12	22.713	24.133	25.650	27.271	29.001	30.850	32.824	34.931	37.180	39.580
13	26.211	28.029	29.984	32.088	34.352	36.786	39.404	42.218	45.244	48.496
14	30.095	32.392	34.882	37.581	40.504	43.672	47.102	50.818	54.841	59.196
15	34.405	37.280	40.417	43.842	47.580	51.659	56.109	60.965	66.260	72.035
16	39.190	42.753	46.671	50.980	55.717	60.925	66.648	72.938	79.850	87.442
17	44.500	48.883	53.738	59.117	65.075	71.673	78.978	87.067	96.021	105.930
18	50.396	55.749	61.724	68.393	75.836	84.140	93.404	103.739	115.265	128.116
19	56.939	63.439	70.748	78.968	88.211	98.603	110.283	123.412	138.165	154.739
20	64.202	72.052	80.946	91.024	102.443	115.379	130.031	146.626	165.417	186.687
21	72.264	81.698	92.468	104.767	118.809	134.840	153.136	174.019	197.846	225.024
22	81.213	92.502	105.489	120.434	137.630	157.414	180.169	206.342	236.436	271.028
23	91.147	104.602	120.203	138.295	159.274	183.600	211.798	244.483	282.359	326.234
24	102.173	118.154	136.829	158.656	184.166	213.976	248.803	289.490	337.007	392.480
25	114.412	133.333	155.616	181.867	212.790	249.212	292.099	342.598	402.038	471.976
30	119.018	241.330	293.192	356.778	434.738	530.306	647.423	790.932	966.698	1181.865
35	341.583	431.658	546.663	693.552	881.152	1120.699	1426.488	1816.607	2314.173	2948.294
40	581.812	767.080	1013.667	1341.979	1779.048	2360.724	3134.412	4163.094	5529.711	7343.715
45	986.613	1358.208	1874.086	2590.464	3585.031	4965.191	6879.008	9531.248	13203.105	18280.914
50	1668.723	2399.975	3459.344	4994.301	7217.488	10435.449	15088.805	21812.273	31514.492	45496.094

THE PRESENT VALUE OF ONE DOLLAR DISCOUNTED ANNUALLY FOR N YEARS

Year	1%	2%	3%	4%	5%	6%	7%	8%	9%	10%
1	.990	.980	.971	.962	.952	.943	.935	.926	.917	.909
2	.980	.961	.943	.925	.907	.890	.873	.857	.842	.826
3	.971	.942	.915	.889	.864	.840	.816	.794	.772	.751
4	.961	.924	.888	.855	.823	.792	.763	.735	.708	.683
5	.951	.906	.863	.822	.784	.747	.713	.681	.650	.621
6	.942	.888	.837	.790	.746	.705	.666	.630	.596	.564
7	.933	.871	.813	.760	.711	.665	.623	.583	.547	.513
8	.923	.853	.789	.731	.677	.627	.582	.540	.502	.467
9	.914	.837	.766	.703	.645	.592	.544	.500	.460	.424
10	.905	.820	.744	.676	.614	.558	.508	.463	.422	.386
11	.896	.804	.722	.650	.585	.527	.475	.429	.388	.350
12	.887	.789	.701	.615	.557	.497	.444	.397	.356	.319
13	.879	.773	.681	.601	.530	.469	.415	.368	.326	.290
14	.870	.758	.661	.577	.505	.442	.388	.340	.299	.263
15	.861	.743	.642	.555	.481	.417	.362	.315	.275	.239
16	.853	.728	.623	.534	.458	.394	.339	.292	.252	.218
17	.844	.714	.605	.513	.436	.371	.317	.270	.231	.198
18	.836	.700	.587	.494	.416	.350	.296	.250	.212	.180
19	.828	.686	.570	.475	.396	.331	.277	.232	.194	.164
20	.820	.673	.554	.456	.377	.312	.258	.215	.178	.149
21	.811	.660	.538	.439	.359	.294	.242	.199	.164	.135
22	.803	.647	.522	.422	.342	.278	.226	.184	.150	.123
23	.795	.634	.507	.406	.326	.262	.211	.170	.138	.112
24	.788	.622	.492	.390	.310	.247	.197	.158	.126	.102
25	.780	.610	.478	.375	.295	.233	.184	.146	.116	.092
30	.742	.552	.412	.308	.231	.174	.131	.099	.075	.057
35	.706	.500	.355	.253	.181	.130	.094	.068	.049	.036
40	.672	.453	.307	.208	.142	.097	.067	.046	.032	.022
45	.639	.410	.264	.171	.111	.073	.048	.031	.021	.014
50	.608	.372	.228	.141	.087	.054	.034	.021	.013	.009

Year	11%	12%	13%	14%	15%	16%	17%	18%	19%	20%
1	.901	.893	.885	.877	.870	.862	.855	.847	.840	.833
2	.812	.797	.783	.769	.756	.743	.731	.718	.706	.694
3	.731	.712	.693	.675	.658	.641	.624	.609	.593	.579
4	.659	.636	.613	.592	.572	.552	.534	.516	.499	.482
5	.593	.567	.543	.519	.497	.476	.456	.437	.419	.402
6	.535	.507	.480	.456	.432	.410	.390	.370	.352	.335
7	.482	.452	.425	.400	.376	.354	.333	.314	.296	.279
8	.434	.404	.376	.351	.327	.305	.285	.266	.249	.233
9	.391	.361	.333	.308	.284	.263	.243	.225	.209	.194
10	.352	.322	.295	.270	.247	.227	.208	.191	.176	.162
11	.317	.287	.261	.237	.215	.195	.178	.162	.148	.135
12	.286	.257	.231	.208	.187	.168	.152	.137	.124	.112
13	.258	.229	.204	.182	.163	.145	.130	.116	.104	.093
14	.232	.205	.181	.160	.141	.125	.111	.099	.088	.078
15	.209	.183	.160	.140	.123	.108	.095	.084	.074	.065
16	.188	.163	.141	.123	.107	.093	.081	.071	.062	.054
17	.170	.146	.125	.108	.093	.080	.069	.060	.052	.045
18	.153	.130	.111	.095	.081	.069	.059	.051	.044	.038
19	.138	.116	.098	.083	.070	.060	.051	.043	.037	.031
20	.124	.104	.087	.073	.061	.051	.043	.037	.031	.026
21	.112	.093	.077	.064	.053	.044	.037	.031	.026	.022
22	.101	.083	.068	.056	.046	.038	.032	.026	.022	.018
23	.091	.074	.060	.049	.040	.033	.027	.022	.018	.015
24	.082	.066	.053	.043	.035	.028	.023	.019	.015	.013
25	.074	.059	.047	.038	.030	.024	.020	.016	.013	.010
30	.044	.033	.026	.020	.015	.012	.009	.007	.005	.004
35	.026	.019	.014	.010	.008	.006	.004	.003	.002	.002
40	.015	.011	.008	.005	.004	.003	.002	.001	.001	.001
45	.009	.006	.004	.003	.002	.001	.001	.001	.000	.000
50	.005	.003	.002	.001	.001	.001	.000	.000	.000	.000

THE PRESENT VALUE OF AN ANNUITY OF
ONE DOLLAR DISCOUNTED ANNUALLY FOR N YEARS

Year	1%	2%	3%	4%	5%	6%	7%	8%	9%	10%
1	.990	.980	.971	.962	.952	.943	.935	.926	.917	.909
2	1.970	1.942	1.913	1.886	1.859	1.833	1.808	1.783	1.759	1.736
3	2.941	2.884	2.829	2.775	2.723	2.673	2.624	2.577	2.531	2.487
4	3.902	3.808	3.717	3.630	3.546	3.465	3.387	3.312	3.240	3.170
5	4.853	4.713	4.580	4.452	4.329	4.212	4.100	3.993	3.890	3.791
6	5.795	5.601	5.417	5.242	5.076	4.917	4.767	4.623	4.486	4.355
7	6.728	6.472	6.230	6.002	5.786	5.582	5.389	5.206	5.033	4.868
8	7.652	7.326	7.020	6.733	6.463	6.210	5.971	5.747	5.535	5.335
9	8.566	8.162	7.786	7.435	7.108	6.802	6.515	6.247	5.995	5.759
10	9.471	8.983	8.530	8.111	7.722	7.360	7.024	6.710	6.418	6.145
11	10.368	9.787	9.253	8.760	8.306	7.887	7.499	7.139	6.805	6.495
12	11.255	10.575	9.954	9.385	8.863	8.384	7.943	7.536	7.161	6.814
13	12.134	11.348	10.635	9.986	9.394	8.853	8.358	7.904	7.487	7.103
14	13.004	12.106	11.296	10.563	9.899	9.295	8.746	8.244	7.786	7.367
15	13.865	12.849	11.938	11.118	10.380	9.712	9.108	8.560	8.061	7.606
16	14.718	13.578	12.561	11.652	10.838	10.106	9.447	8.851	8.313	7.824
17	15.562	14.292	13.166	12.166	11.274	10.477	9.763	9.122	8.544	8.022
18	16.398	14.992	13.754	12.659	11.690	10.828	10.059	9.372	8.756	8.201
19	17.226	15.679	14.324	13.134	12.085	11.158	10.336	9.604	8.950	8.365
20	18.046	16.352	14.878	13.590	12.462	11.470	10.594	9.818	9.129	8.514
21	18.857	17.011	15.415	14.029	12.821	11.764	10.836	10.017	9.292	8.649
22	19.661	17.658	15.937	14.451	13.163	12.042	11.061	10.201	9.442	8.772
23	20.456	18.292	16.444	14.857	13.489	12.303	11.272	10.371	9.580	8.883
24	21.244	18.914	16.936	15.247	13.799	12.550	11.469	10.529	9.707	8.985
25	22.023	19.524	17.413	15.622	14.094	12.783	11.654	10.675	9.823	9.077
30	25.808	22.397	19.601	17.292	15.373	13.765	12.409	11.258	10.274	9.427
35	29.409	24.999	21.487	18.665	16.374	14.498	12.948	11.655	10.567	9.644
40	32.835	27.356	23.115	19.793	17.159	15.046	13.332	11.925	10.757	9.779
45	36.095	29.490	24.519	20.720	17.774	15.456	13.606	12.108	10.881	9.863
50	39.197	31.424	25.730	21.482	18.256	15.762	13.801	12.234	10.962	9.915

Year	11%	12%	13%	14%	15%	16%	17%	18%	19%	20%
1	.901	.893	.885	.877	.870	.862	.855	.847	.840	.833
2	1.713	1.690	1.668	1.647	1.626	1.605	1.585	1.566	1.547	1.528
3	2.444	2.402	2.361	2.322	2.283	2.246	2.210	2.174	2.140	2.106
4	3.102	3.037	2.974	2.914	2.855	2.798	2.743	2.690	2.639	2.589
5	3.696	3.605	3.517	3.433	3.352	3.274	3.199	3.127	3.058	2.991
6	4.231	4.111	3.998	3.889	3.784	3.685	3.589	3.498	3.410	3.326
7	4.712	4.564	4.423	4.288	4.160	4.039	3.922	3.812	3.706	3.605
8	5.146	4.968	4.799	4.639	4.487	4.344	4.207	4.078	3.954	3.837
9	5.537	5.328	5.132	4.946	4.772	4.607	4.451	4.303	4.163	4.031
10	5.889	5.650	5.426	5.216	5.019	4.833	4.659	4.494	4.339	4.192
11	6.207	5.938	5.687	5.453	5.234	5.029	4.836	4.656	4.487	4.327
12	6.492	6.194	5.918	5.660	5.421	5.197	4.988	4.793	4.611	4.439
13	6.750	6.424	6.122	5.842	5.583	5.342	5.118	4.910	4.715	4.533
14	6.982	6.628	6.303	6.002	5.724	5.468	5.229	5.008	4.802	4.611
15	7.191	6.811	6.462	6.142	5.847	5.575	5.324	5.902	4.876	4.675
16	7.379	6.974	6.604	6.265	5.954	5.669	5.405	5.162	4.938	4.730
17	7.549	7.120	6.729	6.373	6.047	5.749	5.475	5.222	4.990	4.775
18	7.702	7.250	6.840	6.467	6.128	5.818	5.534	5.273	5.033	4.812
19	7.839	7.366	6.938	6.550	6.198	5.877	5.585	5.316	5.070	4.843
20	7.963	7.469	7.025	6.623	6.259	5.929	5.628	5.353	5.101	4.870
21	8.075	7.562	7.102	6.687	6.312	5.973	5.665	5.384	5.127	4.891
22	8.176	7.645	7.170	6.743	6.359	6.011	5.696	5.410	5.149	4.909
23	8.266	7.718	7.230	6.792	6.399	6.044	5.723	5.432	5.167	4.925
24	8.348	7.784	7.283	6.835	6.434	6.073	5.747	5.451	5.182	4.937
25	8.422	7.843	7.330	6.873	6.464	6.097	5.766	5.467	5.195	4.948
30	8.694	8.055	7.496	7.003	6.566	6.177	5.829	5.517	5.235	4.979
35	8.855	8.176	7.586	7.070	6.617	6.215	5.858	5.539	5.251	4.992
40	8.951	8.244	7.634	7.105	6.642	6.233	5.871	5.548	5.258	4.997
45	9.008	8.283	7.661	7.123	6.654	6.242	5.877	5.552	5.621	4.999
50	9.042	8.305	7.675	7.133	6.661	6.246	5.880	5.554	5.262	4.999

Appendix II

OPTIONAL TABLE FOR 31.5-YEAR NONRESIDENTIAL REAL PROPERTY

If the Recovery Year is:	And the Month in the First Recovery Year the Property is Placed in Service is:											
	1	2	3	4	5	6	7	8	9	10	11	12
	the Depreciation Rate is:											
1	3.042	2.778	2.513	2.249	1.984	1.720	1.455	1.190	0.926	0.661	0.397	0.132
2	3.175	3.175	3.175	3.175	3.175	3.175	3.175	3.175	3.175	3.175	3.175	3.175
3	3.175	3.175	3.175	3.175	3.175	3.175	3.175	3.175	3.175	3.175	3.175	3.175
4	3.175	3.175	3.175	3.175	3.175	3.175	3.175	3.175	3.175	3.175	3.175	3.175
5	3.175	3.175	3.175	3.175	3.175	3.175	3.175	3.175	3.175	3.175	3.175	3.175
6	3.175	3.175	3.175	3.175	3.175	3.175	3.175	3.175	3.175	3.175	3.175	3.175
7	3.175	3.175	3.175	3.175	3.175	3.175	3.175	3.175	3.175	3.175	3.175	3.175
8	3.175	3.174	3.175	3.174	3.175	3.174	3.175	3.175	3.175	3.175	3.175	3.175
9	3.174	3.175	3.174	3.175	3.174	3.175	3.174	3.175	3.174	3.175	3.174	3.175
10	3.175	3.174	3.175	3.174	3.175	3.174	3.175	3.174	3.175	3.174	3.175	3.174
11	3.174	3.175	3.174	3.175	3.174	3.175	3.174	3.175	3.174	3.175	3.174	3.175
12	3.175	3.174	3.175	3.174	3.175	3.174	3.175	3.174	3.175	3.174	3.175	3.174
13	3.174	3.175	3.174	3.175	3.174	3.175	3.174	3.175	3.174	3.175	3.174	3.175
14	3.175	3.174	3.175	3.174	3.175	3.174	3.175	3.174	3.175	3.174	3.175	3.174
15	3.174	3.175	3.174	3.175	3.174	3.175	3.174	3.175	3.174	3.175	3.174	3.175
16	3.175	3.174	3.175	3.174	3.175	3.174	3.175	3.174	3.175	3.174	3.175	3.174
17	3.174	3.175	3.174	3.175	3.174	3.175	3.174	3.175	3.174	3.175	3.174	3.175
18	3.175	3.174	3.175	3.174	3.175	3.174	3.175	3.174	3.175	3.174	3.175	3.174
19	3.174	3.175	3.174	3.175	3.174	3.175	3.174	3.175	3.174	3.175	3.174	3.175
20	3.175	3.174	3.175	3.174	3.175	3.174	3.175	3.174	3.175	3.174	3.175	3.174
21	3.174	3.175	3.174	3.175	3.174	3.175	3.174	3.175	3.174	3.175	3.174	3.175
22	3.175	3.174	3.175	3.174	3.175	3.174	3.175	3.174	3.175	3.174	3.175	3.174
23	3.174	3.175	3.174	3.175	3.174	3.175	3.174	3.175	3.174	3.175	3.174	3.175
24	3.175	3.174	3.175	3.174	3.175	3.174	3.175	3.174	3.175	3.174	3.175	3.174
25	3.174	3.175	3.174	3.175	3.174	3.175	3.174	3.175	3.174	3.175	3.174	3.175
26	3.175	3.174	3.175	3.174	3.175	3.174	3.175	3.174	3.175	3.174	3.175	3.174
27	3.174	3.175	3.174	3.175	3.174	3.175	3.174	3.175	3.174	3.175	3.174	3.175
28	3.175	3.174	3.175	3.174	3.175	3.174	3.175	3.174	3.175	3.174	3.175	3.174
29	3.174	3.175	3.174	3.175	3.174	3.175	3.174	3.175	3.174	3.175	3.174	3.175
30	3.175	3.174	3.175	3.174	3.175	3.174	3.175	3.174	3.175	3.174	3.175	3.174
31	3.174	3.175	3.174	3.175	3.174	3.175	3.174	3.175	3.174	3.175	3.174	3.175
32	1.720	1.984	2.249	2.513	2.778	3.042	3.175	3.174	3.175	3.174	3.175	3.174
33	0.000	0.000	0.000	0.000	0.000	0.000	0.132	0.397	0.661	0.926	1.190	1.455

OPTIONAL TABLE FOR 27.5-YEAR RESIDENTIAL RENTAL PROPERTY

If the Recovery Year is:	And the Month in the First Recovery Year the Property is Placed in Service is:											
	1	2	3	4	5	6	7	8	9	10	11	12
	the Depreciation Rate is:											
1	3.485%	3.182%	2.879%	2.576%	2.273%	1.970%	1.667%	1.364%	1.061%	0.758%	0.455%	0.152%
2–9	3.636	3.636	3.636	3.636	3.636	3.636	3.636	3.636	3.636	3.636	3.636	3.636
10	3.637	3.637	3.637	3.637	3.637	3.637	3.636	3.636	3.636	3.636	3.636	3.636
11	3.636	3.636	3.636	3.636	3.636	3.636	3.637	3.637	3.637	3.637	3.637	3.637
12	3.637	3.637	3.637	3.637	3.637	3.637	3.636	3.636	3.636	3.636	3.636	3.636
13	3.636	3.636	3.636	3.636	3.636	3.636	3.637	3.637	3.637	3.637	3.637	3.637
14	3.637	3.637	3.637	3.637	3.637	3.637	3.636	3.636	3.636	3.636	3.636	3.636
15	3.636	3.636	3.636	3.636	3.636	3.636	3.637	3.637	3.637	3.637	3.637	3.637
16	3.637	3.637	3.637	3.637	3.637	3.637	3.636	3.636	3.636	3.636	3.636	3.636
17	3.636	3.636	3.636	3.636	3.636	3.636	3.637	3.637	3.637	3.637	3.637	3.637
18	3.637	3.637	3.637	3.637	3.637	3.637	3.636	3.636	3.636	3.636	3.636	3.636
19	3.636	3.636	3.636	3.636	3.636	3.636	3.637	3.637	3.637	3.637	3.637	3.637
20	3.637	3.637	3.637	3.637	3.637	3.637	3.636	3.636	3.636	3.636	3.636	3.636
21	3.636	3.636	3.636	3.636	3.636	3.636	3.637	3.637	3.637	3.637	3.637	3.637
22	3.637	3.637	3.637	3.637	3.637	3.637	3.636	3.636	3.636	3.636	3.636	3.636
23	3.636	3.636	3.636	3.636	3.636	3.636	3.637	3.637	3.637	3.637	3.637	3.637
24	3.637	3.637	3.637	3.637	3.637	3.637	3.636	3.636	3.636	3.636	3.636	3.636
25	3.636	3.636	3.636	3.636	3.636	3.636	3.637	3.637	3.637	3.637	3.637	3.637
26	3.637	3.637	3.637	3.637	3.637	3.637	3.636	3.636	3.636	3.636	3.636	3.636
27	3.636	3.636	3.636	3.636	3.636	3.636	3.637	3.637	3.637	3.637	3.637	3.637
28	1.970	2.273	2.576	2.879	3.182	3.485	3.636	3.636	3.636	3.636	3.636	3.636
29	0.000	0.000	0.000	0.000	0.000	0.000	0.152	0.455	0.758	1.061	1.364	1.667

CHECKLIST FOR EVALUATING FRANCHISES

A. FRANCHISE—GENERAL

1. IS THE PRODUCT OR SERVICE:

	Yes	No
a. Considered reputable	⎯	⎯
b. Part of a growing market	⎯	⎯
c. Needed in your area	⎯	⎯
d. Of interest to you	⎯	⎯
e. Safe	⎯	⎯
f. Protected	⎯	⎯
g. Covered by guarantee	⎯	⎯

2. IS THE FRANCHISE:

a.	Local	⎯	⎯
	Regional	⎯	⎯
	National	⎯	⎯
	International	⎯	⎯
b.	Full time	⎯	⎯
	Part time	⎯	⎯
	Full time possible in future	⎯	⎯

3. EXISTING FRANCHISES:

a. How long was the company in business before the first franchise was awarded? _____ years.

b. What date was the company founded and what date was the first franchise awarded? Company founded _____. First franchise awarded _____.

c. Number currently in operation or under construction? _____.
   Information on those to contact:

   Franchise #1: Owner _____

   Address _____

   _____

   Telephone _____

   Date Started _____

CHECKLIST FOR EVALUATING FRANCHISES *(Continued)*

Franchise #2:   Owner _____

Address _____

_____

Telephone _____

Date Started _____

Franchise #3:   Owner _____

Address _____

_____

Telephone _____

Date Started _____

Franchise #4:   Owner _____

Address _____

_____

Telephone _____

Date Started _____

4. WHY HAVE FRANCHISES FAILED?

a. How many franchises have failed? _____. How many of these have been in the last two years? _____.

b. Why have franchises failed?

Franchisor Reasons: _____

_____

_____

_____

Better Business Bureau Reasons: _____

_____

_____

_____

Franchisee Reasons: _____

_____

_____

_____

CHECKLIST FOR EVALUATING FRANCHISES *(Continued)*

5. FRANCHISE IN LOCAL MARKET AREA

   a. Has a franchise ever been awarded in this area? _____. If so and if it is still in operation:

   Owner _____
   Address _____
   Telephone _____ Date Started _____

   If so and if it is no longer in operation:

   Person involved _____
   Address _____
   Date Started _____ Date Ended _____
   Reasons for failure _____
   _____

   How many inquiries have you had for your franchise from my area in the past six months? _____.

6. COMPETITION?

   a. What is my competition? _____
   _____
   _____

7. ARE ALL FRANCHISES INDEPENDENTLY OWNED?

   a. Of the total outlets, _____ are franchised, and _____ are company owned.

   b. If some outlets are company owned did they start out this way _____ or were they repurchased from a franchisee _____. Date of the most recent company acquisition _____.

8. FRANCHISE DISTRIBUTION PATTERN:

   a. Is the franchise exclusive _____ or nonexclusive _____.

   b. Is the franchise a distributorship _____ or a dealership _____. If it is a dealership who is the distributor in my area:

   Name _____
   Address _____
   How long has he been a distributor _____

CHECKLIST FOR EVALUATING FRANCHISES *(Continued)*

9. FRANCHISE OPERATIONS:

    a. What facilities are required and do I lease or build. Operated out of home _____

	Build	Lease
Office	_____	_____
Building	_____	_____
Manufacturing facility	_____	_____
Warehouse	_____	_____

    b. Getting started. . . . who is responsible for what?

	Franchisor	Franchisee
Feasibility study	_____	_____
Design	_____	_____
Construction	_____	_____
Furnishing	_____	_____
Financing	_____	_____

B. FRANCHISE COMPANY

    1. THE COMPANY:

        a. What is the name and address of the parent company if different than the franchise company:

        Name _____

        Address _____

        b. Is the parent company public _____ or private _____?

        c. If the company is public, where is the stock traded:

        New York Stock Exchange _____

        American Exchange _____

        Over the Counter _____

        d. If the company is private the president is _____. The following bank can be used as a reference:

        Name _____

        Address _____

        Person to contact _____

CHECKLIST FOR EVALUATING FRANCHISES *(Continued)*

C. FINANCIAL AND LEGAL

   1. a. Lawyer Name _____
       Address _____
       Telephone _____

     b. Financial Name _____
       Address _____
       Telephone _____

     c. Management Name _____
       Address _____
       Telephone _____

   2. TOTAL FRANCHISE COST:

     a. How much money is required to get started?

Item	Amount
Franchise start up	$_____
First year operating	$_____
First year personal	$_____
TOTAL	$_____

     b. What do I have to pay the franchisor to get started? $_____.

Item	Amount
Franchise fee	$_____
Services	$_____
Product	$_____
Real estate	$_____
Equipment	$_____
TOTAL	$_____

     c. Is any of the initial franchise cost refundable? _____. If so, on what
       basis? _____
       _____.

   3. FINANCING:

     a. Is part of the initial cost to the franchisee financed? _____. If so, how much
       $_____, this represents _____% of the total initial cost.

CHECKLIST FOR EVALUATING FRANCHISES *(Continued)*

b. What is the interest rate? _____%. When does financing have to be paid back? _____.

4. FORECAST OF INCOME AND EXPENSES:

a. Is a forecast of income and expenses provided? _____.

Is it:
Based on actual franchisee operations? _____.
Based on a franchisor outlet? _____.
Purely estimated? _____.

b. If a forecast is provided does it:

	Yes	No
Related to your market area	____	____
Meet your personal goals	____	____
Provide adequate return on your investment	____	____
Provide for adequate promotion and personnel	____	____

5. ARE ALL DETAILS COVERED IN A WRITTEN FRANCHISE CONTRACT?

Yes _____ No _____ (get copy for lawyer and accountant review)

a. What to look for—are these included?

	Yes	No
Franchise fee	____	____
Termination	____	____
Selling and renewal	____	____
Advertising and promotion	____	____
Patent and liability protection	____	____
Home office services	____	____
Commissions and royalties	____	____
Training	____	____
Financing	____	____
Territory	____	____
Exclusive vs. nonexclusive	____	____

CHECKLIST FOR EVALUATING FRANCHISES *(Continued)*

D. TRAINING

1. INITIAL TRAINING:

a. Does the franchisor provide formal initial training? _____. If so, how long does it last? _____.

b. Cost

	Yes	No
Included in franchise cost	_____	_____
Includes all materials	_____	_____
Includes transportation	_____	_____
Includes room and board	_____	_____

If not included in franchise cost what is the total cost including all costs outlined above? $_____.

c. What does the training course include?

	Yes	No
Franchise operations	_____	_____
Sales	_____	_____
Finance	_____	_____
Promotion	_____	_____
Personnel	_____	_____
Management	_____	_____
Manufacturing and maintenance	_____	_____
Other _____		
_____	_____	_____

d. How do you train your initial staff? Is a training program provided? _____. Does the franchisor make available a staff member from the home office to assist? _____. What materials are included in the staff training program? _____
_____
_____
_____.

2. CONTINUING TRAINING:

a. What is the continuing program? Is there any cost? _____. If so, how much $_____. Are there any special materials or equipment required? _____. If so, what? _____. What is the cost to the franchisee? $_____.

CHECKLIST FOR EVALUATING FRANCHISES *(Continued)*

E. <u>MARKETING</u>

1. How is the product or service sold?

	Yes	No
In home—appointment	——	——
In home—cold calls	——	——
Telephone	——	——
In store or place of business	——	——
At business—appointment	——	——
At business—cold calls	——	——
Mail	——	——
Other _____		
_____	——	——

2. How do you get the sales leads?

	Yes	No
Franchisor	——	——
Franchisee	——	——
Both	——	——
Advertising	——	——
Direct mail	——	——
Telephone	——	——
Trade shows	——	——
Other _____		
_____	——	——

3. Who are the prospects for the products or services?
   Outline a brief profile: _____
   _____.

4. What is the national advertising program of the franchisor?

   a. What is the national advertising budget? $_____.

   b. What are the primary advertising media?

       Television _____
       Radio _____
       Outdoor _____
       Newspaper _____
       Magazine _____
       Direct mail _____

CHECKLIST FOR EVALUATING FRANCHISES *(Continued)*

5. What kind of advertising and promotion support is available for the franchisee?

	Yes	No
Is a packaged advertising program available?	____	____
Is there a coop advertising program?	____	____
Is there a grand opening package?	____	____

6. Should you have an advertising agency? _____.

F. HOME OFFICE SUPPORT

1. PRINCIPALS AND DIRECTORS:

a. Who are the key persons involved in the day to day operations of the business:

Name	Title	Background
_____	_____	_____
_____	_____	_____
_____	_____	_____
_____	_____	_____
_____	_____	_____

b. Who are the directors (do not include those from a. above)?

Appendix III

3-YEAR PROPERTY

Year	Half-Year Convention	Mid-Quarter Convention			
		First Quarter	Second Quarter	Third Quarter	Fourth Quarter
1	33.33%	58.33%	41.67%	25%	8.33%
2	44.45	27.78	38.89	50	61.11
3	14.81	12.35	14.14	16.67	20.37
4	7.41	1.54	5.30	8.33	10.19

5-YEAR PROPERTY

Year	Half-Year Convention	Mid-Quarter Convention			
		First Quarter	Second Quarter	Third Quarter	Fourth Quarter
1	20%	35%	25%	15%	5%
2	32	26	30	34	38
3	19.2	15.6	18	20.4	22.8
4	11.52	11.01	11.37	12.24	13.68
5	11.52	11.01	11.37	11.30	10.94
6	5.76	1.38	4.26	7.06	9.58

7-YEAR PROPERTY

Year	Half-Year Convention	Mid-Quarter Convention			
		First Quarter	Second Quarter	Third Quarter	Fourth Quarter
1	14.29%	25.00%	17.85%	10.71%	3.57%
2	24.49	21.43	23.47	25.51	27.55
3	17.49	15.31	16.67	18.22	19.68
4	12.49	10.93	11.97	13.02	14.06
5	8.93	8.75	8.87	9.30	10.04
6	8.92	8.74	8.87	8.85	8.73
7	8.93	8.75	8.87	8.86	8.73
8	4.46	1.09	3.3[4]	5.53	7.64

Source: Internal Revenue Service

Index